Managing Information Technology

Managing Information Technology

Liam Lewis

Larsen & Keller
www.larsen-keller.com

Managing Information Technology
Liam Lewis
ISBN: 978-1-64172-379-4 (Hardback)

 Larsen & Keller

Published by Larsen and Keller Education,
5 Penn Plaza,
19th Floor,
New York, NY 10001, USA

Cataloging-in-Publication Data

Managing information technology / Liam Lewis.
    p. cm.
Includes bibliographical references and index.
ISBN 978-1-64172-379-4
1. Management information systems. 2. Information technology. 3. Information technology--Management.
I. Lewis, Liam.
T58.6 .M36 2020
658.403 8--dc23

For more information regarding Larsen and Keller Education and its products, please visit the publisher's website www.larsen-keller.com

TABLE OF CONTENTS

This book is a culmination of my many years of practice in this field. I attribute the success of this book to my support group. I would like to thank my parents who have showered me with unconditional love and support and my peers and professors for their constant guidance.

The discipline of information technology management deals with the management of all the information technology resources of an organization. A few of such resources are computer hardware, software, data, networks and data centre facilities and the staff that is hired to maintain them. Some of the responsibilities which fall under information technology management are budgeting, change management, organizing and controlling. It also includes various other aspects such as software design, network planning and tech support, etc. A few of the major disciplines within this field are business/IT alignment, IT governance, IT financial management, sourcing and IT configuration management. This textbook presents the complex subject of information technology management in the most comprehensible and easy to understand language. Some of the diverse topics covered herein address the varied branches that fall under this category. This book, with its detailed analyses and data, will prove immensely beneficial to professionals and students involved in this area at various levels.

The details of chapters are provided below for a progressive learning:

Chapter – Introduction

Information technology refers to the usage of computer in saving, sending and manipulating data in the diverse areas of computing. Prioritizing and managing IT resources is defined as information technology management. This is an introductory chapter which will briefly introduce all the significant aspects of information technology.

Chapter – Information Management

The process of gathering, storing, organizing and maintaining all types of information is called information management. Some of the aspects that fall under its domain are information lifecycle management, IT service management, IT risk management, information processing, etc. This chapter closely examines these aspects of information management to provide an extensive understanding of the subject.

Chapter – Information System and its Types

The organizational systems which are used to process, store and distribute information are termed as information systems. Different types of information systems are transaction processing system, management information system, decision support system, etc. This chapter discusses these different types of information systems in detail.

Chapter – Data Management

Data management consists of managing and maintaining information as a valuable resource. It comprises many fields such as data quality management, data modeling, data architecture, data integration, data processing, data security, data retrieval, database management system, etc. The topics elaborated in this chapter will help in gaining a better perspective about these aspects of data management.

Chapter – Information Technology Network

A network in computing is a group of interconnected devices used to communicate with one another. Its major components are networking hardware, network topology, wireless network, internet protocol address, etc. All these diverse components of information technology network have been carefully analyzed in this chapter.

Chapter – Information Technology Infrastructure

Information technology infrastructure is an element of information technology which deals with hardware, software and networking components. It can be categorized as converged infrastructure, hyper-converged infrastructure, dynamic infrastructure, information infrastructure, software-defined infrastructure, etc. This chapter has been carefully written to provide an easy understanding of the various infrastructures of information technology.

Chapter – Diverse Aspects of Information Technology

Information technology has a wide range of applications which include information retrieval, data mining, information extraction, data storage, ontology, strategic management, content management, information architecture, etc. These diverse applications of information technology have been thoroughly discussed in this chapter.

Liam Lewis

Introduction

Information technology refers to the usage of computer in saving, sending and manipulating data in the diverse areas of computing. Prioritizing and managing IT resources is defined as information technology management. This is an introductory chapter which will briefly introduce all the significant aspects of information technology.

INFORMATION TECHNOLOGY

The terms "information technology" and "IT" are widely used in business and the field of computing. People use the terms generically when referring to various kinds of computer-related work, which sometimes confuses their meaning.

A 1958 article in Harvard Business Review referred to information technology as consisting of three basic parts: computational data processing, decision support, and business software. This time period marked the beginning of IT as an officially defined area of business; in fact, this article probably coined the term.

Over the ensuing decades, many corporations created so-called "IT departments" to manage the computer technologies related to their business. Whatever these departments worked on became the de facto definition of Information Technology, one that has evolved over time. Today, IT departments have responsibilities in areas like computer tech support, business computer network and database administration, business software deployment, and information security.

Especially during the dot-com boom of the 1990s, Information Technology also became associated with aspects of computing beyond those owned by IT departments. This broader definition of IT includes areas like software development, computer systems architecture, and project management.

Issues and Challenges in Information Technology

- As computing systems and capabilities continue expanding worldwide, "data overload" has become an increasingly critical issue for many IT professionals. Efficiently processing huge amounts of data to produce useful business intelligence requires large amounts of processing power, sophisticated software, and human analytic skills.

- Teamwork and communication skills have also become essential for most businesses to manage the complexity of IT systems. Many IT professionals are responsible for providing service to business users who are not trained in computer networking or other information technologies but who are instead interested in simply using IT as a tool to get their work done efficiently.

- System and network security issues are a primary concern for many business executives, as any security incident can potentially damage a company's reputation and cost large sums of money.

Computer Networking and Information Technology

Because networks play a central role in the operation of many companies, business computer networking topics tend to be closely associated with Information Technology. Networking trends that play a key role in IT include:

- Network capacity and performance: The popularity of online video has greatly increased the demand for network bandwidth both on the Internet and on IT networks. New types of software applications that support richer graphics and deeper interaction with computers also tend to generate larger amounts of data and hence network traffic. Information technology teams must plan appropriately not just for their company's current needs but also this future growth.

- Mobile and wireless usages: IT network administrators must now support a wide array of smartphones and tablets in addition to traditional PCs and workstations. IT environments tend to require high-performance wireless hotspots with roaming capability. In larger office buildings, deployments are carefully planned and tested to eliminate dead spots and signal interference.

- Cloud services: Whereas IT shops in the past maintained their own server farms for hosting email and business databases, some have migrated to cloud computing environments where third-party hosting providers maintain the data. This change in computing model dramatically changes the patterns of traffic on a company network.

IT Software and Hardware

IT includes several layers of physical equipment (hardware), virtualization and management or automation tools, operating systems and applications (software) used to perform essential functions. User devices, peripherals and software, such as laptops, smartphones or even recording equipment, can be included in the IT domain. IT can also refer to the architectures, methodologies and regulations governing the use and storage of data.

Business applications include databases like SQL Server, transactional systems such as real-time order entry, email servers like Exchange, Web servers like Apache, customer relationship management and enterprise resource planning systems. These applications execute programmed instructions to manipulate, consolidate, disperse or otherwise affect data for a business purpose.

Computer servers run business applications. Servers interact with client users and other servers across one or more business networks. Storage is any kind of technology that holds information as data. Information can take any form including file data, multimedia, telephony data and Web data, data from sensors or future formats. Storage includes volatile random access memory (RAM) as well as non-volatile tape, hard disk and solid-state flash drives.

IT architectures have evolved to include virtualization and cloud computing, where physical resources are abstracted and pooled in different configurations to meet application requirements. Clouds may be distributed across locations and shared with other IT users, or contained within a corporate data center, or some combination of both deployments.

INFORMATION AND COMMUNICATIONS TECHNOLOGY

ICT, or information and communications technology (or technologies), is the infrastructure and components that enable modern computing.

Although there is no single, universal definition of ICT, the term is generally accepted to mean all devices, networking components, applications and systems that combined allow people and organizations (i.e., businesses, nonprofit agencies, governments and criminal enterprises) to interact in the digital world.

Components of an ICT System

ICT encompasses both the internet-enabled sphere as well as the mobile one powered by wireless networks. It also includes antiquated technologies, such as landline telephones, radio and television broadcast -- all of which are still widely used today alongside cutting-edge ICT pieces such as artificial intelligence and robotics.

ICT is sometimes used synonymously with IT (for information technology); however, ICT is generally used to represent a broader, more comprehensive list of all components related to computer and digital technologies than IT.

The list of ICT components is exhaustive, and it continues to grow. Some components, such as computers and telephones, have existed for decades. Others, such as smartphones, digital TVs and robots, are more recent entries.

ICT commonly means more than its list of components, though. It also encompasses the application of all those various components. It's here that the real potential, power and danger of ICT can be found.

ICT's Societal and Economic Impact

ICT is leveraged for economic, societal and interpersonal transactions and interactions. ICT has drastically changed how people work, communicate, learn and live. Moreover, ICT continues to revolutionize all parts of the human experience as first computers and now robots do many of the tasks once handled by humans. For example, computers once answered phones and directed calls to the appropriate individuals to respond; now robots not only can answer the calls, but they can often more quickly and efficiently handle callers' requests for services.

ICT's importance to economic development and business growth has been so monumental, in fact, that it's credited with ushering in what many have labeled the Fourth Industrial Revolution.

ICT also underpins broad shifts in society, as individuals en masse are moving from personal, face-to-face interactions to ones in the digital space. This new era is frequently termed the Digital Age.

For all its revolutionary aspects, though, ICT capabilities aren't evenly distributed. Simply put, richer countries and richer individuals enjoy more access and thus have a greater ability to seize on the advantages and opportunities powered by ICT.

Consider, for example, some findings from the World Bank. In 2016, it stated that more than 75% of people worldwide have access to a cellphone. However, internet access through either mobile or fixed broadband remains prohibitively expensive in many countries due to a lack of ICT infrastructure. Furthermore, the World Bank estimated that out of the global population of 7.4 billion people, more than 4 billion don't have access to the internet. Additionally, it estimated that only 1.1 billion people have access to high-speed internet.

In the United States and elsewhere, this discrepancy in access to ICT has created the so-called digital divide.

The World Bank, numerous governmental authorities and non-government organizations (NGOs) advocate policies and programs that aim to bridge the digital divide by providing greater access to ICT among those individuals and populations struggling to afford it.

These various institutions assert that those without ICT capabilities are left out of the multiple opportunities and benefits that ICT creates and will therefore fall further behind in socio-economic terms.

The United Nations considers one of its Sustainable Development Goals (SDG) to "significantly increase access to information and communications technology and strive to provide universal and affordable access to the internet in least developed countries by 2020."

Economic advantages are found both within the ICT market as well as in the larger areas of business and society as a whole.

Within the ICT market, the advancement of ICT capabilities has made the development and delivery of various technologies cheaper for ICT vendors and their customers while also providing new market opportunities. For instance, telephone companies that once had to build and maintain miles of telephone lines have shifted to more advanced networking materials and can provide telephone, television and internet services; consumers now enjoy more choices in delivery and price points as a result.

The Significance of ICT in Enterprises

For businesses, advances within ICT have brought a slew of cost savings, opportunities and conveniences. They range from highly automated businesses processes that have cut costs, to the big data revolution where organizations are turning the vast trove of data generated by ICT into insights that drive new products and services, to ICT-enabled transactions such as internet shopping and telemedicine and social media that give customers more choices in how they shop, communicate and interact.

But ICT has also created problems and challenges to organizations and individuals alike -- as well as to society as a whole. The digitization of data, the expanding use of high-speed internet and the growing global network together have led to new levels of crime, where so-called bad actors can hatch electronically enabled schemes or illegally gain access to systems to steal money, intellectual property or private information or to disrupt systems that control critical infrastructure. ICT has also brought automation and robots that displace workers who are unable to transfer their skills to new positions. And ICT has allowed more and more people to limit their interactions with others, creating what some people fear is a population that could lose some of what makes it human.

INFORMATION TECHNOLOGY MANAGEMENT

Information technology management (IT management) is the process whereby all resources related to information technology are managed according to an organization's priorities and needs. This includes tangible resources like networking hardware, computers and people, as well as intangible resources like software and data. The central aim of IT management is to generate value through the use of technology. To achieve this, business strategies and technology must be aligned.

Information technology management includes many of the basic functions of management, such as staffing, organizing, budgeting and control, but it also has functions that are unique to IT, such as software development, change management, network planning and tech support.

Generally, IT is used by organizations to support and compliment their business operations.

References

- Introduction-information-technology: lifewire.com, retrieved 5 February, 2019
- It, definition: techtarget.com, retrieved 26 July, 2019
- Ict-information-and-communications-technology-or-technologies, definition: techtarget.com, retrieved 21 may, 2019
- Information-technology-management-it-management, definition: techtarget.com, retrieved 8 January, 2019

Information Management

The process of gathering, storing, organizing and maintaining all types of information is called information management. Some of the aspects that fall under its domain are information lifecycle management, IT service management, IT risk management, information processing, etc. This chapter closely examines these aspects of information management to provide an extensive understanding of the subject.

Information management (IM) is the process of collecting, storing, managing and maintaining information in all its forms. Information management is a broad term that incorporates policies and procedures for centrally managing and sharing information among different individuals, organizations and/or information systems throughout the information life cycle.

Information management may also be called information asset management.

Information management is generally an enterprise information system concept, where an organization produces, owns and manages a suite of information. The information can be in the form of physical data (such as papers, documents and books), or digital data assets. Information management deals with the level and control of an organization's governance over its information assets. Information management is typically achieved through purpose-built information management systems and by supporting business processes and guidelines. Moreover, IM also focuses on how that information is shared and delivered to various recipients, including individuals and different computing devices such as an organization's website, computers, servers, applications and/or mobile devices.

According to a process view of information management, IM is a continuous cycle of six closely related activities:

- Identification of information needs;

- Acquisition and creation of information;

- Analysis and interpretation of information;

- Organization and storage of information;

- Information access and dissemination;

- Information use.

The term 'information management' is used ambiguously in the literatures of several fields: in computer science and its applications it is used as a synonym for information technology management or as identical to 'data management', where the emphasis is on the structures underlying quantitative data and their relationship to the design of databases.

In business or management studies it has similar connotations to technology management, with an emphasis on the relationship of information technology to business performance and competitiveness.

In the field of librarianship and information science it is identified with the 'emerging market' for information workers (managers), whose perception of information embraces data, organizational intelligence, competitive intelligence, external information resources of all kinds and the associated technology (manual or machine) for handling these different sources. Compared with the other areas, information management in this latter context is more widely concerned with the meaning of information for the information user and with information retrieval issues.

INFORMATION LIFECYCLE MANAGEMENT

Information lifecycle management (ILM) refers to strategies for administering storage systems on computing devices.

ILM is the practice of applying certain policies to effective information management. This practice had its basis in the management of information in paper or other physical forms (microfilm, negatives, photographs, audio or video recordings and other assets).

ILM includes every phase of a "record" from its beginning to its end. And while it is generally applied to information that rises to the classic definition of a record (and thus related to records management), it applies to all informational assets. During its existence, information can become a record by being identified as documenting a business transaction or as satisfying a business need. In this sense ILM has been part of the overall approach of enterprise content management.

However, in a more general perspective the term "business" must be taken in a broad sense, and not forcibly tied to direct commercial or enterprise contexts. While most records are thought of as having a relationship to enterprise business, not all do. Much recorded information serves to document an event or a critical point in history. Examples of these are birth, death, medical/health and educational records. e-Science, for example, is an area where ILM has become relevant.

In 2004, the Storage Networking Industry Association, on behalf of the information technology (IT) and information storage industries, attempted to assign a new broader definition to Information Lifecycle Management (ILM). The oft-quoted definition that it released that October at the Storage Networking World conference in Orlando, Florida, stated that "ILM consists of the policies, processes, practices, and tools used to align the business value of information with the most appropriate and cost-effective IT infrastructure from the time information is conceived through its final disposition." In this view, information is aligned with business processes through management policies and service levels associated with applications, metadata, information, and data.

Operational

Operational aspects of ILM include backup and data protection; disaster recovery, restore, and restart; archiving and long-term retention; data replication; and day-to-day processes and procedures necessary to manage a storage architecture.

Infrastructure

Infrastructure facets of ILM include the logical and physical architectures; the applications dependent upon the storage platforms; security of storage; and data center constraints. Within the application realm, the relationship between applications and the production, test, and development requirements are generally most relevant for ILM.

Functionality

For the purposes of business records, there are five phases identified as being part of the lifecycle continuum along with one exception. These are:

- Creation and Receipt,

- Distribution,

- Use,

- Maintenance,

- Disposition.

Creation and Receipt deals with records from their point of origination. This could include their creation by a member of an organization at varying levels or receipt of information from an external source. It includes correspondence, forms, reports, drawings, computer input/output, or other sources.

Distribution is the process of managing the information once it has been created or received. This includes both internal and external distribution, as information that leaves an organization becomes a record of a transaction with others.

Use takes place after information is distributed internally, and can generate business decisions, document further actions, or serve other purposes.

Maintenance is the management of information. This can include processes such as filing, retrieval and transfers. While the connotation of 'filing' presumes the placing of information in a prescribed container and leaving it there, there is much more involved. Filing is actually the process of arranging information in a predetermined sequence and creating a system to manage it for its useful existence within an organization. Failure to establish a sound method for filing information makes its retrieval and use nearly impossible. Transferring information refers to the process of responding to requests, retrieval from files and providing access to users authorized by the organization to have access to the information. While removed from the files, the information is tracked by the use of various processes to ensure it is returned and/or available to others who may need access to it.

Disposition is the practice of handling information that is less frequently accessed or has met its assigned retention periods. Less frequently accessed records may be considered for relocation to an 'inactive records facility' until they have met their assigned retention period. "Although a small percentage of organizational information never loses its value, the value of most information tends to decline over time until it has no further value to anyone for any purpose. The value of nearly all business information is greatest soon after it is created and generally remains active for only a short time -one to three years or so- after which its importance and usage declines. The record then makes its life cycle transition to a semi-active and finally to an inactive state." Retention periods are based on the creation of an organization-specific retention schedule, based on research of the regulatory, statutory and legal requirements for management of information for the industry in which the organization operates. Additional items to consider when establishing a retention period are any business needs that may exceed those requirements and consideration of the potential historic, intrinsic or enduring value of the information. If the information has met all of these needs and is no longer considered to be valuable, it should be disposed of by means appropriate for the content. This may include ensuring that others cannot obtain access to outdated or obsolete information as well as measures for protection privacy and confidentiality.'

Long-term records are those that are identified to have a continuing value to an organization. Based on the period assigned in the retention schedule, these may be held for periods of 25 years or longer, or may even be assigned a retention period of "indefinite" or "permanent". The term "permanent" is used much less frequently outside of the Federal Government, as it is not feasible to establish a requirement for such a retention period. There is a need to ensure records of a continuing value are managed using methods that ensure they remain persistently accessible for length of the time they are retained. While this is relatively easy to accomplish with paper or microfilm based records by providing appropriate environmental conditions and adequate protection from potential hazards, it is less simple for electronic format records. There are unique concerns related to ensuring the format they are generated/captured in remains viable and the media they are stored on remains accessible. Media is subject to both degradation and obsolescence over its lifespan, and therefore, policies and procedures must be established for the periodic conversion and migration of information stored electronically to ensure it remains accessible for its required retention periods.

Exceptions occur with non-recurring issues outside the normal day-to-day operations. One example of this is a legal hold, litigation hold or legal freeze is requested by an attorney. What follows is that the records manager will place a legal hold inside the records management application which will stop the files from being enqueued for disposition.

STRATEGIC INFORMATION MANAGEMENT

Strategic information management means that an organization uses the data that it collects through computer systems and other means in deliberate ways. This kind of management approach is a powerful way to maintain a competitive advantage for private companies and a way to achieve objectives such as efficiency and customer satisfaction for public and nonprofit organizations.

Strategic information management is a salient feature in the world of information technology (IT). In a nutshell, strategic information management helps businesses and organizations categorize, store, process and transfer the information they create and receive. It also offers tools for helping companies apply metrics and analytical tools to their information repositories, allowing them to recognize opportunities for growth and pinpoint ways to improve operational efficiency.

Automation

IT professionals design strategic information management systems to automate the management of incoming and outgoing information to the greatest possible degree. While each company has its own unique IT needs, strategic information management systems typically include built-in controls that filter, sort, categorize and store information in easy-to-manage categories.

Customization

Strategic information management systems are typically customized to meet the unique needs of each individual company. Incoming and outgoing data can be sorted and cross-referenced according to a wide range of individually specified controls and parameters, which include the company's business verticals and horizontals, individual clients, demographics, geographic location and business function.

Organization and Access

Strategic information management systems are extensively categorized, allowing for an optimal level of organization. Access controls can be as strict or as lax as the client wants, allowing for company-wide access to information databases or limiting information accessibility to key personnel. User-specific controls can also be set, in case employees need access to certain information but management wants to limit their access to sensitive data.

Benefits

The benefits of strategic information management can be felt from the executive level right down to the functional staff level. It can help businesses expand their operations into new areas, set goals, measure performance and improve overall productivity.

Risks

Some of the risks involved with strategic information management systems include implementation challenges, incompatibility with client databases and human error. As with other IT management techniques, data protection and information security is also an ongoing concern.

IT SERVICE MANAGEMENT

IT service management (ITSM) refers to the entirety of activities – directed by policies, organized and structured in processes and supporting procedures – that are performed by an organization to design, plan, deliver, operate and control information technology (IT) services offered to customers.

Differing from more technology-oriented IT management approaches like network management and IT systems management, IT service management is characterized by adopting a process approach towards management, focusing on customer needs and IT services for customers rather than IT systems, and stressing continual improvement. The CIO WaterCoolers' annual ITSM report states that business uses ITSM "mostly in support of customer experience (35%) and service quality (48%)."

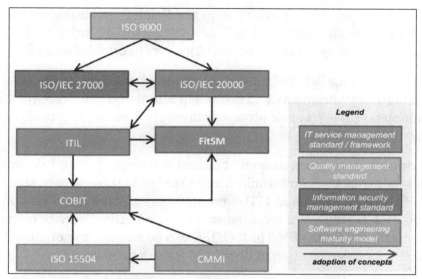

Relationships between ITSM frameworks and other management standards.

As a discipline, ITSM has ties and common interests with other IT and general management approaches, information security management and software engineering. Consequently, IT service management frameworks have been influenced by other standards and adopted concepts from them, e.g. CMMIISO 9000 or ISO/IEC 27000.

Professional Organizations

There are international, chapter-based professional associations, such as the IT Service Management Forum (itSMF), and HDI. The main goal of these organizations is to foster the exchange of experiences and ideas between users of ITSM frameworks. To this end, national and local itSMF and HDI chapters (LIGs or local interest groups for itSMF) organize conferences and workshops. Some of them also contribute to the translations of ITSM framework documents into their respective languages or publish own ITSM guides. There are several certifications for service management like ITIL 2011 foundation.

Information Technology Infrastructure Library

IT service management is often equated with the Information Technology Infrastructure Library (ITIL), even though there are a variety of standards and frameworks contributing to the overall ITSM discipline. ITIL originated as an official publication of United Kingdom government agencies (first CCTA, later OGC, then the Cabinet Office). In January 2014, ownership of ITIL was transferred to Axelos, a joint venture of the UK government and Capita, an international business process outsourcing and professional services company.

Other Frameworks

Other frameworks for ITSM and overlapping disciplines include:

- Business Process Framework (eTOM) is a process framework for telecommunications service providers.

- COBIT (Control Objectives for Information and Related Technologies) is an IT Governance framework that specifies control objectives, metrics and maturity models. Recent versions have aligned the naming of select control objectives to established ITSM process names.

- FitSM is a standard for lightweight service management. It contains several parts, including e.g. auditable requirements and document templates, which are published under Creative Common licenses. Its basic process framework is in large parts aligned to that of ISO/IEC 20000.

- ISO/IEC 20000 is an international standard for managing and delivering IT services. Its process model bears many similarities to that of ITIL version 2, since BS 15000 (precursor of ISO/IEC 20000) and ITIL were mutually aligned up to version 2 of ITIL. ISO/IEC 20000 defines minimum requirements for an effective "service management system" (SMS). Conformance of the SMS to ISO/IEC can be audited and organizations can achieve an ISO/IEC 20000 certification of their SMS for a defined scope.

- MOF (Microsoft Operations Framework) includes, in addition to a general framework of service management functions, guidance on managing services based on Microsoft technologies.

Tools

Execution of ITSM processes in an organization, especially those processes that are more workflow-driven ones, can benefit significantly from being supported with specialized software tools.

ITSM tools are often marketed as ITSM suites, which support a whole set of ITSM processes. At their core is usually a workflow management system for handling incidents, service requests, problems and changes. They usually also include a tool for a configuration management database. The ability of these suites to enable easy linking between incident, service request, problem and change records with each other and with records of configuration items from the CMDB, can be a great advantage.

ITSM tools are also commonly referred to as ITIL tools. More than 100 tools are self-proclaimed ITSM or ITIL tools. Software vendors such as Axios Systems, OTRS and Marval (software), whose ITSM tools fulfill defined functional requirements to support a set of ITIL processes, can obtain official approval, allowing them to use Axelos trademarks and an "ITIL process compliant" logo, under Axelos' ITIL Software Endorsement scheme.

Service Desk

A Service Desk is a primary IT function within the discipline of IT service management (ITSM) as defined by the Information Technology Infrastructure Library (ITIL). It is intended to provide a Single Point of Contact ("SPOC") to meet the communication needs of both users and IT staff, and also to satisfy both Customer and IT Provider objectives. "User" refers to the actual user of the service, while "Customer" refers to the entity that is paying for service.

The ITIL approach considers the service desk to be the central point of contact between service providers and users/customers on a day-to-day basis. It is also a focal point for reporting *incidents* (disruptions or potential disruptions in service availability or quality) and for users making *service requests* (routine requests for services).

ITIL regards a call centre, contact centre or a help desk as limited kinds of service desk which provide only a portion of what a service desk can offer. A service desk has a more broad and user-centered approach which is designed to provide the user with an informed single point of contact for all IT requirements. A service desk seeks to facilitate the integration of business processes into the service management infrastructure. In addition to actively monitoring and owning Incidents and user questions, and providing the communications channel for other service management disciplines with the user community, a service desk also provides an interface for other activities such as customer change requests, third parties (e.g. maintenance contracts), and software licensing.

IT RISK MANAGEMENT

IT risk management is the application of risk management methods to information technology in order to manage IT risk, i.e.:

> The business risk associated with the use, ownership, operation, involvement, influence and adoption of IT within an enterprise or organization.

IT risk management can be considered a component of a wider enterprise risk management system.

The establishment, maintenance and continuous update of an Information Security Management System (ISMS) provide a strong indication that a company is using a systematic approach for the identification, assessment and management of information security risks.

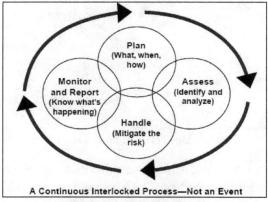

Risk Management Elements.

Different methodologies have been proposed to manage IT risks, each of them divided into processes and steps.

According to the Risk IT framework, this encompasses not only the negative impact of operations and service delivery which can bring destruction or reduction of the value of the organization, but also the benefit enabling risk associated to missing opportunities to use technology to enable or enhance business or the IT project management for aspects like overspending or late delivery with adverse business impact.

Because risk is strictly tied to uncertainty, decision theory should be applied to manage risk as a science, i.e. rationally making choices under uncertainty.

Generally speaking, risk is the product of likelihood times impact (Risk = Likelihood * Impact).

The measure of an IT risk can be determined as a product of threat, vulnerability and asset values:

> Risk = Threat * Vulnerability * Asset

A more current Risk management framework for IT Risk would be the TIK framework:

> Risk = ((Vulnerability * Threat)/Counter Measure) * Asset Value at Risk

The *process* of risk management is an ongoing iterative process. It must be repeated indefinitely. The business environment is constantly changing and new threats and vulnerabilities emerge every day. The choice of countermeasures (controls) used to manage risks must strike a balance between productivity, cost, effectiveness of the countermeasure, and the value of the informational asset being protected.

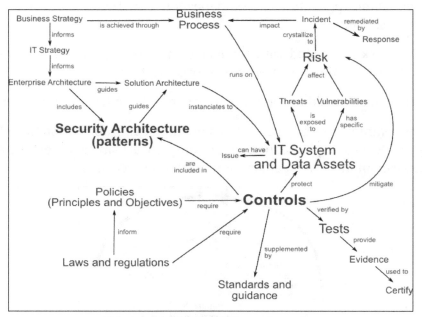

Relationships between IT security entity.

The Certified Information Systems Auditor Review Manual 2006 produced by ISACA, an international professional association focused on IT Governance, provides the following definition of risk management: "Risk management is the process of identifying vulnerabilities and threats to the information resources used by an organization in achieving business objectives, and deciding what countermeasures, if any, to take in reducing risk to an acceptable level, based on the value of the information resource to the organization."

Risk management is the process that allows IT managers to balance the operational and economic costs of protective measures and achieve gains in mission capability by protecting the IT systems and data that support their organizations' missions. This process is not unique to the IT environment; indeed it pervades decision-making in all areas of our daily lives.

The head of an organizational unit must ensure that the organization has the capabilities needed to accomplish its mission. These mission owners must determine the security capabilities that their IT systems must have to provide the desired level of mission support in the face of real world threats. Most organizations have tight budgets for IT security; therefore, IT security spending must be reviewed as thoroughly as other management decisions. A well-structured risk management methodology, when used effectively, can help management identify appropriate controls for providing the mission-essential security capabilities.

Risk management in the IT world is quite a complex, multi faced activity, with a lot of relations with other complex activities. The picture to the right shows the relationships between different related terms.

The American National Information Assurance Training and Education Center defines risk management in the IT field as:

- The total process to identify, control, and minimize the impact of uncertain events. The objective of the risk management program is to reduce risk and obtain and maintain DAA approval. The process facilitates the management of security risks by each level of management throughout the system life cycle. The approval process consists of three elements: risk analysis, certification, and approval.

- An element of managerial science concerned with the identification, measurement, control, and minimization of uncertain events. An effective risk management program encompasses the following four phases:

  ○ A Risk assessment, as derived from an evaluation of threats and vulnerabilities.

  ○ Management decision.

  ○ Control implementation.

  ○ Effectiveness review.

- The total process of identifying, measuring, and minimizing uncertain events affecting AIS resources. It includes risk analysis, cost benefit analysis, safeguard selection, security test and evaluation, safeguard implementation, and systems review.

- The total process of identifying, controlling, and eliminating or minimizing uncertain events that may affect system resources. It includes risk analysis, cost benefit analysis, selection, implementation and test, security evaluation of safeguards, and overall security review.

Risk Management as Part of Enterprise Risk Management

Some organizations have, and many others should have, a comprehensive Enterprise risk management (ERM) in place. The four objective categories addressed, according to Committee of Sponsoring Organizations of the Treadway Commission (COSO) are:

- Strategy: High-level goals, aligned with and supporting the organization's mission.

- Operations: Effective and efficient use of resources.

- Financial Reporting: Reliability of operational and financial reporting.

- Compliance: Compliance with applicable laws and regulations.

According to the Risk IT framework by ISACA, IT risk is transversal to all four categories. The IT risk should be managed in the framework of Enterprise risk management: Risk appetite and Risk sensitivity of the whole enterprise should guide the IT risk management process. ERM should provide the context and business objectives to IT risk management.

Risk Management Methodology

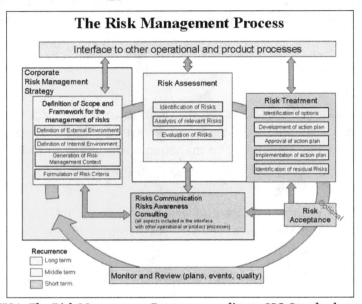

ENISA: The Risk Management Process, according to ISO Standard 13335.

Whilst a methodology does not describe specific methods ; nevertheless it does specify several processes (constitute a generic framework) that need to be followed. These processes may be broken down in sub-processes, they may be combined, or their sequence may change. A risk management exercise must carry out these processes in one form or another, The following table compares the processes foreseen by three leading standards. The ISACA Risk IT framework is more recent.

The term methodology means an organized set of principles and rules that drive action in a particular field of knowledge.

The overall comparison is illustrated in the following table.

Risk management constituent processes			
ISO/IEC 27005:2008	BS 7799-3:2006	NIST SP 800-39	Risk IT
Context establishment	Organizational context	Frame	RG and RE Domains more precisely • RG1.2 Propose IT risk tolerance, • RG2.1 Establish and maintain accountability for IT risk management, • RG2.3 Adapt IT risk practices to enterprise risk practices, • RG2.4 Provide adequate resources for IT risk management, • RE2.1 Define IT risk analysis scope.

Risk assessment	Risk assessment	Assess	RE2 process includes: • RE2.1 Define IT risk analysis scope. • RE2.2 Estimate IT risk. • RE2.3 Identify risk response options. • RE2.4 Perform a peer review of IT risk analysis. In general, the elements as described in the ISO 27005 process are all included in Risk IT; however, some are structured and named differently.
Risk treatment	Risk treatment and management decision making.	Respond	• RE 2.3 Identify risk response options. • RR2.3 Respond to discovered risk exposure and opportunity.
Risk acceptance			RG3.4 Accept IT risk
Risk communication	Ongoing risk management activities.		• RG1.5 Promote IT risk-aware culture. • RG1.6 Encourage effective communication of IT risk. • RE3.6 Develop IT risk indicators.
Risk monitoring and review		Monitor	• RG2 Integrate with ERM. • RE2.4 Perform a peer review of IT risk analysis. • RG2.5 Provide independent assurance over IT risk management.

Due to the probabilistic nature and the need of cost benefit analysis, IT risks are managed following a process that according to NIST SP 800-30 can be divided in the following steps:

• Risk assessment.

• Risk mitigation.

• Evaluation and assessment.

Effective risk management must be totally integrated into the Systems Development Life Cycle.

Information risk analysis conducted on applications, computer installations, networks and systems under development should be undertaken using structured methodologies.

Context Establishment

This step is the first step in ISO ISO/IEC 27005 framework. Most of the elementary activities are foreseen as the first sub process of Risk assessment according to NIST SP 800-30. This step implies the acquisition of all relevant information about the organization and the determination of the basic criteria, purpose, scope and boundaries of risk management activities and the organization in charge of risk management activities. The purpose is usually the compliance with legal requirements and provide evidence of due diligence supporting an ISMS that can be certified. The scope can be an incident reporting plan, a business continuity plan.

Another area of application can be the certification of a product.

Criteria include the risk evaluation, risk acceptance and impact evaluation criteria. These are conditioned by:

• Legal and regulatory requirements.

- The strategic value for the business of information processes.

- Stakeholder expectations.

- Negative consequences for the reputation of the organization.

Establishing the scope and boundaries, the organization should be studied: its mission, its values, its structure; its strategy, its locations and cultural environment. The constraints (budgetary, cultural, political, technical) of the organization are to be collected and documented as guide for next steps.

Organization for Security Management

The set up of the organization in charge of risk management is foreseen as partially fulfilling the requirement to provide the resources needed to establish, implement, operate, monitor, review, maintain and improve an ISMS. The main roles inside this organization are:

- Senior Management.

- Chief information officer (CIO).

- System and Information owners.

- The business and functional managers.

- The Information System Security Officer (ISSO) or Chief information security officer (CISO).

- IT Security Practitioners.

- Security Awareness Trainers.

Risk Assessment

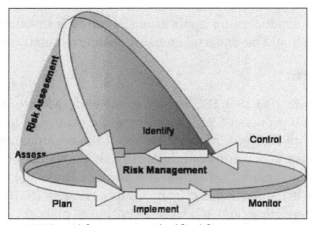

ENISA: Risk assessment inside risk management.

Risk Management is a recurrent activity that deals with the analysis, planning, implementation, control, and monitoring of implemented measurements and the enforced security policy. On the contrary, Risk Assessment is executed at discrete time points (e.g. once a year, on demand, etc.) and – until the performance of the next assessment – provides a temporary view of assessed risks and while parameterizing the entire Risk Management process. This view of the relationship of Risk Management to Risk Assessment is depicted in figure as adopted from OCTAVE.

Risk assessment is often conducted in more than one iteration, the first being a high-level assessment to identify high risks, while the other iterations detailed the analysis of the major risks and other risks.

According to National Information Assurance Training and Education Center risk assessment in the IT field is:

- A study of the vulnerabilities, threats, likelihood, loss or impact, and theoretical effectiveness of security measures. Managers use the results of a risk assessment to develop security requirements and specifications.

- The process of evaluating threats and vulnerabilities, known and postulated, to determine expected loss and establish the degree of acceptability to system operations.

- An identification of a specific ADP facility's assets, the threats to these assets, and the ADP facility's vulnerability to those threats.

- An analysis of system assets and vulnerabilities to establish an expected loss from certain events based on estimated probabilities of the occurrence of those events. The purpose of a risk assessment is to determine if countermeasures are adequate to reduce the probability of loss or the impact of loss to an acceptable level.

- A management tool which provides a systematic approach for determining the relative value and sensitivity of computer installation assets, assessing vulnerabilities, assessing loss expectancy or perceived risk exposure levels, assessing existing protection features and additional protection alternatives or acceptance of risks and documenting management decisions. Decisions for implementing additional protection features are normally based on the existence of a reasonable ratio between cost/benefit of the safeguard and sensitivity/value of the assets to be protected. Risk assessments may vary from an informal review of a small scale microcomputer installation to a more formal and fully documented analysis (i. e., risk analysis) of a large scale computer installation. Risk assessment methodologies may vary from qualitative or quantitative approaches to any combination of these two approaches.

ISO 27005 Framework

Risk assessment receives as input the output of the previous step Context establishment; the output is the list of assessed risks prioritized according to risk evaluation criteria. The process can be divided into the following steps:

- Risk analysis, further divided in:
  - Risk identification,
  - Risk estimation,
  - Risk evaluation.

The following table compares these ISO 27005 processes with Risk IT framework processes:

Risk assessment constituent processes	
ISO 27005	Risk IT
Risk analysis	• RE2 Analyse risk comprises more than what is described by the ISO 27005 process step. RE2 has as its objective developing useful information to support risk decisions that take into account the business relevance of risk factors. • RE1 Collect data serves as input to the analysis of risk (e.g., identifying risk factors, collecting data on the external environment).
Risk identification	This process is included in RE2.2 Estimate IT risk. The identification of risk comprises the following elements: • Risk scenarios • Risk factors
Risk estimation	RE2.2 Estimate IT risk
Risk evaluation	RE2.2 Estimate IT risk

The ISO/IEC 27002:2005 Code of practice for information security management recommends the following be examined during a risk assessment:

- Security policy,
- Organization of information security,
- Asset management,
- Human resources security,
- Physical and environmental security,
- Communications and operations management,
- Access control,
- Information systems acquisition, development and maintenance,
- Information security incident management,
- Business continuity management,
- Regulatory compliance.

Risk Identification

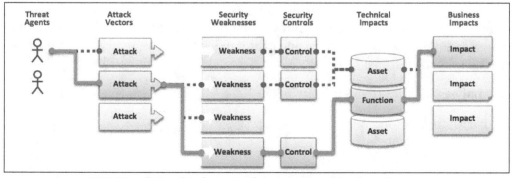

OWASP: relationship between threat agent and business impact.

Risk identification states what could cause a potential loss; the following are to be identified:

- Assets, primary (i.e. Business processes and related information) and supporting (i.e. hardware, software, personnel, site, organization structure),

- Threats,

- Existing and planned security measures,

- Vulnerabilities,

- Consequence,

- Related business processes.

The output of sub process is made up of:

- List of asset and related business processes to be risk managed with associated list of threats, existing and planned security measures.

- List of vulnerabilities unrelated to any identified threats.

- List of incident scenarios with their consequences.

Risk Estimation

There are two methods of risk assessment in information security field, quantitative and qualitative.

Purely quantitative risk assessment is a mathematical calculation based on security metrics on the asset (system or application). For each risk scenario, taking into consideration the different risk factors a Single loss expectancy (SLE) is determined. Then, considering the probability of occurrence on a given period basis, for example the annual rate of occurrence (ARO), the Annualized Loss Expectancy is determined as the product of ARO and SLE. It is important to point out that the values of assets to be considered are those of all involved assets, not only the value of the directly affected resource.

For example, if you consider the risk scenario of a Laptop theft threat, you should consider the value of the data (a related asset) contained in the computer and the reputation and liability of the company (other assets) deriving from the loss of availability and confidentiality of the data that could be involved. It is easy to understand that intangible assets (data, reputation, liability) can be worth much more than physical resources at risk (the laptop hardware in the example). Intangible asset value can be huge, but is not easy to evaluate: this can be a consideration against a pure quantitative approach.

Qualitative risk assessment (three to five steps evaluation, from Very High to Low) is performed when the organization requires a risk assessment be performed in a relatively short time or to meet a small budget, a significant quantity of relevant data is not available, or the persons performing the assessment don't have the sophisticated mathematical, financial, and risk assessment expertise required. Qualitative risk assessment can be performed in a shorter period of time and with less data. Qualitative risk assessments are typically performed through interviews of a sample of personnel from all relevant groups within an organization charged with the security of the asset being assessed. Qualitative risk assessments are descriptive versus measurable. Usually a qualitative classification is done followed by a quantitative evaluation of the highest risks to be compared to the costs of security measures.

Risk estimation has as input the output of risk analysis and can be split in the following steps:

- Assessment of the consequences through the valuation of assets.

- Assessment of the likelihood of the incident (through threat and vulnerability valuation).

- Assign values to the likelihood and consequence of the risks.

The output is the list of risks with value levels assigned. It can be documented in a risk register.

Risks arising from security threats and adversary attacks may be particularly difficult to estimate. This difficulty is made worse because, at least for any IT system connected to the Internet, any adversary with intent and capability may attack because physical closeness or access is not necessary. Some initial models have been proposed for this problem.

During risk estimation there are generally three values of a given asset, one for the loss of one of the CIA properties: Confidentiality, Integrity, Availability.

Risk Evaluation

The risk evaluation process receives as input the output of risk analysis process. It compares each risk level against the risk acceptance criteria and prioritise the risk list with risk treatment indications.

NIST SP 800 30 Framework

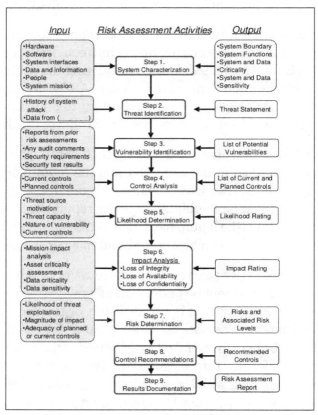

Risk assessment according NIST SP 800-30.

To determine the likelihood of a future adverse event, threats to an IT system must be in conjunction with the potential vulnerabilities and the controls in place for the IT system. Impact refers to the magnitude of harm that could be caused by a threat's exercise of vulnerability. The level of impact is governed by the potential mission impacts and produces a relative value for the IT assets and resources affected (e.g., the criticality sensitivity of the IT system components and data). The risk assessment methodology encompasses nine primary steps:

- Step 1: System Characterization.

- Step 2: Threat Identification.

- Step 3: Vulnerability Identification.

- Step 4: Control Analysis.

- Step 5: Likelihood Determination.

- Step 6: Impact Analysis.

- Step 7: Risk Determination.

- Step 8: Control Recommendations.

- Step 9: Results Documentation.

Risk Mitigation

Risk mitigation, the second process according to SP 800-30, the third according to ISO 27005 of risk management, involves prioritizing, evaluating, and implementing the appropriate risk-reducing controls recommended from the risk assessment process. Because the elimination of all risk is usually impractical or close to impossible, it is the responsibility of senior management and functional and business managers to use the least-cost approach and implement the most appropriate controls to decrease mission risk to an acceptable level, with minimal adverse impact on the organization's resources and mission.

ISO 27005 Framework

The risk treatment process aim at selecting security measures to:

- Reduce

- Retain

- Avoid

- Transfer

Risk and produce a risk treatment plan, that is the output of the process with the residual risks subject to the acceptance of management.

There are some list to select appropriate security measures, but is up to the single organization to choose the most appropriate one according to its business strategy, constraints of the environment and circumstances. The choice should be rational and documented. The importance of accepting a risk that is too costly to reduce is very high and led to the fact that risk acceptance is considered a separate process.

Risk transfer apply were the risk has a very high impact but is not easy to reduce significantly the likelihood by means of security controls. The insurance premium should be compared against the mitigation costs, eventually evaluating some mixed strategy to partially treat the risk. Another option is to outsource the risk to somebody more efficient to manage the risk.

Risk avoidance describe any action where ways of conducting business are changed to avoid any risk occurrence. For example, the choice of not storing sensitive information about customers can be an avoidance for the risk that customer data can be stolen.

The residual risks, i.e. the risk remaining after risk treatment decision have been taken, should be estimated to ensure that sufficient protection is achieved. If the residual risk is unacceptable, the risk treatment process should be iterated.

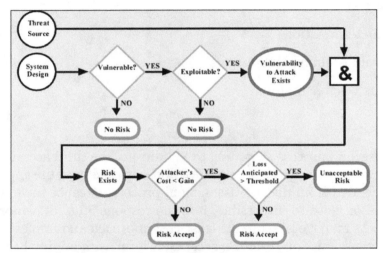

Risk mitigation action point according to NIST SP 800-30.

Risk mitigation is a systematic methodology used by senior management to reduce mission risk. Risk mitigation can be achieved through any of the following risk mitigation options:

- Risk Assumption: To accept the potential risk and continue operating the IT system or to implement controls to lower the risk to an acceptable level.

- Risk Avoidance: To avoid the risk by eliminating the risk cause and/or consequence (e.g., forgo certain functions of the system or shut down the system when risks are identified).

- Risk Limitation: To limit the risk by implementing controls that minimize the adverse impact of a threat's exercising a vulnerability (e.g., use of supporting, preventive, detective controls).

- Risk Planning: To manage risk by developing a risk mitigation plan that prioritizes, implements, and maintains controls.

- Research and Acknowledgement: To lower the risk of loss by acknowledging the vulnerability or flaw and researching controls to correct the vulnerability.

- Risk Transference: To transfer the risk by using other options to compensate for the loss, such as purchasing insurance.

Address the greatest risks and strive for sufficient risk mitigation at the lowest cost, with minimal impact on other mission capabilities.

Risk Communication

Risk communication is a horizontal process that interacts bidirectionally with all other processes of risk management. Its purpose is to establish a common understanding of all aspect of risk among all the organization's stakeholder. Establishing a common understanding is important, since it influences decisions to be taken. The Risk Reduction Overview method is specifically designed for this process. It presents a comprehensible overview of the coherence of risks, measures and residual risks to achieve this common understanding.

Risk Monitoring and Review

Risk management is an ongoing, never ending process. Within this process implemented security measures are regularly monitored and reviewed to ensure that they work as planned and that changes in the environment rendered them ineffective. Business requirements, vulnerabilities and threats can change over the time.

Regular audits should be scheduled and should be conducted by an independent party, i.e. somebody not under the control of whom is responsible for the implementations or daily management of ISMS.

IT Evaluation and Assessment

Security controls should be validated. Technical controls are possible complex systems that are to tested and verified. The hardest part to validate is people knowledge of procedural controls and the effectiveness of the real application in daily business of the security procedures.

Vulnerability assessment, both internal and external, and Penetration test are instruments for verifying the status of security controls.

Information technology security audit is an organizational and procedural control with the aim of evaluating security. The IT systems of most organization are evolving quite rapidly. Risk management should cope with these changes through change authorization after risk re-evaluation of the affected systems and processes and periodically review the risks and mitigation actions.

Monitoring system events according to a security monitoring strategy, an incident response plan and security validation and metrics are fundamental activities to assure that an optimal level of security is obtained. It is important to monitor the new vulnerabilities, apply procedural and technical security controls like regularly updating software, and evaluate other kinds of controls to deal with zero-day attacks.

The attitude of involved people to benchmark against best practice and follow the seminars of professional associations in the sector are factors to assure the state of art of an organization IT risk management practice.

Integrating Risk Management into System Development Life Cycle

Effective risk management must be totally integrated into the SDLC. An IT system's SDLC has five phases: Initiation, development or acquisition, implementation, operation or maintenance, and disposal. The risk management methodology is the same regardless of the SDLC phase for which the assessment is being conducted. Risk management is an iterative process that can be performed during each major phase of the SDLC.

Table: Integration of Risk Management into the SDLC.

SDLC Phases	Phase Characteristics	Support from Risk Management Activities.
Phase 1: Initiation	The need for an IT system is expressed and the purpose and scope of the IT system is documented.	Identified risks are used to support the development of the system requirements, including security requirements, and a security concept of operations (strategy).
Phase 2: Development or Acquisition	The IT system is designed, purchased, programmed, developed, or otherwise constructed.	The risks identified during this phase can be used to support the security analyses of the IT system that may lead to architecture and design tradeoffs during system development.
Phase 3: Implementation	The system security features should be configured, enabled, tested, and verified.	The risk management process supports the assessment of the system implementation against its requirements and within its modeled operational environment. Decisions regarding risks identified must be made prior to system operation.
Phase 4: Operation or Maintenance	The system performs its functions. Typically the system is being modified on an ongoing basis through the addition of hardware and software and by changes to organizational processes, policies, and procedures.	Risk management activities are performed for periodic system reauthorization (or reaccreditation) or whenever major changes are made to an IT system in its operational, production environment (e.g., new system interfaces).
Phase 5: Disposal	This phase may involve the disposition of information, hardware, and software. Activities may include moving, archiving, discarding, or destroying information and sanitizing the hardware and software	Risk management activities are performed for system components that will be disposed of or replaced to ensure that the hardware and software are properly disposed of, that residual data is appropriately handled, and that system migration is conducted in a secure and systematic manner

Early integration of security in the SDLC enables agencies to maximize return on investment in their security programs, through:

- Early identification and mitigation of security vulnerabilities and misconfigurations, resulting in lower cost of security control implementation and vulnerability mitigation;

- Awareness of potential engineering challenges caused by mandatory security controls;

- Identification of shared security services and reuse of security strategies and tools to reduce development cost and schedule while improving security posture through proven methods and techniques;

- Facilitation of informed executive decision making through comprehensive risk management in a timely manner.

This guide focuses on the information security components of the SDLC. First, descriptions of the key security roles and responsibilities that are needed in most information system developments are provided. Second, sufficient information about the SDLC is provided to allow a person who is unfamiliar with the SDLC process to understand the relationship between information security and the SDLC. The document integrates the security steps into the linear, sequential (a.k.a. waterfall) SDLC. The five-step SDLC cited in the document is an example of one method of development and is not intended to mandate this methodology. Lastly, SP 800-64 provides insight into IT projects and initiatives that are not as clearly defined as SDLC-based developments, such as service-oriented architectures, cross-organization projects, and IT facility developments.

Security can be incorporated into information systems acquisition, development and maintenance by implementing effective security practices in the following areas:

- Security requirements for information systems.

- Correct processing in applications.

- Cryptographic controls.

- Security of system files.

- Security in development and support processes.

- Technical vulnerability management.

Information systems security begins with incorporating security into the requirements process for any new application or system enhancement. Security should be designed into the system from the beginning. Security requirements are presented to the vendor during the requirements phase of a product purchase. Formal testing should be done to determine whether the product meets the required security specifications prior to purchasing the product.

Correct processing in applications is essential in order to prevent errors and to mitigate loss, unauthorized modification or misuse of information. Effective coding techniques include validating input and output data, protecting message integrity using encryption, checking for processing errors, and creating activity logs.

Applied properly, cryptographic controls provide effective mechanisms for protecting the confidentiality, authenticity and integrity of information. An institution should develop policies on the use of encryption, including proper key management. Disk Encryption is one way to protect data at rest. Data in transit can be protected from alteration and unauthorized viewing using SSL certificates issued through a Certificate Authority that has implemented a Public Key Infrastructure.

System files used by applications must be protected in order to ensure the integrity and stability of the application. Using source code repositories with version control, extensive testing, production back-off plans, and appropriate access to program code are some effective measures that can be used to protect an application's files.

Security in development and support processes is an essential part of a comprehensive quality assurance and production control process, and would usually involve training and continuous oversight by the most experienced staff.

Applications need to be monitored and patched for technical vulnerabilities. Procedures for applying patches should include evaluating the patches to determine their appropriateness, and whether or not they can be successfully removed in case of a negative impact.

Risk Managements Methods

It is quite hard to list most of the methods that at least partially support the IT risk management process. Efforts in this direction were done by:

- NIST Description of Automated Risk Management Packages That NIST/NCSC Risk Management Research Laboratory Has Examined, updated 1991

- ENISA in 2006; a list of methods and tools is available on line with a comparison engine. Among them the most widely used are:

  - CRAMM Developed by British government is compliant to ISO/IEC 17799, Gramm–Leach–Bliley Act (GLBA) and Health Insurance Portability and Accountability Act (HIPAA).

  - EBIOS developed by the French government it is compliant with major security standards: ISO/IEC 27001, ISO/IEC 13335, ISO/IEC 15408, ISO/IEC 17799 and ISO/IEC 21287.

  - Standard of Good Practice developed by Information Security Forum (ISF).

  - Mehari developed by Clusif Club de la Sécurité de l'Information Français.

  - TIK IT Risk Framework developed by IT Risk Institute.

  - Octave developed by Carnegie Mellon University, SEI (Software Engineering Institute) The Operationally Critical Threat, Asset, and Vulnerability EvaluationSM (OCTAVE) approach defines a risk-based strategic assessment and planning technique for security.

  - IT-Grundschutz (IT Baseline Protection Manual) developed by Federal Office for Information Security (BSI) (Germany); IT-Grundschutz provides a method for an organization to establish an Information Security Management System (ISMS). It comprises both generic IT security recommendations for establishing an applicable IT security process and detailed technical recommendations to achieve the necessary IT security level for a specific domain.

Enisa report classified the different methods regarding completeness, free availability, tool support; the result is that:

- EBIOS, ISF methods, IT-Grundschutz cover deeply all the aspects (Risk Identification, Risk analysis, Risk evaluation, Risk assessment, Risk treatment, Risk acceptance, Risk communication).

- EBIOS and IT-Grundschutz are the only ones freely available.

- only EBIOS has an open source tool to support it.

The Factor Analysis of Information Risk (FAIR) main document, "An Introduction to Factor Analysis of Information Risk (FAIR)", Risk Management Insight LLC, November 2006; outline that most of the methods above lack of rigorous definition of risk and its factors. FAIR is not another methodology to deal with risk management, but it complements existing methodologies.

FAIR has had a good acceptance, mainly by The Open Group and ISACA.

ISACA developed a methodology, called Risk IT, to address various kind of IT related risks, chiefly security related risks. It is integrated with COBIT, a general framework to manage IT. Risk IT has a broader concept of IT risk than other methodologies, it encompasses not just only the negative impact of operations and service delivery which can bring destruction or reduction of the value of the organization, but also the benefit\value enabling risk associated to missing opportunities to use technology to enable or enhance business or the IT project management for aspects like overspending or late delivery with adverse business impact.

The "Build Security In" initiative of Homeland Security Department of United States, cites FAIR. The initiative Build Security In is a collaborative effort that provides practices, tools, guidelines, rules, principles, and other resources that software developers, architects, and security practitioners can use to build security into software in every phase of its development. So it chiefly address Secure coding.

In 2016, Threat Sketch launched an abbreviated cyber security risk assessment specifically for small organizations. The methodology uses real options to forecast and prioritize a fixed list of high-level threats.

INFORMATION PROCESSING

Information Processing is the acquisition, recording, organization, retrieval, display, and dissemination of information. In recent years, the term has often been applied to computer-based operations specifically.

In popular usage, the term information refers to facts and opinions provided and received during the course of daily life: one obtains information directly from other living beings, from mass media, from electronic data banks, and from all sorts of observable phenomena in the surrounding environment. A person using such facts and opinions generates more information, some of which is communicated to others during discourse, by instructions, in letters and documents, and through other media. Information organized according to some logical relationships is referred to as a body of knowledge, to be acquired by systematic exposure or study. Application of knowledge (or skills) yields expertise, and additional analytic or experiential insights are said to constitute instances of wisdom. Use of the term information is not restricted exclusively to its communication via natural language. Information is also registered and communicated through art and by facial expressions and gestures or by such other physical responses as shivering. Moreover, every living entity is endowed with information in the form of a genetic code. These information phenomena permeate the physical and mental world, and their variety is such that it has defied so far all attempts at a unified definition of information.

Interest in information phenomena increased dramatically in the 20th century, and today they are the objects of study in a number of disciplines, including philosophy, physics, biology, linguistics, information and computer science, electronic and communications engineering, management science, and the social sciences. On the commercial side, the information service industry has become one of the newer industries worldwide. Almost all other industries—manufacturing and service— are increasingly concerned with information and its handling. The different, though often overlapping, viewpoints and phenomena of these fields lead to different (and sometimes conflicting) concepts and "definitions" of information.

Interest in how information is communicated and how its carriers convey meaning has occupied, since the time of pre-Socratic philosophers, the field of inquiry called semiotics, the study of signs and sign phenomena. Signs are the irreducible elements of communication and the carriers of meaning. The American philosopher, mathematician, and physicist Charles S. Peirce is credited with having pointed out the three dimensions of signs, which are concerned with, respectively, the body or medium of the sign, the object that the sign designates, and the interpretant or interpretation of the sign. Peirce recognized that the fundamental relations of information are essentially triadic; in contrast, all relations of the physical sciences are reducible to dyadic (binary) relations. Another American philosopher, Charles W. Morris, designated these three sign dimensions syntactic, semantic, and pragmatic, the names by which they are known today.

Information processes are executed by information processors. For a given information processor, whether physical or biological, a token is an object, devoid of meaning, that the processor recognizes as being totally different from other tokens. A group of such unique tokens recognized by a processor constitutes its basic "alphabet"; for example, the dot, dash, and space constitute the basic token alphabet of a Morse-code processor. Objects that carry meaning are represented by patterns of tokens called symbols. The latter combine to form symbolic expressions that constitute inputs to or outputs from information processes and are stored in the processor memory.

Information processors are components of an information system, which is a class of constructs. An abstract model of an information system features four basic elements: processor, memory, receptor, and effector. The processor has several functions: (1) to carry out elementary information processes on symbolic expressions, (2) to store temporarily in the processor's short-term memory the input and output expressions on which these processes operate and that they generate, (3) to schedule execution of these processes, and (4) to change this sequence of operations in accordance with the contents of the short-term memory. The memory stores symbolic expressions, including those that represent composite information processes, called programs. The two other components, the receptor and the effector, are input and output mechanisms whose functions are, respectively, to receive symbolic expressions or stimuli from the external environment for manipulation by the processor and to emit the processed structures back to the environment.

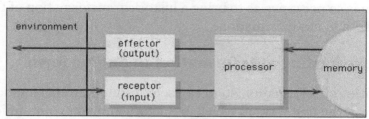

Structure of an information system.

The power of this abstract model of an information-processing system is provided by the ability of its component processors to carry out a small number of elementary information processes: reading; comparing; creating, modifying, and naming; copying; storing; and writing. The model, which is representative of a broad variety of such systems, has been found useful to explicate man-made information systems implemented on sequential information processors.

Because it has been recognized that in nature information processes are not strictly sequential, increasing attention has been focused since 1980 on the study of the human brain as an information processor of the parallel type. The cognitive sciences, the interdisciplinary field that focuses on the study of the human mind, have contributed to the development of neurocomputers, a new class of parallel, distributed-information processors that mimic the functioning of the human brain, including its capabilities for self-organization and learning. So-called neural networks, which are mathematical models inspired by the neural circuit network of the human brain, are increasingly finding applications in areas such as pattern recognition, control of industrial processes, and finance, as well as in many research disciplines.

Elements of Information Processing

Humans receive information with their senses: sounds through hearing; images and text through sight; shape, temperature, and affection through touch; and odours through smell. To interpret the signals received from the senses, humans have developed and learned complex systems of languages consisting of "alphabets" of symbols and stimuli and the associated rules of usage. This has enabled them to recognize the objects they see, understand the messages they read or hear, and comprehend the signs received through the tactile and olfactory senses.

The carriers of information-conveying signs received by the senses are energy phenomena—audio waves, light waves, and chemical and electrochemical stimuli. In engineering parlance, humans are receptors of analog signals; and, by a somewhat loose convention, the messages conveyed via these carriers are called analog-form information, or simply analog information. Until the development of the digital computer, cognitive information was stored and processed only in analog form, basically through the technologies of printing, photography, and telephony.

Although humans are adept at processing information stored in their memories, analog information stored external to the mind is not processed easily. Modern information technology greatly facilitates the manipulation of externally stored information as a result of its representation as digital signals—i.e., as the presence or absence of energy (electricity, light, or magnetism). Information represented digitally in two-state, or binary, form is often referred to as digital information.

Modern information systems are characterized by extensive metamorphoses of analog and digital information. With respect to information storage and communication, the transition from analog to digital information is so pervasive as to bring a historic transformation of the manner in which humans create, access, and use information.

Acquisition and Recording of Information in Analog form

The principal categories of information sources useful in modern information systems are text, video, and voice. One of the first ways in which prehistoric humans communicated was by sound; sounds represented concepts such as pleasure, anger, and fear, as well as objects of the surrounding environment, including food and tools. Sounds assumed their meaning by convention—namely, by the use to which they were consistently put. Combining parts of sound allowed representation of more complex concepts and gradually led to the development of speech and eventually to spoken "natural" languages.

For information to be communicated broadly, it needs to be stored external to human memory; because accumulation of human experience, knowledge, and learning would be severely limited without such storage, the development of writing systems was made necessary.

Civilization can be traced to the time when humans began to associate abstract shapes with concepts and with the sounds of speech that represented them. Early recorded representations were those of visually perceived objects and events, as, for example, the animals and activities depicted in Paleolithic cave drawings. The evolution of writing systems proceeded through the early development of pictographic languages, in which a symbol would represent an entire concept. Such symbols would go through many metamorphoses of shape in which the resemblance between each symbol and the object it stood for gradually disappeared, but its semantic meaning would become more precise. As the conceptual world of humans became larger, the symbols, called ideographs, grew in number. Modern Chinese, a present-day result of this evolutionary direction of a pictographic writing system, has upwards of 50,000 ideographs.

At some point in the evolution of written languages, the method of representation shifted from the pictographic to the phonetic: speech sounds began to be represented by an alphabet of graphic symbols. Combinations of a relatively small set of such symbols could stand for more complex concepts as words, phrases, and sentences. The invention of the written phonetic alphabet is thought to have taken place during the 2nd millennium BC. The pragmatic advantages of alphabetic writing systems over the pictographic became apparent twice in the past millennium after the invention of the movable-type printing press in the 15th century and again with the development of information processing by electronic means since the mid-1940s.

From the time early humans learned to represent concepts symbolically, they used whatever materials were readily available in nature for recording. The Sumerian cuneiform, a wedge-shaped writing system, was impressed by a stylus into soft clay tablets, which were subsequently hardened by drying in the sun or the oven. The earliest Chinese writing, dating to the 2nd millennium BC, is preserved on animal bone and shell, while early writing in India was done on palm leaves and birch bark. Applications of technology yielded other materials for writing. The Chinese had recorded their pictographs on silk, using brushes made from animal hair, long before they invented paper. The Egyptians first wrote on cotton, but they began using papyrus sheets and rolls made from the fibrous lining of the papyrus plant during the 4th millennium BC. The reed brush and a palette of ink were the implements with which they wrote hieroglyphic script. Writing on parchment, a material that was superior to papyrus and was made from the prepared skins of animals, became commonplace about 200 BC, some 300 years after its first recorded use, and the quill pen replaced the reed brush. By the 4th century AD, parchment came to be the principal writing material in Europe.

Paper was invented in China at the beginning of the 2nd century AD, and for some 600 years its use was confined to East Asia. In AD 751 Arab and Chinese armies clashed at the Battle of Talas, near Samarkand; among the Chinese taken captive were some papermakers from whom the Arabs learned the techniques. From the 7th century on, paper became the dominant writing material of the Islamic world. Papermaking finally reached Spain and Sicily in the 12th century, and it took another three centuries before it was practiced in Germany.

With the invention of printing from movable type, typesetting became the standard method of creating copy. Typesetting was an entirely manual operation until the adoption of a typewriter-like keyboard in the 19th century. In fact, it was the typewriter that mechanized the process of recording original text. Although the typewriter was invented during the early 18th century in England, the first practical version, constructed by the American inventor Christopher Latham Sholes, did not appear until 1867. The mechanical typewriter finally found wide use after World War I. Today its electronic variant, the computer video terminal, is used pervasively to record original text.

Recording of original nontextual information was a manual process until the development of photography during the early decades of the 19th century; drawing and carving were the principal early means of recording graphics. Other techniques were developed alongside printing—for example, etching in stone and metal. The invention of film and the photographic process added a new dimension to information acquisition: for the first time, complex visual images of the real world could be captured accurately. Photography provided a method of storing information in less space and more accurately than was previously possible with narrative information.

During the 20th century, versatile electromagnetic media opened up new possibilities for capturing original analog information. Magnetic audio tape is used to capture speech and music, and magnetic videotape provides a low-cost medium for recording analog voice and video signals directly and simultaneously. Magnetic technology has other uses in the direct recording of analog information, including alphanumerics. Magnetic characters, bar codes, and special marks are printed on checks, labels, and forms for subsequent sensing by magnetic or optical readers and conversion to digital form. Banks, educational institutions, and the retail industry rely heavily on this technology. Nonetheless, paper and film continue to be the dominant media for direct storage of textual and visual information in analog form.

Acquisition and Recording of Information in Digital form

The versatility of modern information systems stems from their ability to represent information electronically as digital signals and to manipulate it automatically at exceedingly high speeds. Information is stored in binary devices, which are the basic components of digital technology. Because these devices exist only in one of two states, information is represented in them either as the absence or the presence of energy (electric pulse). The two states of binary devices are conveniently designated by the binary digits, or bits, zero (0) and one (1).

In this manner, alphabetic symbols of natural-language writing systems can be represented digitally as combinations of zeros (no pulse) and ones (pulse). Tables of equivalences of alphanumeric characters and strings of binary digits are called coding systems, the counterpart of writing systems. A combination of three binary digits can represent up to eight such characters; one comprising four digits, up to 16 characters and so on. The choice of a particular coding system depends on the size of the character set to be represented. The widely used systems are the American Standard Code for Information Interchange (ASCII), a seven- or eight-bit code representing the English alphabet, numerals, and certain special characters of the standard computer keyboard; and the corresponding eight-bit Extended Binary Coded Decimal Interchange Code (EBCDIC), used for computers produced by IBM (International Business Machines Corp.) and most compatible systems. The digital representation of a character by eight bits is called a byte.

The seven-bit ASCII code is capable of representing up to 128 alphanumeric and special characters—sufficient to accommodate the writing systems of many phonetic scripts, including Latin and Cyrillic. Some alphabetic scripts require more than seven bits; for example, the Arabic alphabet, also used in the Urdu and Persian languages, has 28 consonantal characters (as well as a number of vowels and diacritical marks), but each of these may have four shapes, depending on its position in the word.

For digital representation of nonalphabetic writing systems, even the eight-bit code accommodating 256 characters is inadequate. Some writing systems that use Chinese characters, for example, have more than 50,000 ideographs (the minimal standard font for the Hanzi system in Chinese and the kanji system in Japanese has about 7,000 ideographs). Digital representation of such scripts can be accomplished in three ways. One approach is to develop a phonetic character set; the Chinese Pinyin, the Korean Hangul, and the Japanese hiragana phonetic schemes all have alphabetic sets similar in number to the Latin alphabet. As the use of phonetic alphabets in Oriental cultures is not yet widespread, they may be converted to ideographic by means of a dictionary lookup. A second technique is to decompose ideographs into a small number of elementary signs called strokes, the sum of which constitutes a shape-oriented, nonphonetic alphabet. The third approach is to use more than eight bits to encode the large numbers of ideographs; for instance, two bytes can represent uniquely more than 65,000 ideographs. Because the eight-bit ASCII code is inadequate for a number of writing systems, either because they are nonalphabetic or because their phonetic scripts possess large numbers of diacritical marks, the computer industry in 1991 began formulating a new international coding standard based on 16 bits.

Recording Media

Punched cards and perforated paper tape were once widely used to store data in binary form. Today they have been supplanted by media based on electromagnetic and electro-optic technologies except in a few special applications.

Present-day storage media are of two types: random- and serial-, or sequential-, access. In random-access media (such as primary memory), the time required for accessing a given piece of data is independent of its location, while in serial-access media the access time depends on the data's location and the position of the read-write head. The typical serial-access medium is magnetic tape. The storage density of magnetic tape has increased considerably over the years, mainly by increases in the number of tracks packed across the width of the tape.

While magnetic tape remains a popular choice in applications requiring low-cost auxiliary storage and data exchange, new tape variants began entering the market of the 1990s. Video recording tape has been adapted for digital storage, and digital audio tape (DAT) surpasses all tape storage devices in offering the highest areal data densities. DAT technology uses a helical-scan recording method in which both the tape and the recording head move simultaneously, which allows extremely high recording densities. Early four-millimetre DAT cassettes had a capacity of up to eight billion bytes (eight gigabytes).

Another type of magnetic storage medium, the magnetic disk, provides rapid, random access to data. This device, developed in 1962, consists of either an aluminum or a plastic platen coated with a metallic material. Information is recorded on a disk by turning the charge of the read-write head on and off, which produces magnetic "dots" representing binary digits in circular tracks. A block of data on a given track can be accessed without having to pass over a large portion of its contents sequentially, as in the case of tape. Data-retrieval time is thus reduced dramatically. Hard disk drives built into personal computers and workstations have storage capacities of up to several gigabytes. Large computers using disk cartridges can provide virtually unlimited mass storage.

During the 1970s the floppy disk—a small, flexible disk—was introduced for use in personal computers and other microcomputer systems. Compared with the storage capacity of the conventional hard disk, that of such a "soft" diskette is low—under three million characters. This medium is used primarily for loading and backing up personal computers.

An entirely different kind of recording and storage medium, the optical disc, became available during the early 1980s. The optical disc makes use of laser technology: digital data are recorded by burning a series of microscopic holes, or pits, with a laser beam into thin metallic film on the surface of a $4^3/_4$-inch (12-centimetre) plastic disc. In this way, information from magnetic tape is encoded on a master disc; subsequently, the master is replicated by a process called stamping. In the read mode, low-intensity laser light is reflected off the disc surface and is "read" by light-sensitive diodes. The radiant energy received by the diodes varies according to the presence of the pits, and this input is digitized by the diode circuits. The digital signals are then converted to analog information on a video screen or in printout form.

Since the introduction of this technology, three main types of optical storage media have become available: (1) rewritable, (2) write-once read-many (WORM), and (3) compact disc read-only memory (CD-ROM). Rewritable discs are functionally equivalent to magnetic disks, although the former are slower. WORM discs are used as an archival storage medium to enter data once and retrieve it many times. CD-ROMs are the preferred medium for electronic distribution of digital libraries and software. To raise storage capacity, optical discs are arranged into "jukeboxes" holding as many as 10 million pages of text or more than one terabyte (one trillion bytes) of image data. The high storage capacities and random access of the magneto-optical, rewritable discs are particularly suited for storing multimedia information, in which text, image, and sound are combined.

Recording Techniques

Digitally stored information is commonly referred to as data, and its analog counterpart is called source data. Vast quantities of nondocument analog data are collected, digitized, and compressed automatically by means of appropriate instruments in fields such as astronomy, environmental monitoring, scientific experimentation and modeling, and national security. The capture of information generated by humankind, in the form of packages of symbols called documents, is accomplished by manual and, increasingly, automatic techniques. Data are entered manually by striking the keys of a keyboard, touching a computer screen, or writing by hand on a digital tablet or its variant, the so-called pen computer. Manual data entry, a slow and error-prone process, is facilitated to a degree by special computer programs that include editing software, with which to insert formatting commands, verify spelling, and make text changes, and document-formatting software, with which to arrange and rearrange text and graphics flexibly on the output page.

It is estimated that 5 percent of all documents in the United States exist in digitized form and that two-thirds of the paper documents cannot be digitized by keyboard transcription because they contain drawings or still images and because such transcription would be highly uneconomical. Such documents are digitized economically by a process called document imaging.

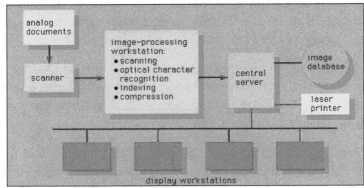

Document imaging.

Document imaging utilizes digital scanners to generate a digital representation of a document page. An image scanner divides the page into minute picture areas called pixels and produces an array of binary digits, each representing the brightness of a pixel. The resulting stream of bits is enhanced and compressed (to as little as 10 percent of the original volume) by a device called an image controller and is stored on a magnetic or optical medium. A large storage capacity is required, because it takes about 45,000 bytes to store a typical compressed text page of 2,500 characters and as much as 1,000,000 bytes to store a page containing an image. Aside from document imaging applications, digital scanning is used for transmission of documents via facsimile, in satellite photography, and in other applications.

An image scanner digitizes an entire document page for storage and display as an image and does not recognize characters and words of text. The stored material therefore cannot be linguistically manipulated by text processing and other software techniques. When such manipulation is desired, a software program performs the optical character recognition (OCR) function by converting each optically scanned character into an electric signal and comparing it with the internally stored representation of an alphabet of characters, so as to select from it the one that matches the scanned character most closely or to reject it as an unidentifiable token. The more sophisticated of present-day OCR programs distinguish shapes, sizes, and pitch of symbols—including handwriting—and learn from experience. A universal OCR machine is not available, however, for even a single alphabet.

Still photographs can be digitized by scanning or transferred from film to a compact digital disc holding more than 100 images. A recent development, the digital camera, makes it possible to bypass the film/paper step completely by capturing the image into the camera's random-access memory or a special diskette and then transferring it to a personal computer. Since both technologies produce a graphics file, in either case the image is editable by means of suitable software.

The digital recording of sound is important because speech is the most frequently used natural carrier of communicable information. Direct capture of sound into personal computers is accomplished by means of a digital signal processor (DSP) chip, a special-purpose device built into the computer to perform array-processing operations. Conversion of analog audio signals to digital recordings is a commonplace process that has been used for years by the telecommunications and entertainment industries. Although the resulting digital sound track can be edited, automatic speech recognition—analogous to the recognition of characters and words in text by means of optical character recognition—is still under development. When perfected, voice recognition is certain to have a tremendous impact on the way humans communicate with recorded information, with computers, and among themselves.

By the beginning of the 1990s, the technology to record (or convert), store in digital form, and edit all visually and aurally perceived signals—text, graphics, still images, animation, motion video, and sound—had thus become available and affordable. These capabilities opened a way for a new kind of multimedia document that employs print, video, and sound to generate more powerful and colourful messages, communicate them securely at electronic speeds, and allow them to be modified almost at will. The traditional business letter, newspaper, journal, and book will no longer be the same.

Inventory of Recorded Information

The development of recording media and techniques enabled society to begin building a store of human knowledge. The idea of collecting and organizing written records is thought to have originated in Sumer about 5,000 years ago; Egyptian writing was introduced soon after. Early collections of Sumerian and Egyptian writings, recorded in cuneiform on clay tablets and in hieroglyphic script on papyrus, contained information about legal and economic transactions. In these and other early document collections (e.g., those of China produced during the Shang dynasty in the 2nd millennium BC and Buddhist collections in India dating to the 5th century BC), it is difficult to separate the concepts of the archive and the library.

From the Middle East the concept of document collections penetrated the Greco-Roman world. Roman kings institutionalized the population and property census as early as the 6th century BC. The great Library of Alexandria, established in the 3rd century BC, is best known as a large collection of papyri containing inventories of property, taxes, and other payments by citizens to their rulers and to each other. It is, in short, the ancient equivalent of today's administrative information systems.

The scholarly splendour of the Islamic world from the 8th to the 13th century AD can in large part be attributed to the maintenance of public and private book libraries. The Bayt al-Ḥikmah ("House of Wisdom"), founded in AD 830 in Baghdad, contained a public library with a large collection of materials on a wide range of subjects, and the 10th-century library of Caliph al-Ḥakam in Cordova, Spain, boasted more than 400,000 books.

Primary and Secondary Literature

The late but rapid development of European libraries from the 16th century on followed the invention of printing from movable type, which spurred the growth of the printing and publishing industries. Since the beginning of the 17th century, literature has become the principal medium for disseminating knowledge. The phrase primary literature is used to designate original information in various printed formats: newspapers, monographs, conference proceedings, learned and trade journals, reports, patents, bulletins, and newsletters. The scholarly journal, the classic medium of scientific communication, first appeared in 1665. Three hundred years later the number of periodical titles published in the world was estimated at more than 60,000, reflecting not only growth in the number of practitioners of science and expansion of its body of knowledge through specialization but also a maturing of the system of rewards that encourages scientists to publish.

The sheer quantity of printed information has for some time prevented any individual from fully absorbing even a minuscule fraction of it. Such devices as tables of contents, summaries, and indexes of various types, which aid in identifying and locating relevant information in primary literature, have been in use since the 16th century and led to the development of what is termed secondary literature during the 19th century. The purpose of secondary literature is to "filter" the primary information sources, usually by subject area, and provide the indicators to this literature in the form of reviews, abstracts, and indexes. Over the past 100 years there has evolved a system of disciplinary, national, and international abstracting and indexing services that acts as a gateway to several attributes of primary literature: authors, subjects, publishers, dates (and languages) of publication, and citations. The professional activity associated with these access-facilitating tools is called documentation.

The quantity of printed materials also makes it impossible, as well as undesirable, for any institution to acquire and house more than a small portion of it. The husbanding of recorded information has become a matter of public policy, as many countries have established national libraries and archives to direct the orderly acquisition of analog-form documents and records. Since these institutions alone are not able to keep up with the output of such documents and records, new forms of cooperative planning and sharing recorded materials are evolving—namely, public and private, national and regional library networks and consortia.

Databases

The emergence of digital technology in the mid-20th century has affected humankind's inventory of recorded information dramatically. During the early 1960s computers were used to digitize text for the first time; the purpose was to reduce the cost and time required to publish two American abstracting journals, the Index Medicus of the National Library of Medicine and the Scientific and Technical Aerospace Reports of the National Aeronautics and Space Administration (NASA). By the late 1960s such bodies of digitized alphanumeric information, known as bibliographic and numeric databases, constituted a new type of information resource. This resource is husbanded outside the traditional repositories of information (libraries and archives) by database "vendors." Advances in computer storage, telecommunications, software for computer sharing, and automated techniques of text indexing and searching fueled the development of an on-line database service industry. Meanwhile, electronic applications to bibliographic control in libraries and archives have led to the development of computerized catalogs and of union catalogs in library networks.

They also have resulted in the introduction of comprehensive automation programs in these institutions.

The explosive growth of communications networks after 1990, particularly in the scholarly world, has accelerated the establishment of the "virtual library." At the leading edge of this development is public-domain information. Residing in thousands of databases distributed worldwide, a growing portion of this vast resource is now accessible almost instantaneously via the Internet, the web of computer networks linking the global communities of researchers and, increasingly, nonacademic organizations. Internet resources of electronic information include selected library catalogs, collected works of the literature, some abstracting journals, full-text electronic journals, encyclopaedias, scientific data from numerous disciplines, software archives, demographic registers, daily news summaries, environmental reports, and prices in commodity markets, as well as hundreds of thousands of e-mail and bulletin-board messages.

The vast inventory of recorded information can be useful only if it is systematically organized and if mechanisms exist for locating in it items relevant to human needs.

Organization and Retrieval of Information

In any collection, physical objects are related by order. The ordering may be random or according to some characteristic called a key. Such characteristics may be intrinsic properties of the objects (e.g., size, weight, shape, or colour), or they may be assigned from some agreed-upon set, such as object class or date of purchase. The values of the key are arranged in a sorting sequence that is dependent on the type of key involved alphanumeric key values are usually sorted in alphabetic sequence, while other types may be sorted on the basis of similarity in class, such as books on a particular subject or flora of the same genus.

In most cases, order is imposed on a set of information objects for two reasons to create their inventory and to facilitate locating specific objects in the set. There also exist other, secondary objectives for selecting a particular ordering, as, for example, conservation of space or economy of effort in fetching objects. Unless the objects in a collection are replicated, any ordering scheme is one-dimensional and unable to meet all the functions of ordering with equal effectiveness. The main approach for overcoming some of the limitations of one-dimensional ordering of recorded information relies on extended description of its content and, for analog-form information, of some features of the physical items. This approach employs various tools of content analysis that subsequently facilitate accessing and searching recorded information.

Description and Content Analysis of Analog-form Records

The collections of libraries and archives, the primary repositories of analog-form information, constitute one-dimensional ordering of physical materials in print (documents), in image form (maps and photographs), or in audio-video format (recordings and videotapes). To break away from the confines of one-dimensional ordering, librarianship has developed an extensive set of attributes in terms of which it describes each item in the collection. The rules for assigning these attributes are called cataloging rules. Descriptive cataloging is the extraction of bibliographic elements (author names, title, publisher, date of publication, etc.) from each item; the assignment of subject categories or headings to such items is termed subject cataloging.

Conceptually, the library catalog is a table or matrix in which each row describes a discrete physical item and each column provides values of the assigned key. When such a catalog is represented digitally in a computer, any attribute can serve as the ordering key. By sorting the catalog on different keys, it is possible to produce a variety of indexes as well as subject bibliographies. More important, any of the attributes of a computerized catalog becomes a search key (access point) to the collection, surpassing the utility of the traditional card catalog.

The most useful access key to analog-form items is subject. The extensive lists of subject headings of library classification schemes provide, however, only a gross access tool to the content of the items. A technique called indexing provides a refinement over library subject headings. It consists of extracting from the item or assigning to it subject and other "descriptors"—words or phrases denoting significant concepts (topics, names) that occur in or characterize the content of the record. Indexing frequently accompanies abstracting, a technique for condensing the full text of a document into a short summary that contains its main ideas (but invariably incurs an information loss and often introduces a bias). Computer-printed, indexed abstracting journals provide a means of keeping users informed of primary information sources.

Description and Content Analysis of Digital-form Information

The description of an electronic document generally follows the principles of bibliographic cataloging if the document is part of a database that is expected to be accessed directly and individually. When the database is an element of a universe of globally distributed database servers that are searchable in parallel, the matter of document naming is considerably more challenging, because several complexities are introduced. The document description must include the name of the database server—i.e., its physical location. Because database servers may delete particular documents, the description must also contain a pointer to the document's logical address (the generating organization). In contrast to their usefulness in the descriptive cataloging of analog documents, physical attributes such as format and size are highly variable in the milieu of electronic documents and therefore are meaningless in a universal document-naming scheme. On the other hand, the data type of the document (text, sound, etc.) is critical to its transmission and use. Perhaps the most challenging design is the "living document"—a constantly changing pastiche consisting of sections electronically copied from different documents, interspersed with original narrative or graphics or voice comments contributed by persons in distant locations, whose different versions reside on different servers. Efforts are under way to standardize the naming of documents in the universe of electronic networks.

Machine Indexing

The subject analysis of electronic text is accomplished by means of machine indexing, using one of two approaches: the assignment of subject descriptors from an unlimited vocabulary (free indexing) or their assignment from a list of authorized descriptors (controlled indexing). A collection of authorized descriptors is called an authority list or, if it also displays various relationships among descriptors such as hierarchy or synonymy, a thesaurus. The result of the indexing process is a computer file known as an inverted index, which is an alphabetic listing of descriptors and the addresses of their occurrence in the document body.

Full-text indexing, the use of every character string (word of a natural language) in the text as an index term, is an extreme case of free-text indexing each word in the document (except function words such as articles and prepositions) becomes an access point to it. Used earlier for the generation of concordances in literary analysis and other computer applications in the humanities, full-text indexing placed great demands on computer storage because the resulting index is at least as large as the body of the text. With decreasing cost of mass storage, automatic full-text indexing capability has been incorporated routinely into state-of-the-art information-management software.

Text indexing may be supplemented by other syntactic techniques so as to increase its precision or robustness. One such method, the Standard Generalized Markup Language (SGML), takes advantage of standard text markers used by editors to pinpoint the location and other characteristics of document elements. In indexing spatial data such as maps and astronomical images, the textual index specifies the search areas, each of which is further described by a set of coordinates defining a rectangle or irregular polygon. These digital spatial document attributes are then used to retrieve and display a specific point or a selected region of the document. There are other specialized techniques that may be employed to augment the indexing of specific document types, such as encyclopaedias, electronic mail, catalogs, bulletin boards, tables, and maps.

Semantic Content Analysis

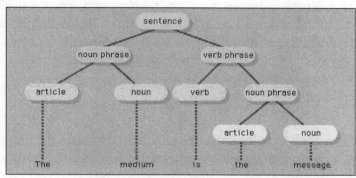

A parsing graph.

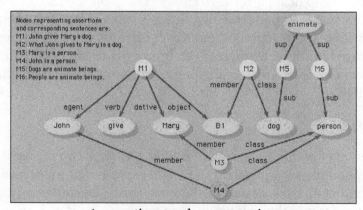

A semantic network representation.

The analysis of digitally recorded natural-language information from the semantic viewpoint is a matter of considerable complexity, and it lies at the foundation of such incipient applications as automatic question answering from a database or retrieval by means of unrestricted natural-language queries. The general approach has been that of computational linguistics to derive representations of the syntactic and semantic relations between the linguistic elements of sentences and larger parts of the document. Syntactic relations are described by parsing (decomposing) the grammar of sentences. For semantic representation, three related formalisms dominate. In a so-called semantic network, conceptual entities such as objects, actions, or events are represented as a graph of linked nodes. "Frames" represent, in a similar graph network, physical or abstract attributes of objects and in a sense define the objects. In "scripts," events and actions rather than objects are defined in terms of their attributes.

Indexing and linguistic analyses of text generate a relatively gross measure of the semantic relationship, or subject similarity, of documents in a given collection. Subject similarity is, however, a pragmatic phenomenon that varies with the observer and the circumstances of an observation (purpose, time, and so forth). A technique experimented with briefly in the mid-1960s, which assigned to each document one or more "roles" (functions) and one or more "links" (pointers to other documents having the same or a similar role), showed potential for a pragmatic measure of similarity; its use, however, was too unwieldy for the computing environment of the day. Some 20 years later, a similar technique became popular under the name "hypertext." In this technique, documents that a person or a group of persons consider related (by concept, sequence, hierarchy, experience, motive, or other characteristics) are connected via "hyperlinks," mimicking the way humans associate ideas. Objects so linked need not be only text; speech and music, graphics and images, and animation and video can all be interlinked into a "hypermedia" database. The objects are stored with their hyperlinks, and a user can easily navigate the network of associations by clicking with a mouse on a series of entries on a computer screen. Another technique that elicits semantic relationships from a body of text is SGML.

Image Analysis

The content analysis of images is accomplished by two primary methods: image processing and pattern recognition. Image processing is a set of computational techniques for analyzing, enhancing, compressing, and reconstructing images. Pattern recognition is an information-reduction process the assignment of visual or logical patterns to classes based on the features of these patterns and their relationships. The stages in pattern recognition involve measurement of the object to identify distinguishing attributes, extraction of features for the defining attributes, and assignment of the object to a class based on these features. Both image processing and pattern recognition have extensive applications in various areas, including astronomy, medicine, industrial robotics, and remote sensing by satellites.

Speech Analysis

The immediate objective of content analysis of digital speech is the conversion of discrete sound elements into their alphanumeric equivalents. Once so represented, speech can be subjected to the same techniques of content analysis as natural-language text—i.e., indexing and linguistic analysis. Converting speech elements into their alphanumeric counterparts is an intriguing problem because the "shape" of speech sounds embodies a wide range of many acoustic characteristics and because the linguistic elements of speech are not clearly distinguishable from one another. The technique used in speech processing is to classify the spectral representations of sound and to match the resulting digital spectrographs against prestored "templates" so as to identify the alphanumeric equivalent of the sound. (The obverse of this technique, the digital-to-analog conversion of such templates into sound, is a relatively straightforward approach to generating synthetic speech).

Speech processing is complex as well as expensive in terms of storage capacity and computational requirements. State-of-the-art speech recognition systems can identify limited vocabularies and parts of distinctly spoken speech and can be programmed to recognize tonal idiosyncrasies of individual speakers. When more robust and reliable techniques become available and the process is made computationally tractable (as is expected with parallel computers), humans will be able to interact with computers via spoken commands and queries on a routine basis. In many situations this may make the keyboard obsolete as a data-entry device.

Storage Structures for Digital-form Information

Digital information is stored in complex patterns that make it feasible to address and operate on even the smallest element of symbolic expression, as well as on larger strings such as words or sentences and on images and sound.

From the viewpoint of digital information storage, it is useful to distinguish between "structured" data, such as inventories of objects that can be represented by short symbol strings and numbers, and "unstructured" data, such as the natural-language text of documents or pictorial images. The principal objective of all storage structures is to facilitate the processing of data elements on the basis of their relationships; the structures thus vary with the type of relationship they represent. The choice of a particular storage structure is governed by the relevance of the relationships it allows to be represented to the information-processing requirements of the task or system at hand.

In information systems whose store consists of unstructured databases of natural-language records, the objective is to retrieve records (or portions thereof) on the basis of the presence in the records of words or short phrases that constitute the query. Since there exists an index as a separate file that provides information about the locations of words and phrases in the database records, the relationships that are of interest (e.g., word adjacency) can be calculated from the index. Consequently, the database text itself can be stored as a simple ordered sequential file of records. The majority of the computations use the index, and they access the text file only to pull out the records or those portions that satisfy the result of the computations. The sequential file structure remains popular, with document-retrieval software intended for use with personal computers and CD-ROM databases.

When relationships between data elements need to be represented as part of the records so as to make more efficient the desired operations on these records, two types of "chained" structures are commonly used: hierarchical and network. In the hierarchical file structure, records are arranged in a scheme resembling a family tree, with records related to one another from top to bottom. In the network file structure, records are arranged in groupings known as sets; these can be connected in any number of ways, giving rise to considerable flexibility. In both hierarchical and network structures, the relationships are shown by means of "pointers" (i.e., identifiers such as addresses or keys) that become part of the records.

Another type of database storage structure, the relational structure, has become increasingly popular since the late 1970s. Its major advantage over the hierarchical and network structures is the ability to handle unanticipated data relationships without pointers. Relational storage structures are two-dimensional tables consisting of rows and columns, much like the conceptual library catalog. The elegance of the relational model lies in its conceptual simplicity, the availability of theoretical underpinnings (relational algebra), and the ability of its associated software to handle data relationships without the use of pointers. The relational model was initially used for databases containing highly structured information. In the 1990s it largely replaced the hierarchical and network models, and it also became the model of choice for large-scale information-management applications, both textual and multimedia.

The feasibility of storing large volumes of full text on an economical medium (the digital optical disc) has renewed interest in the study of storage structures that permit more powerful retrieval and processing techniques to operate on cognitive entities other than words, to facilitate more extensive semantic content and context analysis, and to organize text conceptually into logical units rather than those dictated by printing conventions.

Query Languages

The uses of databases are manifold. They provide a means of retrieving records or parts of records and performing various calculations before displaying the results. The interface by which such manipulations are specified is called the query language. Whereas early query languages were originally so complex that interacting with electronic databases could be done only by specially trained individuals, recent interfaces are more user-friendly, allowing casual users to access database information.

The main types of popular query modes are the menu, the "fill-in-the-blank" technique, and the structured query. Particularly suited for novices, the menu requires a person to choose from several alternatives displayed on the video terminal screen. The fill-in-the-blank technique is one in which the user is prompted to enter key words as search statements. The structured query approach is effective with relational databases. It has a formal, powerful syntax that is in fact a programming language, and it is able to accommodate logical operators. One implementation of this approach, the Structured Query Language (SQL), has the form,

select [field Fa, Fb, . . ., Fn]

from [database Da, Db, . . ., Dn]

where [field Fa = abc] and [field Fb = def].

Structured query languages support database searching and other operations by using commands such as "find," "delete," "print," "sum," and so forth. The sentence like structure of an SQL query resembles natural language except that its syntax is limited and fixed. Instead of using an SQL statement, it is possible to represent queries in tabular form. The technique, referred to as query-by-example (or QBE), displays an empty tabular form and expects the searcher to enter the search specifications into appropriate columns. The program then constructs an SQL-type query from the table and executes it.

The most flexible query language is of course natural language. The use of natural-language sentences in a constrained form to search databases is allowed by some commercial database management software. These programs parse the syntax of the query; recognize its action words and their synonyms; identify the names of files, records, and fields; and perform the logical operations required. Experimental systems that accept such natural-language queries in spoken voice have been developed; however, the ability to employ unrestricted natural language to query unstructured information will require further advances in machine understanding of natural language, particularly in techniques of representing the semantic and pragmatic context of ideas. The prospect of an intelligent conversation between humans and a large store of digitally encoded knowledge is not imminent.

Information Searching and Retrieval

State-of-the-art approaches to retrieving information employ two generic techniques: (1) matching words in the query against the database index (key-word searching) and (2) traversing the database with the aid of hypertext or hypermedia links.

Key-word searches can be made either more general or more narrow in scope by means of logical operators (e.g., disjunction and conjunction). Because of the semantic ambiguities involved in free-text indexing, however, the precision of the key-word retrieval technique—that is, the percentage of relevant documents correctly retrieved from a collection—is far from ideal, and various modifications have been introduced to improve it. In one such enhancement, the search output is sorted by degree of relevance, based on a statistical match between the key words in the query and in the document; in another, the program automatically generates a new query using one or more documents considered relevant by the user. Key-word searching has been the dominant approach to text retrieval since the early 1960s; hypertext has so far been largely confined to personal or corporate information-retrieval applications.

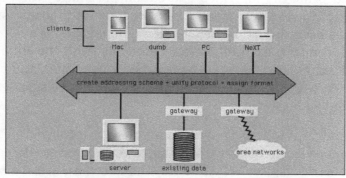

The architecture of a networked information system.

The exponential growth of the use of computer networks in the 1990s presages significant changes in systems and techniques of information retrieval. In a wide-area information service, a number of which began operating at the beginning of the 1990s on the Internet computer network, a user's personal computer or terminal (called a client) can search simultaneously a number of databases maintained on heterogeneous computers (called servers). The latter are located at different geographic sites, and their databases contain different data types and often use incompatible data formats. The simultaneous, distributed search is possible because clients and servers agree on a standard document addressing scheme and adopt a common communications protocol that accommodates all the data types and formats used by the servers. Communication with other wide-area services using different protocols is accomplished by routing through so-called gateways capable of protocol translation. The architecture of a typical networked information system is illustrated in figure. Several representative clients are shown a "dumb" terminal (i.e., one with no internal processor), a personal computer (PC), a Macintosh (Mac), and a NeXT machine. They have access to data on the servers sharing a common protocol as well as to data provided by services that require protocol conversion via the gateways. Network news is such a wide-area service, containing hundreds of news groups on a variety of subjects, by which users can read and post messages.

Evolving information-retrieval techniques, exemplified by an experimental interface to the NASA space shuttle reference manual, combine natural language, hyperlinks, and key-word searching. Other techniques, seeking higher levels of retrieval precision and effectiveness, are studied by researchers involved with artificial intelligence and neural networks. The next major milestone may be a computer program that traverses the seamless information universe of wide-area electronic networks and continuously filters its contents through profiles of organizational and personal interest: the information robot of the 21st century.

Information display

For humans to perceive and understand information, it must be presented as print and image on paper; as print and image on film or on a video terminal; as sound via radio or telephony; as print, sound, and video in motion pictures, on television broadcasts, or at lectures and conferences; or in face-to-face encounters. Except for live encounters and audio information, such displays emanate increasingly from digitally stored data, with the output media being video, print, and sound.

Video

Possibly the most widely used video display device, at least in the industrialized world, is the television set. Designed primarily for video and sound, its image resolution is inadequate for alphanumeric data except in relatively small amounts. Use of the television set in text-oriented information systems has been limited to menu-oriented applications such as videotex, in which information is selected from hierarchically arranged menus (with the aid of a numeric keyboard attachment) and displayed in fixed frames. The television, computer, and communications technologies are, however, converging in a high-resolution digital television set capable of receiving alphanumeric, video, and audio signals.

The computer video terminal is today's ubiquitous interface that transforms computer-stored data into analog form for human viewing. The two basic apparatuses used are the cathode-ray tube (CRT) and the more recent flat-panel display. In CRT displays an electron gun emits beams of electrons on a phosphorus-coated surface; the beams are deflected, forming visible patterns representative of data. Flat-panel displays use one of four different media for visual representation of data: liquid crystal, light-emitting diodes, plasma panels, and electroluminescence. Advanced video display systems enable the user to scroll, page, zoom (change the scale of the details of the display image for enhancement), divide the screen into multiple colours and windows (viewing areas), and in some cases even activate commands by touching the screen instead of using the keyboard. The information capacity of the terminal screen depends on its resolution, which ranges from low (character-addressable) to high (bit-addressable). High resolution is indispensable for the display of graphic and video data in state-of-the-art workstations, such as those used in engineering or information systems design.

Print

Modern society continues to be dominated by printed information. The convenience and portability of print on paper make it difficult to imagine the paperless world that some have predicted. The generation of paper print has changed considerably, however. Although manual typesetting is still practiced for artwork, in special situations, and in some developing countries, electronic means of composing pages for subsequent reproduction by photoduplication and other methods has become commonplace.

Since the 1960s, volume publishing has become an automated process using large computers and high-speed printers to transfer digitally stored data on paper. The appearance of microcomputer-based publishing systems has proved to be another significant advance. Economical enough to allow even small organizations to become in-house publishers, these so-called desktop publishing systems are able to format text and graphics interactively on a high-resolution video screen with the aid of page-description command languages. Once a page has been formatted, the entire image is transferred to an electronic printing or photocomposition device.

Printers

Computer printers are commonly divided into two general classes according to the way they produce images on paper: impact and non-impact. In the first type, images are formed by the print mechanism making contact with the paper through an ink-coated ribbon. The mechanism consists either of print hammers shaped like characters or of a print head containing a row of pins that produce a pattern of dots in the form of characters or other images.

Most non-impact printers form images from a matrix of dots, but they employ different techniques for transferring images to paper. The most popular type, the laser printer, uses a beam of laser light and a system of optical components to etch images on a photoconductor drum from which they are carried via electrostatic photocopying to paper. Light-emitting diode (LED) printers resemble laser printers in operation but direct light from energized diodes rather than a laser onto a photoconductive surface. Ion-deposition printers make use of technology similar to that of photocopiers for producing electrostatic images. Another type of nonimpact printer, the ink-jet printer, sprays electrically charged drops of ink onto the print surface.

Microfilm and Microfiche

Alphanumeric and image information can be transferred from digital computer storage directly to film. Reel microfilm and microfiche (a flat sheet of film containing multiple microimages reduced from the original) were popular methods of document storage and reproduction for several decades. During the 1990s they were largely replaced by optical disc technology.

Voice

In synthetic speech generation, digitally prestored sound elements are converted to analog sound signals and combined to form words and sentences. Digital-to-analog converters are available as inexpensive boards for microcomputers or as software for larger machines. Human speech is the most effective natural form of communication, and so applications of this technology are becoming increasingly popular in situations where there are numerous requests for specific information (e.g., time, travel, and entertainment), where there is a need for repetitive instruction, in electronic voice mail (the counterpart of electronic text mail), and in toys.

Dissemination of Information

The process of recording information by handwriting was obviously laborious and required the dedication of the likes of Egyptian scribes or monks in monasteries around the world. It was only after mechanical means of reproducing writing were invented that information records could be duplicated more efficiently and economically.

The first practical method of reproducing writing mechanically was block printing; it was developed in China during the T'ang dynasty (618–907). Ideographic text and illustrations were engraved in wooden blocks, inked, and copied on paper. Used to produce books as well as cards, charms, and calendars, block printing spread to Korea and Japan but apparently not to the Islamic or European Christian civilizations. European woodcuts and metal engravings date only to the 14th century.

Printing from movable type was also invented in China (in the mid-11th century AD). There and in the bookmaking industry of Korea, where the method was applied more extensively during the 15th century, the ideographic type was made initially of baked clay and wood and later of metal. The large number of typefaces required for pictographic text composition continued to handicap printing in the Orient until the present time.

The invention of character-oriented printing from movable type (1440–50) is attributed to the German printer Johannes Gutenberg. Within 30 years of his invention, the movable-type printing press was in use throughout Europe. Character-type pieces were metallic and apparently cast from metallic molds; paper and vellum (calfskin parchment) were used to carry the impressions. Gutenberg's technique of assembling individual letters by hand was employed until 1886, when the German-born American printer Ottmar Mergenthaler developed the Linotype, a keyboard-driven device that cast lines of type automatically. Typesetting speed was further enhanced by the Monotype technique, in which a perforated paper ribbon, punched from a keyboard, was used to operate a type-casting machine. Mechanical methods of typesetting prevailed until the 1960s. Since that time they have been largely supplanted by the electronic and optical printing techniques.

Unlike the use of movable type for printing text, early graphics were reproduced from wood relief engravings in which the non-printing portions of the image were cut away. Musical scores, on the other hand, were reproduced from etched stone plates. At the end of the 18th century, the German printer Aloys Senefelder developed lithography, a planographic technique of transferring images from a specially prepared surface of stone. In offset lithography the image is transferred from zinc or aluminum plates instead of stone, and in photoengraving such plates are superimposed with film and then etched.

The first successful photographic process, the daguerreotype, was developed during the 1830s. The invention of photography, aside from providing a new medium for capturing still images and later video in analog form, was significant for two other reasons. First, recorded information (textual and graphic) could be easily reproduced from film, and, second, the image could be enlarged or reduced. Document reproduction from film to film has been relatively unimportant, because both printing and photocopying are cheaper. The ability to reduce images, however, has led to the development of the microform, the most economical method of disseminating analog-form information.

Another technique of considerable commercial importance for the duplication of paper-based information is photocopying, or dry photography. Printing is most economical when large numbers of copies are required, but photocopying provides a fast and efficient means of duplicating records in small quantities for personal or local use. Of the several technologies that are in use, the most popular process, xerography, is based on electrostatics.

While the volume of information issued in the form of printed matter continues unabated, the electronic publishing industry has begun to disseminate information in digital form. The digital optical disc is developing as an increasingly popular means of issuing large bodies of archival information—for example, legislation, court and hospital records, encyclopaedias and other reference works, referral databases, and libraries of computer software. Full-text databases, each containing digital page images of the complete text of some 400 periodicals stored on CD-ROM, entered the market in 1990. The optical disc provides the mass production technology for publication in machine-readable form. It offers the prospect of having large libraries of information available in virtually every school and at many professional workstations.

The coupling of computers and digital telecommunications is also changing the modes of information dissemination. High-speed digital satellite communications facilitate electronic printing at remote sites; for example, the world's major newspapers and magazines transmit electronic page copies to different geographic locations for local printing and distribution. Updates of catalogs, computer software, and archival databases are distributed via e-mail, a method of rapidly forwarding and storing bodies of digital information between remote computers.

Indeed, a large-scale transformation is taking place in modes of formal as well as informal communication. For more than three centuries, formal communication in the scientific community has relied on the scholarly and professional periodical, widely distributed to tens of thousands of libraries and to tens of millions of individual subscribers. In 1992 a major international publisher announced that its journals would gradually be available for computer storage in digital form; and in that same year the State University of New York at Buffalo began building a completely electronic, paperless library. The scholarly article, rather than the journal, is likely to become the basic unit of formal communication in scientific disciplines; digital copies of such an article will be transmitted electronically to subscribers or, more likely, on demand to individuals and organizations who learn of its existence through referral databases and new types of alerting information services. The Internet already offers instantaneous public access to vast resources of non-commercial information stored in computers around the world.

Similarly, the traditional modes of informal communications—various types of face-to-face encounters such as meetings, conferences, seminars, workshops, and classroom lectures—are being supplemented and in some cases replaced by e-mail, electronic bulletin boards (a technique of broadcasting newsworthy textual and multimedia messages between computer users), and electronic teleconferencing and distributed problem-solving (a method of linking remote persons in real time by voice-and-image communication and special software called "groupware"). These technologies are forging virtual societal networks—communities of geographically dispersed individuals who have common professional or social interests.

References

- Information-management, definition: techopedia.com, retrieved 13 may, 2019

- Katsicas, sokratis k. (2009). "35". In vacca, john (ed.). Computer and information security handbook. Morgan kaufmann publications. Elsevier inc. P. 605. Isbn 978-0-12-374354-1

- Characteristics-strategic-information-management: bizfluent.com, retrieved 25 February, 2019

- Caballero, albert (2009). "14". In vacca, john (ed.). Computer and information security handbook. Morgan kaufmann publications. Elsevier inc. P. 232. Isbn 978-0-12-374354-1.s

- Information-processing, technology: britannica.com, retrieved 16 January, 2019

- Spring, j.; kern, s.; summers, a. (2015-05-01). "global adversarial capability modeling". 2015 apwg symposium on electronic crime research (ecrime): 1–21. Doi:10.1109/ecrime.2015.7120797. Isbn 978-1-4799-8909-6

Information System and its Types

The organizational systems which are used to process, store and distribute information are termed as information systems. Different types of information systems are transaction processing system, management information system, decision support system, etc. This chapter discusses these different types of information systems in detail.

INFORMATION SYSTEM

An information system (IS) refers to a collection of multiple pieces of equipment involved in the dissemination of information. Hardware, software, computer system connections and information, information system users, and the system's housing are all part of an IS.

There are several types of information systems, including the following common types:

- Operations support systems, including transaction processing systems.
- Management information systems.
- Decision support systems.
- Executive information systems.

An information system commonly refers to a basic computer system but may also describe a telephone switching or environmental controlling system. The IS involves resources for shared or processed information, as well as the people who manage the system. People are considered part of the system because without them, systems would not operate correctly.

There are many types of information systems, depending on the need they are designed to fill. An operations support system, such as a transaction processing system, converts business data (financial transactions) into valuable information. Similarly, a management information system uses database information to output reports, helping users and businesses make decisions based on extracted data.

In a decision support system, data is pulled from various sources and then reviewed by managers, who make determinations based on the compiled data. An executive information system is useful for examining business trends, allowing users to quickly access custom strategic information in summary form, which can be reviewed in more detail.

There are some general types of information systems. For example, a database management system (DBMS) is a combination of software and data that makes it possible to organize and analyze data. DBMS software is typically not designed to work with a specific organization or a specific type of analysis. Rather, it is a general-purpose information system. Another example is an electronic spreadsheet. This is a tool for basic data analysis based on formulas that define relationships among the data. For example, you can use a spreadsheet to calculate averages for a set of values or to plot the trend of a value over time.

In contrast, there are a number of specialized information systems that have been specifically designed to support a particular process within an organization or to carry out very specific analysis tasks. For example, enterprise resource planning (ERP) is an information system used to integrate the management of all internal and external information across an entire organization. Another example is a geographic information system (GIS), which is used to manage and analyze all types of geographical data. Expert systems are another example of information systems. An experts system is designed to solve complex problems by following the reasoning of an expert.

Components of Information Systems

While information systems may differ in how they are used within an organization, they typically contain the following components:

- Hardware: Computer-based information systems use computer hardware, such as processors, monitors, keyboard and printers.

- Software: These are the programs used to organize, process and analyze data.

- Databases: Information systems work with data, organized into tables and files.

- Network: Different elements need to be connected to each other, especially if many different people in an organization use the same information system.

- Procedures: These describe how specific data are processed and analyzed in order to get the answers for which the information system is designed.

The first four components are part of the general information technology (IT) of an organization. Procedures, the fifth component, are very specific to the information needed to answer a specific question.

Information System Development

Information technology departments in larger organizations tend to strongly influence the development, use, and application of information technology in the business. A series of methodologies and processes can be used to develop and use an information system. Many developers use a systems engineering approach such as the system development life cycle (SDLC), to systematically develop an information system in stages. The stages of the system development lifecycle are planning, system analysis and requirements, system design, development, integration and testing, implementation and operations and maintenance. Recent research aims at enabling and measuring the ongoing, collective development of such systems within an organization by the entirety of human actors themselves. An information system can be developed in house (within the organization) or outsourced. This can be accomplished by outsourcing certain components or the entire system. A specific case is the geographical distribution of the development team (offshoring, global information system).

A computer-based information system, following a definition of Langefors, is a technologically implemented medium for:

- Recording, storing, and disseminating linguistic expressions,

- As well as for drawing conclusions from such expressions.

Geographic information systems, land information systems, and disaster information systems are examples of emerging information systems, but they can be broadly considered as spatial information systems. System development is done in stages which include:

- Problem recognition and specification.

- Information gathering.

- Requirements specification for the new system.

- System design.

- System construction.

- System implementation.

- Review and maintenance.

TRANSACTION PROCESSING SYSTEM

Transaction processing is a way of computing that divides work into individual, indivisible operations, called transactions. A transaction processing system (TPS) is a software system, or software/hardware combination, that supports transaction processing.

Transaction Processing System Features

The following features are considered important in evaluating transaction processing systems.

Performance

Fast performance with a rapid response time is critical. Transaction processing systems are usually measured by the number of transactions they can process in a given period of time.

Continuous Availability

The system must be available during the time period when the users are entering transactions. Many organizations rely heavily on their TPS; a breakdown will disrupt operations or even stop the business.

Data Integrity

The system must be able to handle hardware or software problems without corrupting data.

Multiple users must be protected from attempting to change the same piece of data at the same time, for example two operators cannot sell the same seat on an airplane.

Ease of Use

Often users of transaction processing systems are casual users. The system should be simple for them to understand, protect them from data-entry errors as much as possible, and allow them to easily correct their errors.

Modular Growth

The system should be capable of growth at incremental costs, rather than requiring a complete replacement. It should be possible to add, replace, or update hardware and software components without shutting down the system.

Types of Transaction Processing

Processing in a Batch

Transactions may be collected and processed as in batch processing. Transactions will be collected and later updated as a batch when it's convenient or economical to process them. Historically, this was the most common method as the information technology did not exist to allow real-time processing.

Processing in Real-time

This is the immediate processing of data. It provides instant confirmation of a transaction. It may involve a large number of users who are simultaneously performing transactions which change data. Because of advances in technology (such as the increase in the speed of data transmission and larger bandwidth), real-time updating is possible.

Databases for Transaction Processing

A database is an organized collection of data. Databases offer fast retrieval times for non-structured requests as in a typical transaction processing application.

Databases for transaction processing may be constructed using hierarchical, network, or relational structures.

- Hierarchical structure: Organizes data in a series of levels. Its top-to-bottom-like structure consists of nodes and branches; each child node has branches and is only linked to one higher level parent node.

- Network structure: Network structures also organizes data using nodes and branches. But, unlike hierarchical, each child node can be linked to multiple, higher parent nodes.

- Relational structure: A relational database organizes its data in a series of related tables. This gives flexibility as relationships between the tables are built.

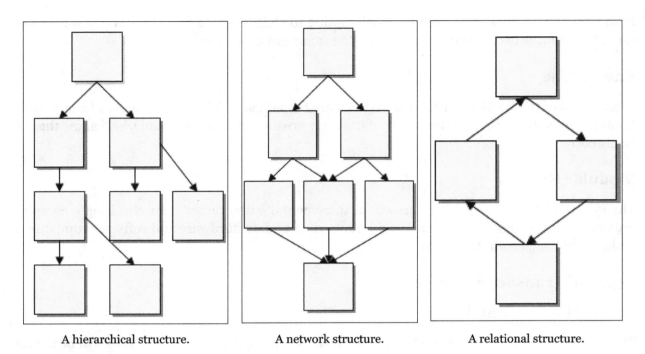

A hierarchical structure.   A network structure.   A relational structure.

The following features are desirable in a database system used in transaction processing systems:

- Good data placement: The database should be designed to access patterns of data from many simultaneous users.

- Short transactions: Short transactions enables quick processing. This avoids concurrency and paces the systems.

- Real-time backup: Backup should be scheduled between low times of activity to prevent lag of the server.

- High normalization: This lowers redundant information to increase the speed and improve concurrency, this also improves backups.

- Archiving of historical data: Uncommonly used data are moved into other databases or backed up tables. This keeps tables small and also improves backup times.

- Good hardware configuration: Hardware must be able to handle many users and provide quick response times.

Backup Procedures

Since business organizations have become very dependent on transaction processing, a breakdown may disrupt the business' regular routine and stop its operation for a certain amount of time. In order to prevent data loss and minimize disruptions there have to be well-designed backup and recovery procedures. The recovery process can rebuild the system when it goes down.

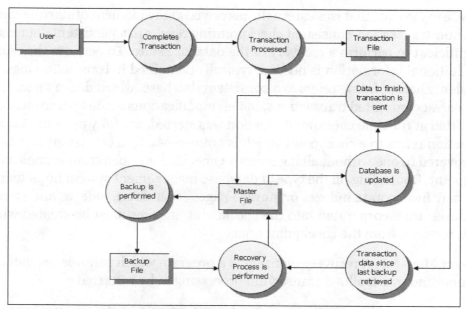

A Dataflow Diagram of backup and recovery procedures.

Recovery Process

A TPS may fail for many reasons such as system failure, human errors, hardware failure, incorrect or invalid data, computer viruses, software application errors or natural or man-made disasters. As it's not possible to prevent all failures, a TPS must be able to detect and correct errors when they occur and cope with failures. A TPS will go through a recovery of the database which may involve the backup, journal, checkpoint, and recovery manager:

- Journal: A journal maintains an audit trail of transactions and database changes. Transaction logs and Database change logs are used, a transaction log records all the essential data for each transactions, including data values, time of transaction and terminal number. A database change log contains before and after copies of records that have been modified by transactions.

- Checkpoint: The purpose of checkpointing is to provide a snapshot of the data within the database. A checkpoint, in general, is any identifier or other reference that identifies the state of the database at a point in time. Modifications to database pages are performed in memory and are not necessarily written to disk after every update. Therefore, periodically, the database system must perform a checkpoint to write these updates which are held in-memory to the storage disk. Writing these updates to storage disk creates a point in time in which the database system can apply changes contained in a transaction log during recovery after an unexpected shut down or crash of the database system. If a checkpoint is interrupted and a recovery is required, then the database system must start recovery from a previous successful checkpoint. Checkpointing can be either transaction-consistent or non-transaction-consistent (called also fuzzy checkpointing). Transaction-consistent checkpointing produces a persistent database image that is sufficient to recover the database to the state that was externally perceived at the moment of starting the checkpointing. A non-transaction-consistent checkpointing results in a persistent database image that is insufficient to perform a recovery of the database state. To perform the database recovery, additional information is needed, typically contained in transaction logs. Transaction consistent checkpointing refers to a consistent database, which doesn't necessarily include all the latest committed transactions, but all modifications made by transactions, that were committed at the time checkpoint creation was started, are fully present. A non-consistent transaction refers to a checkpoint which is not necessarily a consistent database, and can't be recovered to one without all log records generated for open transactions included in the checkpoint. Depending on the type of database management system implemented a checkpoint may incorporate indexes or storage pages (user data), indexes and storage pages. If no indexes are incorporated into the checkpoint, indexes must be created when the database is restored from the checkpoint image.

- Recovery Manager: A recovery manager is a program which restores the database to a correct condition which allows transaction processing to be restarted.

Depending on how the system failed, there can be two different recovery procedures used. Generally, the procedures involves restoring data that has been collected from a backup device and then running the transaction processing again. Two types of recovery are *backward recovery* and *forward recovery*:

- Backward recovery: Used to undo unwanted changes to the database. It reverses the changes made by transactions which have been aborted.

- Forward recovery: It starts with a backup copy of the database. The transaction will then reprocess according to the transaction journal that occurred between the time the backup was made and the present time.

Types of Back-up Procedures

Grandfather-father-son

This procedure involves taking complete backups of all data at regular intervals – daily, weekly, monthly, or whatever is appropriate. Multiple generations of backup are retained, often three which gives rise to the name. The most recent backup is the son, the previous the father, and the oldest backup is the grandfather. This method is commonly used for a *batch transaction processing system* with a magnetic tape. If the system fails during a batch run, the master file is recreated by restoring the son backup and then restarting the batch. However, if the son backup fails, is corrupted or destroyed, then the previous generation of backup (the father) is used. Likewise, if that fails, then the generation of backup previous to the father (i.e. the grandfather) is required. Of course the older the generation, the more the data may be out of date. Organize only of records that have changed. For example, a full backup could be performed weekly, and partial backups taken nightly. Recovery using this scheme involves restoring the last full backup and then restoring all partial backups in order to produce an up-to-date database. This process is quicker than taking only complete backups, at the expense of longer recovery time.

Backup Plus Journal

This technique is also used in conjunction with regular complete backups. The master file is backed up at regular intervals. Completed transactions since the last backup are stored separately and are called journals, or journal files. The master file can be recreated by restoring the last complete backup and then reprocessing transactions from the journal files. This will produce the most up-to-date copy of the database, but recovery may take longer because of the time required to process a volume of journal records.

Advantages

- Batch or real-time processing available.

- Reduction in processing time, lead time and order cycle time.

- Reduction in inventory, personnel and ordering costs.

- Increase in productivity and customer satisfaction.

MANAGEMENT INFORMATION SYSTEM

A management information system (MIS) is an information system used for decision-making, and for the coordination, control, analysis, and visualization of information in an organization.

The study of management information systems examines people, processes and technology in an organizational context.

In a corporate setting, the ultimate goal of the use of a management information system is to increase the value and profits of the business.

While it can be contested that the history of management information systems date as far back as companies using ledgers to keep track of accounting, the modern history of MIS can be divided into five *eras* originally identified by Kenneth C. Laudon and Jane Laudon:

- First Era: Mainframe and minicomputer computing.

- Second Era: Personal computers.

- Third Era: Client/server networks.

- Fourth Era: Enterprise computing.

- Fifth Era: Cloud computing.

The first era (mainframe and minicomputer computing) was ruled by IBM and their mainframe computers for which they supplied both the hardware and software. These computers would often take up whole rooms and require teams to run them. As technology advanced, these computers were able to handle greater capacities and therefore reduce their cost. Smaller, more affordable minicomputers allowed larger businesses to run their own computing centers in-house / on-site / on-premises.

The second era (personal computers) began in 1965 as microprocessors started to compete with mainframes and minicomputers and accelerated the process of decentralizing computing power from large data centers to smaller offices. In the late 1970s, minicomputer technology gave way to personal computers and relatively low-cost computers were becoming mass market commodities, allowing businesses to provide their employees access to computing power that ten years before would have cost tens of thousands of dollars. This proliferation of computers created a ready market for interconnecting networks and the popularization of the Internet. The first microprocessor — a four-bit device intended for a programmable calculator — was introduced in 1971 and microprocessor-based systems were not readily available for several years. The MITS Altair 8800 was the first commonly known microprocessor-based system, followed closely by the Apple I and II. It is arguable that the microprocessor-based system did not make significant inroads into minicomputer use until 1979, when VisiCalc prompted record sales of the Apple II on which it ran.

The third era (client/server networks) arose as technological complexity increased, costs decreased, and the end-user (now the ordinary employee) required a system to share information with other employees within an enterprise. Computers on a common network shared information on a server. This lets thousands and even millions of people access data simultaneously on networks referred to as Intranets.

The fourth era (enterprise computing) enabled by high speed networks, consolidated the original department specific software applications into integrated software platforms referred to as enterprise software. This new platform tied all aspects of the business enterprise together offering rich information access encompassing the complete management structure.

Management

While management information systems can be used by any and every level of management, the decision of which systems to implement generally falls upon the chief information officers (CIO) and chief technology officers (CTO). These officers are generally responsible for the overall technology strategy of an organization including evaluating how new technology can help their organization. They act as decision makers in the implementation process of new MIS.

Once decisions have been made, IT directors, including MIS directors, are in charge of the technical implementation of the system. They are also in charge of implementing the policies affecting the MIS (either new specific policies passed down by the CIOs or CTOs or policies that align the new systems with the organizations overall IT policy). It is also their role to ensure the availability of data and network services as well as the security of the data involved by coordinating IT activities.

Upon implementation, the assigned users will have the appropriate access to relevant information. It is important to note that not everyone inputting data into MIS need necessarily be management level. It is common practice to have inputs to MIS be inputted by non-managerial employees though they rarely have access to the reports and decision support platforms offered by these systems.

Types

The following are types of information systems used to create reports, extract data, and assist in the decision making processes of middle and operational level managers.

- Decision support systems (DSS) are computer program applications used by middle and higher management to compile information from a wide range of sources to support problem solving and decision making. A DSS is used mostly for semi-structured and unstructured decision problems.

- Executive information systems (EIS) is a reporting tool that provides quick access to summarized reports coming from all company levels and departments such as accounting, human resources and operations.

- Marketing information systems are management Information Systems designed specifically for managing the marketing aspects of the business.

- Accounting information systems are focused accounting functions.

- Human resource management systems are used for personnel aspects.

- Office automation systems (OAS) support communication and productivity in the enterprise by automating workflow and eliminating bottlenecks. OAS may be implemented at any and all levels of management.

- School Information Management Systems (SIMS) cover school administration, often including teaching and learning materials.

- Enterprise resource planning (ERP) software facilitates the flow of information between all business functions inside the boundaries of the organization and manage the connections to outside stakeholders.

- Local Databases, can be small, simplified tools for managers and are considered to be a primal or base level version of a MIS.

Advantages and Disadvantages

The following are some of the benefits that can be attained using MIS:

- Improve an organization's operational efficiency, add value to existing products, engender innovation and new product development, and help managers make better decisions.

- Companies are able to identify their strengths and weaknesses due to the presence of revenue reports, employee performance records etc. Identifying these aspects can help a company improve its business processes and operations.

- Giving an overall picture of the company.

- Acting as a communication and planning tool.

- The availability of customer data and feedback can help the company to align its business processes according to the needs of its customers. The effective management of customer data can help the company to perform direct marketing and promotion activities.

- MIS can help a company gain a competitive advantage.

- MIS reports can help with decision-making as well as reduce downtime for actionable items.

Some of the disadvantages of MIS systems:

- Retrieval and dissemination are dependent on technology hardware and software.

- Potential for inaccurate information.

Enterprise Applications

- Enterprise systems—also known as enterprise resource planning (ERP) systems: Provide integrated software modules and a unified database that personnel use to plan, manage, and control core business processes across multiple locations. Modules of ERP systems may include finance, accounting, marketing, human resources, production, inventory management, and distribution.

- Supply chain management (SCM) systems enable more efficient management of the supply chain by integrating the links in a supply chain. This may include suppliers, manufacturers, wholesalers, retailers, and final customers.

- Customer relationship management (CRM) systems help businesses manage relationships with potential and current customers and business partners across marketing, sales, and service.

- Knowledge management system (KMS) helps organizations facilitate the collection, recording, organization, retrieval, and dissemination of knowledge. This may include documents, accounting records, unrecorded procedures, practices, and skills. Knowledge management (KM) as a system covers the process of knowledge creation and acquisition from internal processes and the external world. The collected knowledge is incorporated in organizational policies and procedures, and then disseminated to the stakeholders.

STRATEGIC INFORMATION SYSTEM

Strategic information systems (SIS) are information systems that are developed in response to corporate business initiative. They are intended to give competitive advantage to the organization. They may deliver a product or service that is at a lower cost, that is differentiated, that focuses on a particular market segment, or is innovative.

Strategic information management (SIM) is a salient feature in the world of information technology (IT). In a nutshell, SIM helps businesses and organizations categorize, store, process and transfer the information they create and receive. It also offers tools for helping companies apply metrics and analytical tools to their information repositories, allowing them to recognize opportunities for growth and pinpoint ways to improve operational efficiency.

Some of the key ideas of storefront writers are summarized. These include Michael E. Porter's Competitive Advantage and the Value Chain, Charles Wiseman's Strategic Perspective View and the Strategic Planning Process, F. Warren McFarlan's Competitive Strategy with examples of Information Service's Roles, and Gregory Parson's Information Technology Management at the industry, firm, and at the strategy level.

A SIS is a computer system that implements business strategies; they are those systems where information services resources are applied to strategic business opportunities in such a way that the computer systems affect the organization's products and business operations. Strategic information systems are always systems that are developed in response to corporate business initiative. The ideas in several well-known cases came from information services people, but they were directed at specific corporate business thrusts. In other cases, the ideas came from business operational people, and Information Services supplied the technological capabilities to realize profitable results.

Most information systems are looked on as support activities to the business. They mechanize operations for better efficiency, control, and effectiveness, but they do not, in themselves, increase corporate profitability. They are simply used to provide management with sufficient dependable information to keep the business running smoothly, and they are used for analysis to plan new directions. Strategic information systems, on the other hand, become an integral and necessary part of the business, and they affect the profitability and growth of a company. They open up new markets and new businesses. They directly affect the competitive stance of the organization, giving it an advantage against the competitors.

Most literature on strategic information systems emphasizes the dramatic breakthroughs in computer systems, such as American Airlines' Sabre System and American Hospital Supply's terminals in customer offices. These, and many other highly successful approaches are most attractive to think about, and it is always possible that an equivalent success may be attained in an organization. There are many possibilities for strategic information systems, however, which may not be dramatic breakthroughs, but which will certainly become a part of corporate decision making and will, increase corporate profitability. The development of any strategic information systems always enhances the image of information Services in the organization, and leads to information management having a more participatory role in the operation of the organization.

Three General Types of Information Systems

The three general types of information systems that are developed and in general use are financial systems, operational systems, and strategic systems. These categories are not mutually exclusive and, in fact, they always overlap to some degree. Well-directed financial systems and operational systems may well become the strategic systems for a particular organization.

- Financial systems are the basic computerization of the accounting, budgeting, and finance operations of an organization. These are similar and ubiquitous in all organizations because the computer has proven to be ideal for the mechanization and control or financial systems; these include the personnel systems because the headcount control and payroll of a company is of prime financial concern. Financial systems should be one of the bases of all other systems because they give a common, controlled measurement of all operations and projects, and can supply trusted numbers for indicating departmental or project success. Organizational planning must be tied to financial analysis. There is always a greater opportunity to develop strategic systems when the financial systems are in place, and required figures can be readily retrieved from them.

- Operational systems, or services systems, help control the details of the business. Such systems will vary with each type of enterprise. They are the computer systems that operational managers need to help run the business on a routing basis. They may be useful but mundane systems that simply keep track of inventory, for example, and print out reorder points and cost allocations. On the other hand, they may have a strategic perspective built into them, and may handle inventory in a way that dramatically affects profitability. A prime example of this is the American Hospital Supply inventory control system installed on customer premises. Where the great majority of inventory control systems simply smooth the operations and give adequate cost control, this well-known hospital system broke through with a new version of the use of an operational system for competitive advantage. The great majority of operational systems for which many large and small computer systems have been purchased, however, simply help to manage and automate the business. They are important and necessary, but can only be put into the "strategic" category it they substantially affect the profitability of the business. All businesses should have both long-range and short-range planning of operational systems to ensure that the possibilities of computer usefulness will be seized in a reasonable time. Such planning will project analysis and costing, system development life cycle considerations, and specific technology planning, such as for computers, databases, and communications. There must be computer capacity planning, technology forecasting, and personnel performance planning. Operational systems, then, are those that keep the organization operating under control and most cost effectively. Any of them may be changed to strategic systems if they are viewed with strategic vision.

- Strategic systems are those that link business and computer strategies. They are the systems where new business strategies has been developed and they can be realized using Information Technology. They may be systems where new computer technology has been made available on the market, and planners with an entrepreneurial spirit perceive how the new capabilities can quickly gain competitive advantage. They may be systems where operational management people and Information Services people have brainstormed together over business problems, and have realized that a new competitive thrust is possible when computer methods are applied in a new way. There is general agreement that strategic systems are those information systems that may be used gaining competitive advantage. As to how is competitive advantage is gained, different writers list different possibilities, but none of them claim that there may not be other openings to move through.

Gaining Competitive Advantage

Some of the more common ways of thinking about gaining competitive advantage are:

- Deliver a product or a service at a lower cost: This does not necessarily mean the lowest cost, but simply a cost related to the quality of the product or service that will be both attractive in the marketplace and will yield sufficient return on investment. The cost considered is not simply the data processing cost, but is the overall cost of all corporate activities for the delivery of that product or service. There are many operational computer systems that have given internal cost saving and other internal advantages, but they cannot be thought of as strategic until those savings can be translated to a better competitive position in the market.

- Deliver a product or service that is differentiated: Differentiation means the addition of unique features to a product or service that are competitive attractive in the market. Generally such features will cost something to produce, and so they will be the setting point, rather than the cost itself. Seldom does a lowest cost product also have the best differentiation. A strategic system helps customers to perceive that they are getting some extras for which they will willingly pay.

- Focus on a specific market segment: The idea is to identify and create market niches that have not been adequately filled. Information technology is frequently able to provide the capabilities of defining, expanding, and filling a particular niche or segment. The application would be quite specific to the industry.

- Innovation: Develop products or services through the use of computers that are new and appreciably from other available offerings. Examples of this are automatic credit card handing at service stations, and automatic teller machines at banks. Such innovative approaches not only give new opportunities to attract customers, but also open up entirely new fields of business so that their use has very elastic demand.

Almost any data processing system may be called "strategic" if it aligns the computer strategies with the business strategies of the organization, and there is close cooperation in its development between the information services people and operational business managers. There should be an explicit connection between the organization's business plan and its systems plan to provide better support of the organization's goals and objectives, and closer management control of the critical information systems.

Many organizations that have done substantial work with computers since the 1950s have long used the term "strategic planning" for any computer developments that are going to directly affect the conduct of their business. Not included are budget, or annual planning and the planning of developing Information Services facilities and the many "housekeeping" tasks that are required in any corporation. Definitely included in strategic planning are any information systems that will be used by operational management to conduct the business more profitably. A simple test would be to ask whether the president of the corporation, or some senior vice presidents, would be interested in the immediate outcome of the systems development because they felt it would affect their profitability. If the answer is affirmative, then the system is strategic.

Strategic systems, thus, attempt to match Information Services resources to strategic business opportunities where the computer systems will affect the products and the business operations. Planning for strategic systems is not defined by calendar cycles or routine reporting. It is defined by the effort required to affect the competitive environment and the strategy of a firm at the point in time that management wants to move on the idea.

Effective strategic systems can only be accomplished, of course, if the capabilities are in place for the routine basic work of gathering data, evaluating possible equipment and software, and managing the routine reporting of project status. The calendarized planning and operational work is absolutely necessary as a base from which a strategic system can be planned and developed when a priority situation arises. When a new strategic need becomes apparent, Information Services should have laid the groundwork to be able to accept the task of meeting that need.

Strategic systems that are dramatic innovations will always be the ones that are written about in the literature. Consultants in strategic systems must have clearly innovative and successful examples to attract the attention of senior management. It should be clear, however, that most Information Services personnel will have to leverage the advertised successes to again funding for their own systems. These systems may not have an Olympic effect on an organization, but they will have a good chance of being clearly profitable. That will be sufficient for most operational management, and will draw out the necessary funding and support. It helps to talk about the possibilities of great breakthroughs, if it is always kept in mind that there are many strategic systems developed and installed that are successful enough to be highly praised within the organization and offer a competitive advantage, but will not be written up in the Harvard Business Review.

Another way of characterizing strategic information systems is to point out some of the key ideas of the foremost apostles of such systems.

Models for Strategic Information System

Porter's Competitive Advantage

Michael E. Porter, Professor of Business Administration, Harvard Business School, has addressed his ideas in two keystone books. *Competitive Strategy: Techniques for Analyzing Industries and Competitors*, and his newer book, *Competitive Advantage*, present a framework for helping firms actually create and sustain a competitive advantage in their industry in either cost or differentiation. Dr. Porter's theories on competitive advantage are not tied to information systems, but are used by others to involve information services technologies. In his book, Dr. Porter says that there are two central questions in competitive strategy:

- How structurally attractive is the industry?

- What is the firm's relative position in the industry?

Neither of these question is sufficient alone to guide strategic choices. Both can be influenced by competitor behavior, and both can be shaped by a firm's actions. It is imperative that these questions be answered by analysis, which will be the starting point for good strategic thinking, and will open up possibilities for the role of information systems. Industry profitability is a function of five basic competitive forces:

- The threat of new entrants.

- The threat of substitute products or services.

- The bargaining power of suppliers.

- The bargaining power of buyers.

- The intensity of the rivalry among existing competitors.

Porter's books give techniques for getting a handle on the possible average profitability of an industry over time. The analysis of these forces is the base for estimating a firm's relative position and competitive advantage. In any industry, the sustained average profitability of competitors varies widely. The problem is to determine how a business can outperform the industry average and attain a sustainable competitive advantage. It is possible that the answer lies in information technology together with good management. Porter claims that the principal types of competitive advantage are low cost producer, differentiation, and focus.

A firm has a competitive advantage if it is able to deliver its product or service at a lower cost than its competitors. If the quality of its product is satisfactory, this will translate into higher margins and higher returns. Another advantage is gained if the firm is able to differentiate itself in some way. Differentiation leads to offering something that is both unique and is desired, and translates into a premium price. Again, this will lead to higher margins and superior performance.

It seems that two types of competitive advantage, lower cost and differentiation, are mutually exclusive. To get lower cost, you sacrifice uniqueness. To get a premium price, there must be extra cost involved in the process. To be a superior performer, however, you must go for competitive advantage in either cost or differentiation.

Another point of Porter's is that competitive advantage is gained through a strategy based on scope. It is necessary to look at the breadth of a firm's activities, and narrow the competitive scope to gain focus in either an industry segment, a geographic area, a customer type, and so on. Competitive advantage is most readily gained by defining the competitive scope in which the firm is operating, and concentrating on it.

Based on these ideas of type and scope, Porter gives a useful tool for analysis which he calls the value chain. This value chain gives a framework on which a useful analysis can be hung. The basic notion is that to understand competitive advantage in any firm, one cannot look at the firm as a whole. It is necessary to identify the specific activities which the firm performs to do business. Each firm is a collection of the things that it does that all add up to the product being delivered to the customer. These activities are numerous and are unique to every industry, but it is only in these activities where cost advantage or differentiation can be gained. The basic idea is that the firm's activities can be divided into nine generic types. Five are the primary activities, which are the activities that create the product, market it and deliver it; four are the support activities that cross between the primary activities.

The primary activities are:

- Inbound logistics: Which includes the receipt and storage of material, and the general management of supplies.

- Operations: Which are the manufacturing steps or the service steps.

- Outbound logistics: Which are associated with collecting, storing, and physically distributing the product to buyers. In some companies this is a significant cost, and buyers value speed and consistency.

- Marketing and sales includes customer relations, order entry, and price management.

- After-sales services covers the support of the product in the field, installation, customer training, and so on.

The support activities are not directed to the customer, but they allow the firm to perform its primary activities. The four generic types of support activities are:

- Procurement: Which includes the contracting for and purchase of raw materials, or any items used by the enterprise. Part of procurement is in the purchasing department, but it is also spread throughout the organization.

- Technology development may simply cover operational procedures, or many be involved with the use of complex technology. Today, sophisticated technology is pervasive, and cuts across all activities; it is not just an R&D function.

- Human resource management is the recruiting, training, and development of people. Obviously, the cuts across every other activity.

- Firm infrastructure is a considerable part of the firm, including the accounting department, the legal department, the planning department, government relations, and so on.

The basic idea is that competitive advantage grows out of the firm's ability to perform these activities either less expensively than its competitors, or in a unique way. Competitive advantage should be linked precisely to these specific activities, and not thought of broadly at a firm-wide level. This is an attractive way of thinking for most information services people, as it is, fundamentally, the systems analysis approach. Computer people are trained to reduce systems to their components, look for the best application for each component, then put together an interrelated system.

Information technology is also pervasive throughout all parts of the value chain. Every activity that the firm performs has the potential to embed information technology because it involves information processing. As information technology moves away from repetitive transaction processing and permeates all activities in the value chain, it will be in a better position to be useful in gaining competitive advantage. Porter emphasizes what he call the linkages between the activities that the firm performs. No activities in a firm are independent, yet each department is managed separately. It is most important to understand the cost linkages that are involved so that the firm may get an overall optimization of the production rather than departmental optimizations. A typical linkage might be that if more is spent in procurement, less is spent in operations. If more testing is done in operations, after-sales service costs will be lower.

Multi-functional coordination is crucial to competitive advantage, but it is often difficult to see. Insights into linkages give the ability to have overall optimization. Any strategic information system must be analyzed across all departments in the organization.

Cost and Competitive Advantage

Cost leadership is one of Porter's two types of competitive advantage. The cost leader delivers a product of acceptable quality at the lowest possible cost. It attempts to open up a significant and sustainable cost gap over all other competitors. The cost advantage is achieved through superior position in relation to the key cost drivers. Achieving cost leadership usually requires trade-offs with differentiation. The two are usually incompatible. A firm's relative cost position cannot be understood by viewing the firm as a whole. Overall cost grows out of the cost performing discrete activities. Cost position is determined by the cumulative cost of performing all value activities.

To sustain cost advantage, Porter gives a number of cost drivers which must be understood in detail because the sustainability of cost advantage in an activity depends on the cost drivers of that activity. Again, this type of detail is best obtained by classical systems analysis methods.

Some of the cost drivers which must be analyzed, understood, and controlled are:

- Scale: The appropriate type of scale must be found. Policies must be set to reinforce economies of scale in scale-sensitive activities.

- Learning: The learning curve must be understood and managed. As the organization tries to learn from competitors, it must strive to keep its own learning proprietary.

- Capacity Utilization: Cost can be controlled by the leveling of throughput.

- Linkages: Linkages should be exploited within the value chain. Work with suppliers and channels can reduce costs.

- Interrelationships: Shared activities can reduce costs.

- Integration: The possibilities for integration or de-integration should be examined systematically.

- Timing: If the advantages of being the first mover or a late mover are understood, they can be exploited.

- Policies: Policies that enhance the low-cost position or differentiation should be emphasized.

- Location: When viewed as a whole, the location of individual activities can be optimized.

- Institutional Factors: Institutional factors should be examined to see whether their change may be helpful.

Care must be taken in the evaluation and perception of cost drivers because there are pitfalls if the thinking is incremental and indirect activities are ignored. Even though the manufacturing activities, for example, are obvious candidates for analyses, they should not have exclusive focus. Linkages must be exploited and cross-subsidies avoided.

Porter gives five steps to achieving cost leadership:

- Identify the appropriate value chain and assign costs and assets to it.

- Identify the cost drivers of each value activity and see how they interact.

- Determine the relative costs of competitors and the sources of cost differences.

- Develop a strategy to lower relative cost position through controlling cost drivers or reconfiguring the value chain.

Differentiation Advantage

Differentiation is the second of Porter's two types of competitive advantage. In the differentiation strategy, one or more characteristics that are widely value by buyers are selected. The purpose is to achieve and sustain performance that is superior to any competitor in satisfying those buyer needs. A differentiator selectively adds costs in areas that are important to the buyer. Thus, successful differentiation leads to premium prices, and these lead to above-average profitably if there is approximate cost parity. To achieve this, efficient forms of differentiation must be picked, and costs must be reduced in areas that are irrelevant to the buyer needs. Buyers are like sellers in that they have their own value chains. The product being sold will represent one purchased input, but the seller may affect the buyer's activities in other ways. Differentiation can lower the buyer's cost and improve the buyer's performance, and thus create value, or competitive advantage, for the buyer. The buyer may not be able to assess all the value that a firm provides, but it looks for signals of value, or perceived value.

A few typical factors which may lower the buyer's costs are:

- Less idle time.

- Lower risk of failure.

- Lower installation costs.

- Faster processing time.

- Lower labor costs.

- Longer useful life.

Porter points out that differentiation is usually costly, depending on the cost drivers of the activities involved. A firm must find forms of differentiation where it has a cost advantage in differentiating. Differentiation is achieved by enhancing the sources of uniqueness. These may be found throughout the value chain, and should be signaled to the buyer. The cost of differentiation can be turned to advantage if the less costly sources are exploited and the cost drivers are controlled. The emphasis must be on getting a sustainable cost advantage in differentiating. Efforts must be made to change the buyer's criteria by reconfiguring the value chain to be unique in new ways, and by preemptively responding to changing buyer or channel circumstances. Differentiation will nor work if there is too much uniqueness, or uniqueness that the buyers do not value. The buyer's ability to pay a premium price, the signaling criteria, and the segments important to the buyer must all be understood. Also, there cannot be an over reliance on sources of differentiation that competitors can emulate cheaply or quickly.

Porter lists seven steps to achieving differentiation:

- Determine the identity of the real buyer.

- Understand the buyer's value chain, and the effect of the seller's product on it.

- Determine the purchasing criteria of the buyer.

- Assess possible sources of uniqueness in the firm's value chain.

- Identify the cost of these sources of uniqueness.

- Choose the value activities that create the most valuable differentiation for the buyer relative to the costs incurred.

- Test the chosen differentiation strategy for sustainability.

Focus Strategies for Advantage

Porter's writings also discuss focus strategies. He emphasizes that a company that attempts to completely satisfy every buyer does not have a strategy. Focusing means selecting targets and optimizing the strategies for them. Focus strategies further segment the industry. They may be imitated, but can provide strategic openings. Clearly, multiple generic strategies may be implemented, but internal inconsistencies can then arise, and the distinctions between the focused entities may become blurred. Porter's work is directed towards competitive advantage in general, and is not specific to strategic information systems. The value chain concept has been widely adopted, and the ideas of low cost and differentiation are accepted.

Wiseman's Strategic Perspective View

Wiseman applied the concepts of SIS in work at GTE (Implementors of SIS for competitive advantage) and other companies, and in his consulting work. His book extends Porter's thinking in many practical ways in the Information Systems area, and discusses many examples of strategic systems.

Wiseman emphasizes that companies have begun to use information systems strategically to reap significant competitive advantage. He feels that the significance of these computer-based products and services does not lie in their technological sophistication or in the format of the reports they produce; rather it is found in the role played by these information systems in the firm's planning and implementation in gaining and maintaining competitive advantage.

Wiseman points out that although the use of information systems may not always lead to competitive advantage, it can serve as an important tool in the firm's strategic plan. Strategic systems must not be discovered haphazardly. Those who would be competitive leaders must develop a systematic approach for identifying strategic information systems (SIS) opportunities. Both business management and information management must be involved.

A framework must be developed for identifying SIS opportunities. There will certainly be competitive response, so one should proceed with strategic thrusts based on information technology. These moves are just as important as other strategic thrusts, such as acquisition, geographical expansion, and so on. It is necessary to plan rationally about acquisition, major alliances with other firms, and other strategic thrusts.

IMB'S Business Systems Planning (BSP) and MIT's Critical Success Factor (CSF) methodologies are ways to develop information architectures and to identify conventional information systems, which are primarily used for planning and control purposes. To identify SIS, a new model or framework is needed. The conventional approach works within the perceived structures of the organization. An effective SIS approach arises from the forging of new alliances that expand the horizon of expectation. Such an approach is most difficult to attain, and can only work with top management support. Innovations, however, frequently, come from simply a new look at existing circumstances, from a new viewpoint. Information Services people must start to look systematically at application opportunities related to managers.

Wiseman believes that the range of opportunities is limited by the framework adopted. He contrasts the framework for Conventional IS Opportunities with the framework for Strategic IS Opportunities.

In the conventional view, there are two information system thrusts: to automate the basic processes of the firm, or to satisfy the information needs of managers, professionals, or others. There are three generic targets: strategic planning, management control, and operational control. In this perspective, there are, thus, six generic opportunity areas.

In the strategic view of IS opportunities, there are five strategic information thrusts and three strategic targets. This gives fifteen generic opportunity areas. This opens up the range and perspective of management vision.

Sustainable competitive advantage can mean many things to different firms. Competitive advantage may be with respect to a supplier, a customer, or a rival. It may exist because of a lower price, because of desirable features, or because of the various resources that a firm possesses. Sustainability is also highly relative, depending upon the business. In established businesses, it may refer to years, and the experience that the firm develops may be quite difficult to emulate. In other industries, a lead of a few weeks or months may be all that is necessary.

Wiseman uses the term strategic thrusts for the moves that companies make to gain or maintain some kind of competitive edge, or to reduce the competitive edge of one of the strategic targets. Information technology can be used to support or to shape one or more of these thrusts. Examining the possibilities of these thrusts takes imagination, and it is helped by understanding what other firms have done in similar situations. This is why so many examples are presented in the literature. Analogy is important.

There is no question that there is considerable overlap between conventional information systems and strategic information systems. Systems are complex and a great deal of data is involved. The idea is to look at this complexity in a new light, and see where competitive advantage might possibly be gained. Note that Wiseman takes Porter's three generic categories: low cost producer, differentiation, and focus, and extends them to five categories: differentiation, cost, innovations, growth, and alliance.

Cost may be moves that not only reduces the costs, but also reduces the costs of selected strategic targets so that you will benefit from preferential treatment. A strategic cost thrust may also aim at achieving economies of scale.

Innovation is another strategic thrust that can be supported or shaped by information technology in either product or process. In many financial firms, the innovative product is really an information system. Innovation requires rapid response to opportunities to be successful, but this carries with it the question of considerable risk. There can be no innovation without risk, whether information systems are included or not. Innovation, however, can achieve advantage in product or process that results in a fundamental transformation in the way that type of business is conducted.

Growth achieves an advantage by expansion in volume or geographical distribution. It may also come from product-time diversification. Information systems can be of considerable help in the management of rapid growth.

Alliance gains competitive advantage by gaining growth, differentiation, or cost advantages through marketing agreements, forming joint ventures, or making appropriate acquisitions.

The Strategic Planning Process. Wiseman advocates brainstorming and the systematic search for SIS opportunities. He describes his SIS Planning Process in five phases:

- Introduce the Information Services management to SIS concepts. Give an overview of the process describe cases. Gain approval to proceed with an idea-generation meeting in Information Service.

- Conduct an SIS idea generation meeting with Information Services middle management. Test the SIS idea-generation methodology. Identify significant SIS areas for executive consideration.

- Conduct an SIS idea-generation meeting with senior Information Services management. Identify SIS ideas, and evaluate them together with the ideas from the previous meeting.

- Introduce the top business executives to the SIS concept. Discuss some of the SIS ideas that were considered for the business. Gain approval to proceed with the SIS idea-generation meetings with business planners.

- Conduct an SIS idea-generation meeting with the corporate planners. Identify some SIS ideas and evaluate them together with the ideas that have emerged from the previous meeting.

Wiseman points out that the whole idea is designed to introduce the strategic perspective on information systems, stimulate the systematic search for SIS opportunities, and evaluate and select a set of projects that are expected to secure the greatest competitive advantage for the firm. In the idea-generation meetings of Phases 2, 3, and 5 of the process, there are always seven explicit steps:

- Give a Tutorial on Competitive Strategy: Introduce the concepts of strategic thrusts, strategic targets, and competitive strategy.

- Apply SIS Concepts to Actual Cases: Develop an understanding of SIS possibilities and their strategic thrusts and targets.

- Review the Company's Competitive Position: Try to understand its present business position and its strategies.

- Brainstorm for SIS Opportunities: Generate SIS ideas in small groups.

- Discuss the SIS Opportunities: Use the experience of the group to correlate and condense the SIS ideas.

- Evaluate the SIS Opportunities: Consider the competitive significance of the SIS ideas.

- Detail the SIS Blockbusters: Select the best SIS ideas, and detail their competitive advantages and key implementation issues.

Wiseman says that typical SIS idea-generation meetings will last for days. Each step takes about two hours, at least. The process generates many good SIS ideas, and a few will always be considered worth implementation. Top management begins to focus their attention on SIS opportunities. The ideas that are generated can produce significant competitive advantage.

DECISION SUPPORT SYSTEM

A decision support system (DSS) is an information system that supports business or organizational decision-making activities. DSSs serve the management, operations and planning levels of an organization (usually mid and higher management) and help people make decisions about problems that may be rapidly changing and not easily specified in advance—i.e. unstructured and semi-structured decision problems. Decision support systems can be either fully computerized or human-powered, or a combination of both.

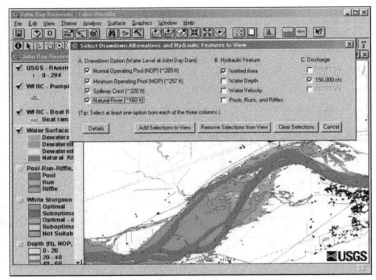

Decision support system for John Day Reservoir.

While academics have perceived DSS as a tool to support decision making processes, DSS users see DSS as a tool to facilitate organizational processes. Some authors have extended the definition of DSS to include any system that might support decision making and some DSS include a decision-making software component; Sprague defines a properly termed DSS as follows:

- DSS tends to be aimed at the less well structured, underspecified problem that upper level managers typically face;

- DSS attempts to combine the use of models or analytic techniques with traditional data access and retrieval functions;

- DSS specifically focuses on features which make them easy to use by non-computer-proficient people in an interactive mode;

- DSS emphasizes flexibility and adaptability to accommodate changes in the environment and the decision making approach of the user.

DSSs include knowledge-based systems. A properly designed DSS is an interactive software-based system intended to help decision makers compile useful information from a combination of raw data, documents, and personal knowledge, or business models to identify and solve problems and make decisions.

Typical information that a decision support application might gather and present includes:

- Inventories of information assets (including legacy and relational data sources, cubes, data warehouses, and data marts),

- Comparative sales figures between one period and the next,

- Projected revenue figures based on product sales assumptions.

Taxonomies

Using the relationship with the user as the criterion, Haettenschwiler differentiates passive, active, and cooperative DSS. A passive DSS is a system that aids the process of decision making, but that cannot bring out explicit decision suggestions or solutions. An active DSS can bring out such decision suggestions or solutions. A cooperative DSS allows for an iterative process between human and system towards the achievement of a consolidated solution, the decision maker (or its advisor) can modify, complete, or refine the decision suggestions provided by the system, before sending them back to the system for validation, and likewise the system again improves, completes, and refines the suggestions of the decision maker and sends them back to them for validation.

Another taxonomy for DSS, according to the mode of assistance, has been created by Daniel Power. He differentiates communication-driven DSS, data-driven DSS, document-driven DSS, knowledge-driven DSS, and model-driven DSS.

- A communication-driven DSS enables cooperation, supporting more than one person working on a shared task; examples include integrated tools like Google Docs or Microsoft SharePoint Workspace.

- A data-driven DSS (or data-oriented DSS) emphasizes access to and manipulation of a time series of internal company data and, sometimes, external data.

- A document-driven DSS manages, retrieves, and manipulates unstructured information in a variety of electronic formats.

- A knowledge-driven DSS provides specialized problem-solving expertise stored as facts, rules, procedures or in similar structures like DeciZone interactive decision trees and flowcharts.

- A model-driven DSS emphasizes access to and manipulation of a statistical, financial, optimization, or simulation model. Model-driven DSS use data and parameters provided by users to assist decision makers in analyzing a situation; they are not necessarily data-intensive. Dicodess is an example of an open-source model-driven DSS generator.

Using scope as the criterion, Power differentiates *enterprise-wide DSS* and *desktop DSS*. An *enterprise-wide DSS* is linked to large data warehouses and serves many managers in the company. A *desktop, single-user DSS* is a small system that runs on an individual manager's PC.

Components

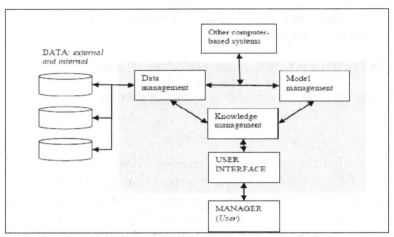

Design of a drought mitigation decision support system.

Three fundamental components of a DSS architecture are:

- The database (or knowledge base),

- The model (i.e., the decision context and user criteria)

- The user interface.

The users themselves are also important components of the architecture.

Development Frameworks

Similarly to other systems, DSS systems require a structured approach. Such a framework includes people, technology, and the development approach.

The Early Framework of Decision Support System consists of four phases:

- Intelligence – Searching for conditions that call for decision;

- Design – Developing and analyzing possible alternative actions of solution;

- Choice – Selecting a course of action among those;

- Implementation – Adopting the selected course of action in decision situation.

DSS technology levels (of hardware and software) may include:

- The actual application that will be used by the user. This is the part of the application that allows the decision maker to make decisions in a particular problem area. The user can act upon that particular problem.

- Generator contains Hardware/software environment that allows people to easily develop specific DSS applications. This level makes use of case tools or systems such as Crystal, Analytica and iThink.

- Tools include lower level hardware/software. DSS generators including special languages, function libraries and linking modules.

An iterative developmental approach allows for the DSS to be changed and redesigned at various intervals. Once the system is designed, it will need to be tested and revised where necessary for the desired outcome.

Classification

There are several ways to classify DSS applications. Not every DSS fits neatly into one of the categories, but may be a mix of two or more architectures.

Holsapple and Whinston classify DSS into the following six frameworks: text-oriented DSS, database-oriented DSS, spreadsheet-oriented DSS, solver-oriented DSS, rule-oriented DSS, and compound DSS. A compound DSS is the most popular classification for a DSS; it is a hybrid system that includes two or more of the five basic structures.

The support given by DSS can be separated into three distinct, interrelated categories: Personal Support, Group Support, and Organizational Support.

DSS components may be classified as:

- Inputs: Factors, numbers, and characteristics to analyze.

- User knowledge and expertise: Inputs requiring manual analysis by the user.

- Outputs: Transformed data from which DSS "decisions" are generated.

- Decisions: Results generated by the DSS based on user criteria.

DSSs which perform selected cognitive decision-making functions and are based on artificial intelligence or intelligent agents technologies are called intelligent decision support systems (IDSS).

The nascent field of decision engineering treats the decision itself as an engineered object, and applies engineering principles such as design and quality assurance to an explicit representation of the elements that make up a decision.

Applications

DSS can theoretically be built in any knowledge domain.

One example is the clinical decision support system for medical diagnosis. There are four stages in the evolution of clinical decision support system (CDSS): the primitive version is standalone and does not support integration; the second generation supports integration with other medical systems; the third is standard-based, and the fourth is service model-based.

DSS is extensively used in business and management. Executive dashboard and other business performance software allow faster decision making, identification of negative trends, and better allocation of business resources. Due to DSS all the information from any organization is represented in the form of charts, graphs i.e. in a summarized way, which helps the management to take strategic decision. For example, one of the DSS applications is the management and development of complex anti-terrorism systems. Other examples include a bank loan officer verifying the credit of a loan applicant or an engineering firm that has bids on several projects and wants to know if they can be competitive with their costs.

A growing area of DSS application, concepts, principles, and techniques is in agricultural production, marketing for sustainable development. For example, the DSSAT4 package, developed through financial support of USAID during the 80s and 90s, has allowed rapid assessment of several agricultural production systems around the world to facilitate decision-making at the farm and policy levels. Precision agriculture seeks to tailor decisions to particular portions of farm fields. There are, however, many constraints to the successful adoption on DSS in agriculture.

DSS are also prevalent in forest management where the long planning horizon and the spatial dimension of planning problems demands specific requirements. All aspects of Forest management, from log transportation, harvest scheduling to sustainability and ecosystem protection have been addressed by modern DSSs. In this context the consideration of single or multiple management objectives related to the provision of goods and services that traded or non-traded and often subject to resource constraints and decision problems. The Community of Practice of Forest Management Decision Support Systems provides a large repository on knowledge about the construction and use of forest Decision Support Systems.

References

- Information-system-is, definition: techopedia.com, retrieved 29 march, 2019

- D'atri a., de marco m., casalino n. (2008). "interdisciplinary aspects of information systems studies", physica-verlag, springer, germany, pp. 1–416, doi:10.1007/978-3-7908-2010-2 isbn 978-3-7908-2009-6

- Taylor, victoria. "supply chain management: the next big thing?". Sept. 12, 2011. Business week. Retrieved 5 march 2014

- What-are-information-systems-definition-types-quiz, lesson, academy: study.com, retrieved 30 April, 2019

- Piccoli, gabriele; pigni, federico (july 2018). Information systems for managers: with cases (edition 4.0 ed.). Prospect press. P. 28. Isbn 978-1-943153-50-3. Retrieved 25 november 2018

- Alter, s (2013). "work system theory: overview of core concepts, extensions, and challenges for the future". Journal of the association for information systems. 14 (2): 72–121. Doi:10.17705/1jais.00323

- "Management information systems". Umassd.edu. University of massachusetts dartmouth. Retrieved 2018-04-11

Data Management

Data management consists of managing and maintaining information as a valuable resource. It comprises many fields such as data quality management, data modeling, data architecture, data integration, data processing, data security, data retrieval, database management system, etc. The topics elaborated in this chapter will help in gaining a better perspective about these aspects of data management.

Data management is the practice of organizing and maintaining data processes to meet ongoing information lifecycle needs. Emphasis on data management began with the electronics era of data processing, but data management methods have roots in accounting, statistics, logistical planning and other disciplines that predate the emergence of corporate computing in the mid-20th century.

Beginning in the 1960s, the Association of Data Processing Service Organizations (ADAPSO) became one of a handful of groups that forwarded best practices for data management, especially in terms of professional training and data quality assurance metrics. Over time, information became more popular than data as a term to describe the objectives of corporate computing -- as seen, for example, in the renaming of ADAPSO as the Information Technology Association of America (ITAA), or the National Microfilm Association renaming as the Association for Information and Image Management (AIIM) -- but the practices of data management continued to evolve.

In the 1970s, the relational database management system began to emerge at the center of data management efforts. Based on relational logic, the relational database provided improved means for assuring consistent data processing and for reducing or managing duplicated data. These traits were key for transactional applications. With the rise of the relational database, relational data modeling, schema creation, deduplication and other techniques advanced to become bigger parts of common data management practice.

The 1980s saw the creation of the Data Management Association International, or DAMA International, chartered to improve data-related education. Data arose again as a leading descriptive term when IT professionals began to build data warehouses that employed relational techniques for offline data analytics that gave business managers a better view of their organizations' key trends for decision-making. Modeling, schema and change management all called for different treatments with the advent of data warehousing that improved organization's views of operations.

Types of Data Management

DAMA International and other groups have worked to advance understanding of various approaches to data management. One such approach, master data management (MDM), for example, is a comprehensive method of enabling an enterprise to link all of its critical data to one file, called a master file, which provides a common point of reference. Data stewardship, data quality management, data governance, MDM and data security management are among the components of many professionals' data management practices. DAMA, among other groups which oversee certifications in data management skills proficiency, has created the DAMA Guide to the Data Management Body of Knowledge, or DAMA DMBOK, which attempts to define a standard industry view of data management functions and methods.

The view of data as a corporate asset, and concern about data-related responsibilities, have increased over time. Data management professionals are charged with finding ways to monetize corporate data -- whether by process streamlining, enhancing existing products or outright data selling.

The effective management of corporate data has grown in importance as businesses are subject to an increasing number of compliance regulations. At the same time, the sheer volume of data that must be managed by organizations has increased so markedly that it is sometimes referred to as big data.

Data Management Tasks

Many data managers are held accountable for corporate data security and legal liability. Stricter financial records and consumer protection requirements are driven by legislation or regulations which include Basel III, the Sarbanes-Oxley Act and Payment Card Industry Data Security Standard (PCI-DSS) policies.

Data privacy-related data management responsibilities have expanded in recent years, especially in the light of high-profile data hacks which occurred at retailer Target in 2013 and Equifax in 2017. A European data standard known as General Data Protection Regulation (GDPR) has also become the focus of data management project planning in Europe and beyond.

As data technologies have expanded, the purview of data management has expanded in turn. Increasing volumes of data and real-time processing of data have ushered in such data frameworks as Hadoop and Spark. The variety of data has grown as well. Unstructured data types have complicated data modeling procedures and ushered in an assortment of databases that do not use SQL, the structured query language closely associated with the use of relational databases. Collectively, the new technologies have come under the banner of big data. Analyst group Gartner has listed in-database analytics, event stream processing, graph databases, key-value stores and distributed ledgers as just some of the data management technologies to watch going forward.

Data Management Challenges

While some companies are good at collecting data, they are not managing it well enough to make sense of it. Simply collecting data is not enough; enterprises and organizations need to understand from the start that data management and data analytics only will be successful when they first put some thought into how they will gain value from their raw data. They can then move beyond raw data collection with efficient systems for processing, storing, and validating data, as well as effective analysis strategies.

Another challenge of data management occurs when companies categorize data and organize it without first considering the answers they hope to glean from the data. Each step of data collection and management must lead toward acquiring the right data and analyzing it in order to get the actionable intelligence necessary for making truly data-driven business decisions.

Data Management Best Practices

The best way to manage data, and eventually get the insights needed to make data-driven decisions, is to begin with a business question and acquire the data that is needed to answer that question. Companies must collect vast amounts of information from various sources and then utilize best practices while going through the process of storing and managing the data, cleaning and mining the data, and then analyzing and visualizing the data in order to inform their business decisions.

It's important to keep in mind that data management best practices result in better analytics. By correctly managing and preparing the data for analytics, companies optimize their Big Data. A few data management best practices organizations and enterprises should strive to achieve include:

- Simplify access to traditional and emerging data.

- Scrub data to infuse quality into existing business processes.

- Shape data using flexible manipulation techniques.

It is with the help of data management platforms that organizations have the ability to gather, sort, and house their information and then repackage it in visualized ways that are useful to marketers. Top performing data management platforms are capable of managing all of the data from all data sources in a central location, giving marketers and executives the most accurate business and customer information available.

Benefits of Data Management and Data Management Platforms

Managing your data is the first step toward handling the large volume of data, both structured and unstructured, that floods businesses daily. It is only through data management best practices that organizations are able to harness the power of their data and gain the insights they need to make the data useful.

In fact, data management via leading data management platforms enables organizations and enterprises to use data analytics in beneficial ways, such as:

- Personalizing the customer experience.

- Adding value to customer interactions.

- Identifying the root causes of marketing failures and business issues in real- time.

- Reaping the revenues associated with data-driven marketing.

- Improving customer engagement.

- Increasing customer loyalty.

DATA QUALITY MANAGEMENT

Data quality management is an administration type that incorporates the role establishment, role deployment, policies, responsibilities and processes with regard to the acquisition, maintenance, disposition and distribution of data. In order for a data quality management initiative to succeed, a strong partnership between technology groups and the business is required.

Information technology groups are in charge of building and controlling the entire environment, that is, architecture, systems, technical establishments and databases. This overall environment acquires, maintains, disseminates and disposes of an organization's electronic data assets.

When considering a business intelligence platform, there are various roles associated with data quality management:

- Project leader and program manager: In charge of supervising individual projects or the business intelligence program. They also manage day-to-day functions depending on the budget, scope and schedule limitations.

- Organization change agent: Assists the organization in recognizing the impact and value of the business intelligence environment, and helps the organization to handle any challenges that arise.

- Data analyst and business analyst: Communicate business needs, which consist of in-depth data quality needs. The data analyst demonstrates these needs in the data model as well as in the prerequisites for the data acquisition and delivery procedures. Collectively, these analysts guarantee that the quality needs are identified and demonstrated in the design, and that these needs are carried to the team of developers.

- Data steward: Handles data as a corporate asset.

An effective data quality management approach has both reactive and proactive elements. The proactive elements include:

- Establishment of the entire governance.

- Identification of the roles and responsibilities.

- Creation of the quality expectations as well as the supporting business strategies.

- Implementation of a technical platform that facilitates these business practices.

The reactive elements include the management of issues in the data located in existing databases.

The 5 Pillars of Data Quality Management

The People

Technology is only as efficient as the individuals who implement it. We may function within a technologically advanced business society, but human oversight and process implementation have not (yet) been rendered obsolete. Therefore, there are several DQM roles that need to be filled, including:

- DQM Program Manager: The program manager role should be filled by a high-level leader who accepts the responsibility of general oversight for business intelligence initiatives. He/ she should also oversee the management of the daily activities involving data scope, project budget and program implementation. The program manager should lead the vision for quality data and ROI.

- Organization Change Manager: The change manager does exactly what the title suggests: organizing. He/she assists the organization by providing clarity and insight into advanced data technology solutions. As quality issues are often highlighted with the use of a dashboard software, the change manager plays an important role in the visualization of data quality.

- Business/Data Analyst: The business analyst is all about the "meat and potatoes" of the business. This individual defines the quality needs from an organizational perspective. These needs are then quantified into data models for acquisition and delivery. This person (or group of individuals) ensures that the theory behind data quality is communicated to the development team.

Data Profiling

Data profiling is an essential process in the DQM lifecycle. It involves:

- Reviewing data in detail.

- Comparing and contrasting the data to its own metadata.

- Running statistical models.

- Reporting the quality of the data.

This process is initiated for the purpose of developing insight into existing data, with the purpose of comparing it to quality goals. It helps businesses develop a starting point in the DQM process and sets the standard for how to improve their information quality. The data quality metrics of complete and accurate data are imperative to this step. Accurate data is looking for disproportionate numbers, and complete data is defining the data body and ensuring that all data points are whole.

Defining Data Quality

The third pillar of DQM is quality itself. "Quality rules" should be created and defined based on business goals and requirements. These are the business/technical rules with which data must comply in order to be considered viable.

Business requirements are likely to take a front seat in this pillar, as critical data elements should depend upon industry. The development of quality rules is essential to the success of any DQM process, as the rules will detect and prevent compromised data from infecting the health of the whole set.

Much like antibodies detecting and correcting viruses within our bodies, data quality rules will correct inconsistencies among valuable data. When teamed together with online BI tools, these rules can be key in predicting trends and reporting analytics.

Data Reporting

DQM reporting is the process of removing and recording all compromising data. This should be designed to follow as a natural process of data rule enforcement. Once exceptions have been identified and captured, they should be aggregated so that quality patterns can be identified.

The captured data points should be modeled and defined based on specific characteristics (e.g., by rule, by date, by source, etc.). Once this data is tallied, it can be connected to an online reporting software to report on the state of quality and the exceptions that exist within a dashboard. If possible, automated and "on-demand" technology solutions should be implemented as well, so dashboard insights can appear in real-time.

Reporting and monitoring are the crux of data quality management ROI, as they provide visibility into the state of data at any moment in real time. By allowing businesses to identify the location and domiciles of data exceptions, teams of data specialists can begin to strategize remediation processes.

Knowledge of where to begin engaging in proactive data adjustments will help businesses move one step closer to recovering their part of the $9.7 billion lost each year to low-quality data.

Data Repair

Data repair is the two-step process of determining:

- The best way to remediate data.

- The most efficient manner in which to implement the change.

The most important aspect of data remediation is the performance of a "root cause" examination to determine why, where, and how the data defect originated. Once this examination has been implemented, the remediation plan should begin.

Data processes that depended upon the previously defective data will likely need to be re-initiated, especially if their functioning was at risk or compromised by the defected data. These processes could include reports, campaigns, or financial documentation.

This is also the point where data quality rules should be reviewed again. The review process will help determine if the rules need to be adjusted or updated, and it will help begin the process of data evolution. Once data is deemed of high-quality, critical business processes and functions should run more efficiently and accurately, with a higher ROI and lower costs.

Measuring Data Quality

To measure data quality, you obviously need data quality metrics. They are also key in assessing your efforts in increasing the quality of your information. Among the various techniques of quality management, data quality metrics must be of a top-notch and clearly defined. These metrics encompass different aspect of quality, that can be summed up with the acronym "ACCIT" standing for Accuracy, Consistency, Completeness, Integrity, and Timeliness.

While data analysis can be quite complex, there are a few basic measurements that all key DQM stakeholders should be aware of. Data quality metrics are essential to provide the best and most solid basis you can have for future analyses. These metrics will also help you track the effectiveness of your quality improvement efforts, which is of course needed to make sure you are on the right tracks.

Accuracy

Refers to business transactions or status changes as they happen in real time. Accuracy should be measured through source documentation (i.e., from the business interactions), but if not available, then through confirmation techniques of an independent nature. It will indicate whether data is void of significant errors.

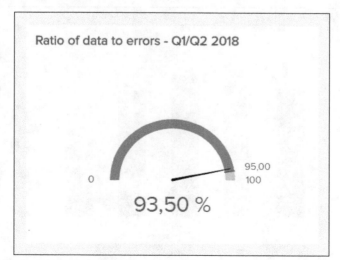

A typical metric to measure accuracy is the ratio of data to errors, that tracks the amount of known errors (like a missing, an incomplete or a redundant entry) relatively to the data set. This ratio should of course increase over time, proving that the quality of your data gets better. There is no specific ratio of data to errors, as it very much depends on the size and nature of your data set – but the higher the better of course. In the example below, we see that the data to error rate is just below the target of 95% of accuracy:

Consistency

Strictly speaking, consistency specifies that two data values pulled from separate data sets should not conflict with each other. However, consistency does not automatically imply correctness.

An example of consistency is for instance a rule that will verify that the sum of employee in each department of a company does not exceed the total number of employee in that organization.

Completeness

Completeness will indicate if there is enough information to draw conclusions. Completeness can be measured by determining whether or not each data entry is a "full" data entry. All available data entry fields must be complete, and sets of data records should not be missing any pertinent information.

For instance, a simple quality metric you can use is the number of empty values within a data set. In an inventory/warehousing context, that means that each line of item refers to a product and each of them must have a product identifier. Until that product identifier is filled, the line item is not valid. You should then monitor that metric over time with the goal to reduce it.

Integrity

Also known as data validation, integrity refers to the structural testing of data to ensure that the data complies with procedures. This means there are no unintended data errors, and it corresponds to its appropriate designation (e.g., date, month and year).

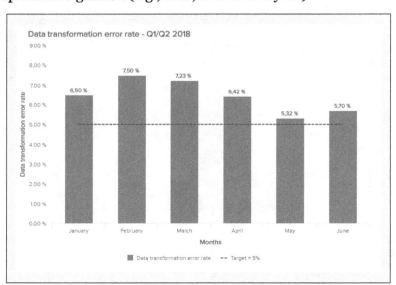

Here, it all comes down to the data transformation error rate. The metric you want to use tracks how many data transformation operations fail relatively to the whole – or in other words, how often the process of taking data stored in one format and converting it to a different one is not successfully performed. In our example below, the transformation error rate is represented over time:

Timeliness

Timeliness corresponds to the expectation for availability and accessibility of information. In other words, it measures the time between when data is expected and the moment when it is readily available for use.

A metric to evaluate timeliness is the data time-to-value. This is essential to measure and optimize this time, as it has many repercussions on the success of a business. The best moment to derive valuable information of data is always now, so the earliest you have access to that information, the better.

Whichever way you choose to improve the quality of your data, you will always need to measure the effectiveness of your efforts. All of these data quality metrics examples make a good assessment of your processes, and shouldn't be left out of the picture. The more you assess, the better you can improve, so it is key to have it under control.

Data Quality Metrics Examples

- Ratio of data to errors: Monitors the number of known data errors compared to the entire data set.

- Number of empty values: Counts the times you have an empty field within a data set.

- Data time-to-value: Evaluates how long it takes you to gain insights from a data set. There are other factors influencing it, yet quality is one of the main reason this time can increase.

- Data transformation error rate: This metric tracks how often a data transformation operation fails.

- Data storage costs: When your storage costs go up while the amount of data you use remains the same, or worse, decreases, it might mean that a significant part of the data stored has a quality to low to be used.

DATA MODELING

Data modeling in software engineering is the process of creating a data model for an information system by applying certain formal techniques.

Data modeling is a process used to define and analyze data requirements needed to support the business processes within the scope of corresponding information systems in organizations. Therefore, the process of data modeling involves professional data modelers working closely with business stakeholders, as well as potential users of the information system.

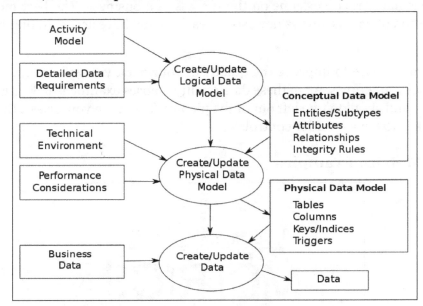

The data modeling process: The figure illustrates the way data models are developed and used today. A conceptual data model is developed based on the data requirements for the application that is being developed, perhaps in the context of an activity model. The data model will normally consist of entity types, attributes, relationships, integrity rules, and the definitions of those objects. This is then used as the start point for interface or database design.

There are three different types of data models produced while progressing from requirements to the actual database to be used for the information system. The data requirements are initially recorded as a conceptual data model which is essentially a set of technology independent specifications about the data and is used to discuss initial requirements with the business stakeholders. The conceptual model is then translated into a logical data model, which documents structures of the data that can be implemented in databases. Implementation of one conceptual data model may require multiple logical data models. The last step in data modeling is transforming the logical data model to a physical data model that organizes the data into tables, and accounts for access, performance and storage details. Data modeling defines not just data elements, but also their structures and the relationships between them.

Data modeling techniques and methodologies are used to model data in a standard, consistent, predictable manner in order to manage it as a resource. The use of data modeling standards is strongly recommended for all projects requiring a standard means of defining and analyzing data within an organization, e.g., using data modeling:

- To assist business analysts, programmers, testers, manual writers, IT package selectors, engineers, managers, related organizations and clients to understand and use an agreed semi-formal model the concepts of the organization and how they relate to one another.

- To manage data as a resource.

- For the integration of information systems.

- For designing databases/data warehouses (aka data repositories).

Data modeling may be performed during various types of projects and in multiple phases of projects. Data models are progressive; there is no such thing as the final data model for a business or application. Instead a data model should be considered a living document that will change in response to a changing business. The data models should ideally be stored in a repository so that they can be retrieved, expanded, and edited over time. Whitten et al. determined two types of data modeling:

- Strategic data modeling: This is part of the creation of an information systems strategy, which defines an overall vision and architecture for information systems. Information technology engineering is a methodology that embraces this approach.

- Data modeling during systems analysis: In systems analysis logical data models are created as part of the development of new databases.

Data modeling is also used as a technique for detailing business requirements for specific databases. It is sometimes called *database modeling* because a data model is eventually implemented in a database.

Data Models

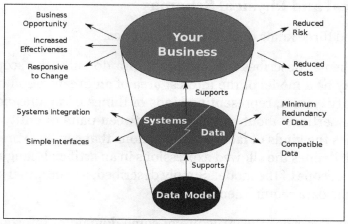

How data models deliver benefit.

Data models provide a framework for data to be used within information systems by providing specific definition and format. If a data model is used consistently across systems then compatibility of data can be achieved. If the same data structures are used to store and access data then different applications can share data seamlessly. The results of this are indicated in the diagram. However, systems and interfaces are often expensive to build, operate, and maintain. They may also constrain the business rather than support it. This may occur when the quality of the data models implemented in systems and interfaces is poor.

Some common problems found in data models are:

- Business rules, specific to how things are done in a particular place, are often fixed in the structure of a data model. This means that small changes in the way business is conducted lead to large changes in computer systems and interfaces. So, business rules need to be implemented in a flexible way that does not result in complicated dependencies, rather the data model should be flexible enough so that changes in the business can be implemented within the data model in a relatively quick and efficient way.

- Entity types are often not identified, or are identified incorrectly. This can lead to replication of data, data structure and functionality, together with the attendant costs of that duplication in development and maintenance. Therefore, data definitions should be made as explicit and easy to understand as possible to minimize misinterpretation and duplication.

- Data models for different systems are arbitrarily different. The result of this is that complex interfaces are required between systems that share data. These interfaces can account for between 25-70% of the cost of current systems. Required interfaces should be considered inherently while designing a data model, as a data model on its own would not be usable without interfaces within different systems.

- Data cannot be shared electronically with customers and suppliers, because the structure and meaning of data has not been standardised. To obtain optimal value from an implemented data model, it is very important to define standards that will ensure that data models will both meet business needs and be consistent.

Conceptual, Logical and Physical Schemas

In 1975 ANSI described three kinds of data-model *instance*:

- Conceptual schema: describes the semantics of a domain (the scope of the model). For example, it may be a model of the interest area of an organization or of an industry. This consists of entity classes, representing kinds of things of significance in the domain, and relationships assertions about associations between pairs of entity classes. A conceptual schema specifies the kinds of facts or propositions that can be expressed using the model. In that sense, it defines the allowed expressions in an artificial "language" with a scope that is limited by the scope of the model. Simply described, a conceptual schema is the first step in organizing the data requirements.

- Logical schema: describes the structure of some domain of information. This consists of descriptions of (for example) tables, columns, object-oriented classes, and XML tags. The logical schema and conceptual schema are sometimes implemented as one and the same.

- Physical schema: describes the physical means used to store data. This is concerned with partitions, CPUs, tablespaces, and the like.

According to ANSI, this approach allows the three perspectives to be relatively independent of each other. Storage technology can change without affecting either the logical or the conceptual schema. The table/column structure can change without (necessarily) affecting the conceptual schema. In each case, of course, the structures must remain consistent across all schemas of the same data model.

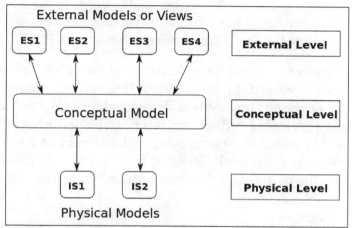

The ANSI/SPARC three level architecture. This shows that a data model can be an external model (or view), a conceptual model, or a physical model. This is not the only way to look at data models, but it is a useful way, particularly when comparing models.

Data Modeling Process

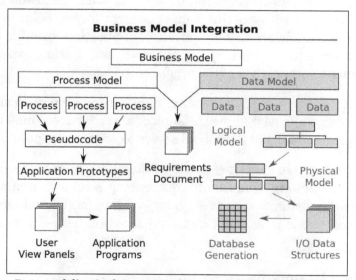

Data modeling in the context of Business Process Integration.

In the context of business process integration, data modeling complements business process modeling, and ultimately results in database generation.

The process of designing a database involves producing the previously described three types of schemas - conceptual, logical, and physical. The database design documented in these schemas are converted through a Data Definition Language, which can then be used to generate a database.

A fully attributed data model contains detailed attributes (descriptions) for every entity within it. The term "database design" can describe many different parts of the design of an overall database system. Principally, and most correctly, it can be thought of as the logical design of the base data structures used to store the data. In the relational model these are the tables and views. In an object database the entities and relationships map directly to object classes and named relationships. However, the term "database design" could also be used to apply to the overall process of designing, not just the base data structures, but also the forms and queries used as part of the overall database application within the Database Management System or DBMS.

In the process, system interfaces account for 25% to 70% of the development and support costs of current systems. The primary reason for this cost is that these systems do not share a common data model. If data models are developed on a system by system basis, then not only is the same analysis repeated in overlapping areas, but further analysis must be performed to create the interfaces between them. Most systems within an organization contain the same basic data, redeveloped for a specific purpose. Therefore, an efficiently designed basic data model can minimize rework with minimal modifications for the purposes of different systems within the organization.

Modeling Methodologies

Data models represent information areas of interest. While there are many ways to create data models, according to Len Silverston only two modeling methodologies stand out, top-down and bottom-up:

- Bottom-up models or View Integration models are often the result of a reengineering effort. They usually start with existing data structures forms, fields on application screens, or reports. These models are usually physical, application-specific, and incomplete from an enterprise perspective. They may not promote data sharing, especially if they are built without reference to other parts of the organization.

- Top-down logical data models, on the other hand, are created in an abstract way by getting information from people who know the subject area. A system may not implement all the entities in a logical model, but the model serves as a reference point or template.

Sometimes models are created in a mixture of the two methods by considering the data needs and structure of an application and by consistently referencing a subject-area model. Unfortunately, in many environments the distinction between a logical data model and a physical data model is blurred. In addition, some case tools don't make a distinction between logical and physical data models.

Entity Relationship Diagrams

There are several notations for data modeling. The actual model is frequently called "Entity relationship model", because it depicts data in terms of the entities and relationships described in the data. An Entity-relationship Model (ERM) is an abstract conceptual representation of structured data. Entity-relationship modeling is a relational schema database modeling method, used in software engineering to produce a type of conceptual data model (or semantic data model) of a system, often a relational database, and its requirements in a top-down fashion.

These models are being used in the first stage of information system design during the requirements analysis to describe information needs or the type of information that is to be stored in a database. The data modeling technique can be used to describe any ontology (i.e. an overview and classifications of used terms and their relationships) for a certain universe of discourse i.e. area of interest.

Several techniques have been developed for the design of data models. While these methodologies guide data modelers in their work, two different people using the same methodology will often come up with very different results. Most notable are:

- Bachman diagrams.

- Barker's notation.

- Chen's Notation.

- Data Vault Modeling.

- Extended Backus–Naur form.

- IDEF1X.

- Object-relational mapping.

- Object-Role Modeling.

- Relational Model.

- Relational Model/Tasmania.

Generic Data Modeling

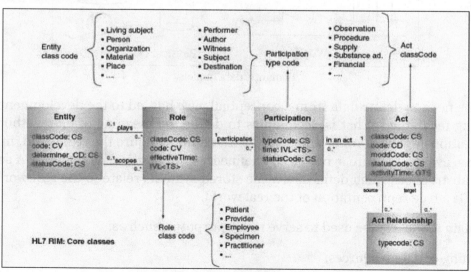

Generic data model.

Generic data models are generalizations of conventional data models. They define standardized general relation types, together with the kinds of things that may be related by such a relation type. The definition of generic data model is similar to the definition of a natural language. For example, a generic data model may define relation types such as a 'classification relation', being a binary relation between an individual thing and a kind of thing (a class) and a 'part-whole relation', being a binary relation between two things, one with the role of part, the other with the role of whole, regardless the kind of things that are related.

Given an extensible list of classes, this allows the classification of any individual thing and to specify part-whole relations for any individual object. By standardization of an extensible list of relation types, a generic data model enables the expression of an unlimited number of kinds of facts and will approach the capabilities of natural languages. Conventional data models, on the other hand, have a fixed and limited domain scope, because the instantiation (usage) of such a model only allows expressions of kinds of facts that are predefined in the model.

Semantic Data Modeling

The logical data structure of a DBMS, whether hierarchical, network, or relational, cannot totally satisfy the requirements for a conceptual definition of data because it is limited in scope and biased toward the implementation strategy employed by the DBMS. That is unless the semantic data model is implemented in the database on purpose, a choice which may slightly impact performance but generally vastly improves productivity.

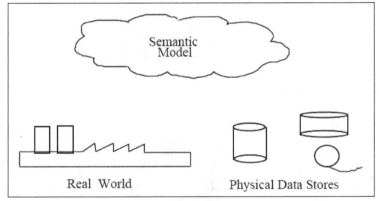

Semantic data models.

Therefore, the need to define data from a conceptual view has led to the development of semantic data modeling techniques. That is, techniques to define the meaning of data within the context of its interrelationships with other data. As illustrated in the figure the real world, in terms of resources, ideas, events, etc., are symbolically defined within physical data stores. A semantic data model is an abstraction which defines how the stored symbols relate to the real world. Thus, the model must be a true representation of the real world.

A semantic data model can be used to serve many purposes, such as:

- Planning of data resources.

- Building of shareable databases.

- Evaluation of vendor software.

- Integration of existing databases.

The overall goal of semantic data models is to capture more meaning of data by integrating relational concepts with more powerful abstraction concepts known from the Artificial Intelligence field. The idea is to provide high level modeling primitives as integral part of a data model in order to facilitate the representation of real world situations.

DATA ARCHITECTURE

In information technology, data architecture is composed of models, policies, rules or standards that govern which data is collected, and how it is stored, arranged, integrated, and put to use in data systems and in organizations. Data is usually one of several architecture domains that form the pillars of an enterprise architecture or solution architecture.

A data architecture should set data standards for all its data systems as a vision or a model of the eventual interactions between those data systems. Data integration, for example, should be dependent upon data architecture standards since data integration requires data interactions between two or more data systems. A data architecture, in part, describes the data structures used by a business and its computer applications software. Data architectures address data in storage, data in use and data in motion; descriptions of data stores, data groups and data items; and mappings of those data artifacts to data qualities, applications, locations etc.

Essential to realizing the target state, Data Architecture describes how data is processed, stored, and utilized in an information system. It provides criteria for data processing operations so as to make it possible to design data flows and also control the flow of data in the system.

The data architect is typically responsible for defining the target state, aligning during development and then following up to ensure enhancements are done in the spirit of the original blueprint.

During the definition of the target state, the Data Architecture breaks a subject down to the atomic level and then builds it back up to the desired form. The data architect breaks the subject down by going through 3 traditional architectural processes:

- Conceptual - represents all business entities.

- Logical - represents the logic of how entities are related.

- Physical - the realization of the data mechanisms for a specific type of functionality.

The "data" column of the Zachman Framework for enterprise architecture –

Layer	View	Data (What)	Stakeholder
1	Scope/Contextual	List of things and architectural standards important to the business	Planner
2	Business Model/Conceptual	Semantic model or Conceptual/Enterprise Data Model	Owner
3	System Model/Logical	Enterprise/Logical Data Model	Designer
4	Technology Model/Physical	Physical Data Model	Builder
5	Detailed Representations	Actual databases	Subcontractor

In this second, broader sense, data architecture includes a complete analysis of the relationships among an organization's functions, available technologies, and data types.

Data architecture should be defined in the planning phase of the design of a new data processing and storage system. The major types and sources of data necessary to support an enterprise should be identified in a manner that is complete, consistent, and understandable. The primary requirement at this stage is to define all of the relevant data entities, not to specify computer hardware items. A data entity is any real or abstracted thing about which an organization or individual wishes to store data.

Physical Data Architecture

Physical data architecture of an information system is part of a technology plan. As its name implies, the technology plan is focused on the actual tangible elements to be used in the implementation of the data architecture design. Physical data architecture encompasses database architecture. Database architecture is a schema of the actual database technology that will support the designed data architecture.

Elements of Data Architecture

Certain elements must be defined during the design phase of the data architecture schema. For example, administrative structure that will be established in order to manage the data resources must be described. Also, the methodologies that will be employed to store the data must be defined. In addition, a description of the database technology to be employed must be generated, as well as a description of the processes that will manipulate the data. It is also important to design interfaces to the data by other systems, as well as a design for the infrastructure that will support common data operations (i.e. emergency procedures, data imports, data backups, external transfers of data).

Without the guidance of a properly implemented data architecture design, common data operations might be implemented in different ways, rendering it difficult to understand and control the flow of data within such systems. This sort of fragmentation is highly undesirable due to the potential increased cost, and the data disconnects involved. These sorts of difficulties may be encountered with rapidly growing enterprises and also enterprises that service different lines of business (e.g. insurance products).

Properly executed, the data architecture phase of information system planning forces an organization to precisely specify and describe both internal and external information flows. These are patterns that the organization may not have previously taken the time to conceptualize. It is therefore possible at this stage to identify costly information shortfalls, disconnects between departments, and disconnects between organizational systems that may not have been evident before the data architecture analysis.

Constraints and Influences

Various constraints and influences will have an effect on data architecture design. These include enterprise requirements, technology drivers, economics, business policies and data processing needs.

Enterprise Requirements

These will generally include such elements as economical and effective system expansion, acceptable performance levels (especially system access speed), transaction reliability, and transparent data management. In addition, the conversion of raw data such as transaction records and image files into more useful information forms through such features as data warehouses is also a common organizational requirement, since this enables managerial decision making and other organizational processes. One of the architecture techniques is the split between managing transaction data and (master) reference data. Another one is splitting data capture systems from data retrieval systems (as done in a data warehouse).

Technology Drivers

These are usually suggested by the completed data architecture and database architecture designs. In addition, some technology drivers will derive from existing organizational integration frameworks and standards, organizational economics, and existing site resources (e.g. previously purchased software licensing). In many cases, the integration of multiple legacy systems requires the use of data virtualization technologies.

Economics

These are also important factors that must be considered during the data architecture phase. It is possible that some solutions, while optimal in principle, may not be potential candidates due to their cost. External factors such as the business cycle, interest rates, market conditions, and legal considerations could all have an effect on decisions relevant to data architecture.

Business Policies

Business policies that also drive data architecture design include internal organizational policies, rules of regulatory bodies, professional standards, and applicable governmental laws that can vary by applicable agency. These policies and rules will help describe the manner in which enterprise wishes to process their data.

Data Processing needs

These include accurate and reproducible transactions performed in high volumes, data warehousing for the support of management information systems (and potential data mining), repetitive periodic reporting, ad hoc reporting, and support of various organizational initiatives as required (i.e. annual budgets, new product development).

DATA INTEGRATION

Data integration involves combining data residing in different sources and providing users with a unified view of them. This process becomes significant in a variety of situations, which include both commercial (such as when two similar companies need to merge their databases) and scientific (combining research results from different bioinformatics repositories, for example) domains. Data integration appears with increasing frequency as the volume (that is, big data) and the need to share existing data explodes. It has become the focus of extensive theoretical work, and numerous open problems remain unsolved. Data integration encourages collaboration between internal as well as external users.

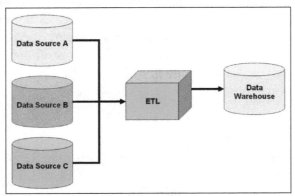

Simple schematic for a data warehouse. The Extract, transform, load (ETL) process extracts information from the source databases, transforms it and then loads it into the data warehouse.

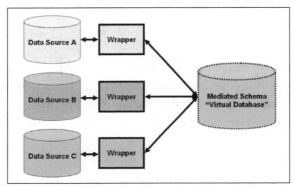

Simple schematic for a data-integration solution. A system designer constructs a mediated schema against which users can run queries.

Issues with combining heterogeneous data sources, often referred to as information silos, under a single query interface have existed for some time. In the early 1980s, computer scientists began designing systems for interoperability of heterogeneous databases. The first data integration system driven by structured metadata was designed at the University of Minnesota in 1991, for the Integrated Public Use Microdata Series (IPUMS). IPUMS used a data warehousing approach, which extracts, transforms, and loads data from heterogeneous sources into a single view schema so data from different sources become compatible. By making thousands of population databases interoperable, IPUMS demonstrated the feasibility of large-scale data integration. The data warehouse approach offers a tightly coupled architecture because the data are already physically reconciled in a single queryable repository, so it usually takes little time to resolve queries.

The data warehouse approach is less feasible for data sets that are frequently updated, requiring the extract, transform, load (ETL) process to be continuously re-executed for synchronization. Difficulties also arise in constructing data warehouses when one has only a query interface to summary data sources and no access to the full data. This problem frequently emerges when integrating several commercial query services like travel or classified advertisement web applications.

As of 2009 the trend in data integration favored loosening the coupling between data and providing a unified query-interface to access real time data over a mediated schema, which allows information to be retrieved directly from original databases. This is consistent with the SOA approach popular in that era. This approach relies on mappings between the mediated schema and the schema of original sources, and transforming a query into specialized queries to match the schema of the original databases. Such mappings can be specified in two ways: as a mapping from entities in the mediated schema to entities in the original sources (the "Global As View" (GAV) approach), or as a mapping from entities in the original sources to the mediated schema (the "Local As View" (LAV) approach). The latter approach requires more sophisticated inferences to resolve a query on the mediated schema, but makes it easier to add new data sources to a (stable) mediated schema.

As of 2010 some of the work in data integration research concerns the semantic integration problem. This problem addresses not the structuring of the architecture of the integration, but how to resolve semantic conflicts between heterogeneous data sources. For example, if two companies merge their databases, certain concepts and definitions in their respective schemas like "earnings" inevitably have different meanings. In one database it may mean profits in dollars (a floating-point number), while in the other it might represent the number of sales (an integer). A common strategy for the resolution of such problems involves the use of ontologies which explicitly define schema terms and thus help to resolve semantic conflicts. This approach represents ontology-based data integration. On the other hand, the problem of combining research results from different bioinformatics repositories requires bench-marking of the similarities, computed from different data sources, on a single criterion such as positive predictive value. This enables the data sources to be directly comparable and can be integrated even when the natures of experiments are distinct.

As of 2011 it was determined that current data modeling methods were imparting data isolation into every data architecture in the form of islands of disparate data and information silos. This data isolation is an unintended artifact of the data modeling methodology that results in the development of disparate data models. Disparate data models, when instantiated as databases, form disparate databases. Enhanced data model methodologies have been developed to eliminate the data isolation artifact and to promote the development of integrated data models. One enhanced data modeling method recasts data models by augmenting them with structural metadata in the form of standardized data entities. As a result of recasting multiple data models, the set of recast data models will now share one or more commonality relationships that relate the structural metadata now common to these data models. Commonality relationships are a peer-to-peer type of entity relationships that relate the standardized data entities of multiple data models. Multiple data models that contain the same standard data entity may participate in the same commonality relationship. When integrated data models are instantiated as databases and are properly populated from a common set of master data, then these databases are integrated.

Since 2011, data hub approaches have been of greater interest than fully structured (typically relational) Enterprise Data Warehouses. Since 2013, data lake approaches have risen to the level of Data Hubs. These approaches combine unstructured or varied data into one location, but do not necessarily require an (often complex) master relational schema to structure and define all data in the Hub.

Example:

Consider a web application where a user can query a variety of information about cities (such as crime statistics, weather, hotels, demographics, etc.). Traditionally, the information must be stored in a single database with a single schema. But any single enterprise would find information of this breadth somewhat difficult and expensive to collect. Even if the resources exist to gather the data, it would likely duplicate data in existing crime databases, weather websites, and census data.

A data-integration solution may address this problem by considering these external resources as materialized views over a virtual mediated schema, resulting in "virtual data integration". This means application-developers construct a virtual schema—the *mediated schema*—to best model the kinds of answers their users want. Next, they design "wrappers" or adapters for each data source, such as the crime database and weather website. These adapters simply transform the local query results (those returned by the respective websites or databases) into an easily processed form for the data integration solution. When an application-user queries the mediated schema, the data-integration solution transforms this query into appropriate queries over the respective data sources. Finally, the virtual database combines the results of these queries into the answer to the user's query.

This solution offers the convenience of adding new sources by simply constructing an adapter or an application software blade for them. It contrasts with ETL systems or with a single database solution, which require manual integration of entire new data set into the system. The virtual ETL solutions leverage virtual mediated schema to implement data harmonization; whereby the data are copied from the designated "master" source to the defined targets, field by field. Advanced data virtualization is also built on the concept of object-oriented modeling in order to construct virtual mediated schema or virtual metadata repository, using hub and spoke architecture.

Each data source is disparate and as such is not designed to support reliable joins between data sources. Therefore, data virtualization as well as data federation depends upon accidental data commonality to support combining data and information from disparate data sets. Because of this lack of data value commonality across data sources, the return set may be inaccurate, incomplete, and impossible to validate.

One solution is to recast disparate databases to integrate these databases without the need for ETL. The recast databases support commonality constraints where referential integrity may be enforced between databases. The recast databases provide designed data access paths with data value commonality across databases.

Theory

The theory of data integration forms a subset of database theory and formalizes the underlying concepts of the problem in first-order logic. Applying the theories gives indications as to the feasibility and difficulty of data integration. While its definitions may appear abstract, they have sufficient generality to accommodate all manner of integration systems, including those that include nested relational / XML databases and those that treat databases as programs. Connections to particular databases systems such as Oracle or DB2 are provided by implementation-level technologies such as JDBC and are not studied at the theoretical level.

Data integration systems are formally defined as a tuple $\langle G, S, M \rangle$ where G is the global (or mediated) schema, S is the heterogeneous set of source schemas, and M is the mapping that maps queries between the source and the global schemas. Both G and S are expressed in languages over alphabets composed of symbols for each of their respective relations. The mapping M consists of assertions between queries over G and queries over S. When users pose queries over the data integration system, they pose queries over G and the mapping then asserts connections between the elements in the global schema and the source schemas.

A database over a schema is defined as a set of sets, one for each relation (in a relational database). The database corresponding to the source schema S would comprise the set of sets of tuples for each of the heterogeneous data sources and is called the *source database*. Note that this single source database may actually represent a collection of disconnected databases. The database corresponding to the virtual mediated schema G is called the *global database*. The global database must satisfy the mapping M with respect to the source database. The legality of this mapping depends on the nature of the correspondence between G and S. Two popular ways to model this correspondence exist: *Global as View* or GAV and *Local as View* or LAV.

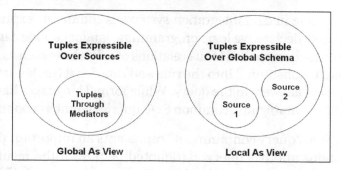

Illustration of tuple space of the GAV and LAV mappings. In GAV, the system is constrained to the set of tuples mapped by the mediators while the set of tuples expressible over the sources may be much larger and richer. In LAV, the system is constrained to the set of tuples in the sources while the set of tuples expressible over the global schema can be much larger. Therefore, LAV systems must often deal with incomplete answers.

GAV systems model the global database as a set of views over S. In this case M associates to each element of G a query over S. Query processing becomes a straightforward operation due to the well-defined associations between G and S. The burden of complexity falls on implementing mediator code instructing the data integration system exactly how to retrieve elements from the source databases. If any new sources join the system, considerable effort may be necessary to update the mediator, thus the GAV approach appears preferable when the sources seem unlikely to change.

In a GAV approach to the example data integration system above, the system designer would first develop mediators for each of the city information sources and then design the global schema around these mediators. For example, consider if one of the sources served a weather website. The designer would likely then add a corresponding element for weather to the global schema. Then the bulk of effort concentrates on writing the proper mediator code that will transform predicates on weather into a query over the weather website. This effort can become complex if some other source also relates to weather, because the designer may need to write code to properly combine the results from the two sources.

On the other hand, in LAV, the source database is modeled as a set of views over   . In this case M associates to each element of S a query over   . Here the exact associations between G and S are no longer well-defined. As is illustrated in the next section, the burden of determining how to retrieve elements from the sources is placed on the query processor. The benefit of an LAV modeling is that new sources can be added with far less work than in a GAV system, thus the LAV approach should be favored in cases where the mediated schema is less stable or likely to change.

In an LAV approach to the example data integration system above, the system designer designs the global schema first and then simply inputs the schemas of the respective city information sources. Consider again if one of the sources serves a weather website. The designer would add corresponding elements for weather to the global schema only if none existed already. Then programmers write an adapter or wrapper for the website and add a schema description of the website's results to the source schemas. The complexity of adding the new source moves from the designer to the query processor.

Query Processing

The theory of query processing in data integration systems is commonly expressed using conjunctive queries and Datalog, a purely declarative logic programming language. One can loosely think of a conjunctive query as a logical function applied to the relations of a database such as " $f(A, B)$ where $A < B$ ". If a tuple or set of tuples is substituted into the rule and satisfies it (makes it true), then we consider that tuple as part of the set of answers in the query. While formal languages like Datalog express these queries concisely and without ambiguity, common SQL queries count as conjunctive queries as well.

In terms of data integration, "query containment" represents an important property of conjunctive queries. A query A contains another query B (denoted $A \supset B$) if the results of applying B are a subset of the results of applying A for any database. The two queries are said to be equivalent if the resulting sets are equal for any database. This is important because in both GAV and LAV systems, a user poses conjunctive queries over a *virtual* schema represented by a set of views, or "materialized" conjunctive queries. Integration seeks to rewrite the queries represented by the views to make their results equivalent or maximally contained by our user's query. This corresponds to the problem of answering queries using views (AQUV).

In GAV systems, a system designer writes mediator code to define the query-rewriting. Each element in the user's query corresponds to a substitution rule just as each element in the global schema corresponds to a query over the source. Query processing simply expands the subgoals of the user's query according to the rule specified in the mediator and thus the resulting query is likely to be equivalent. While the designer does the majority of the work beforehand, some GAV systems such as Tsimmis involve simplifying the mediator description process.

In LAV systems, queries undergo a more radical process of rewriting because no mediator exists to align the user's query with a simple expansion strategy. The integration system must execute a search over the space of possible queries in order to find the best rewrite. The resulting rewrite may not be an equivalent query but maximally contained, and the resulting tuples may be incomplete. As of 2011 the GQR algorithm is the leading query rewriting algorithm for LAV data integration systems.

In general, the complexity of query rewriting is NP-complete. If the space of rewrites is relatively small, this does not pose a problem — even for integration systems with hundreds of sources.

DATA ACCESS

Data access is a generic term referring to a process which has both an IT-specific meaning and other connotations involving access rights in a broader legal and/or political sense. In the former it typically refers to software and activities related to storing, retrieving, or acting on data housed in a database or other repository. Two fundamental types of data access exist:

- Sequential access (as in magnetic tape, for example).

- Random access (as in indexed media).

Data access crucially involves authorization to access different data repositories. Data access can help distinguish the abilities of administrators and users. For example, administrators may have the ability to remove, edit and add data, while general users may not even have "read" rights if they lack access to particular information.

Historically, each repository (including each different database, file system, etc.), might require the use of different methods and languages, and many of these repositories stored their content in different and incompatible formats.

Over the years standardized languages, methods, and formats, have developed to serve as interfaces between the often proprietary, and always idiosyncratic, specific languages and methods. Such standards include SQL (1974), ODBC (ca 1990), JDBC, XQJ, ADO.NET, XML, XQuery, XPath (1999), and Web Services.

Some of these standards enable translation of data from unstructured (such as HTML or free-text files) to structured (such as XML or SQL).

Structures such as connection strings and DBURLs can attempt to standardise methods of connecting to databases.

DATA PROCESSING

Data processing is, generally, "the collection and manipulation of items of data to produce meaningful information." In this sense it can be considered a subset of *information processing*, "the change (processing) of information in any manner detectable by an observer."

The term Data Processing (DP) has also been used to refer to a department within an organization responsible for the operation of data processing applications.

Data Processing Functions

Data processing may involve various processes, including:

- Validation: Ensuring that supplied data is correct and relevant.

- Sorting: "Arranging items in some sequence and/or in different sets."

- Summarization: Reducing detailed data to its main points.

- Aggregation: Combining multiple pieces of data.

- Analysis: The "collection, organization, analysis, interpretation and presentation of data."

- Reporting: List detail or summary data or computed information.

- Classification: Separation of data into various categories.

Applications

Commercial Data Processing

Commercial data processing involves a large volume of input data, relatively few computational operations, and a large volume of output. For example, an insurance company needs to keep records on tens or hundreds of thousands of policies, print and mail bills, and receive and post payments.

Data Analysis

In science and engineering, the terms *data processing* and *information systems* are considered too broad, and the term *data processing* is typically used for the initial stage followed by a data analysis in the second stage of the overall data handling.

Data analysis uses specialized algorithms and statistical calculations that are less often observed in a typical general business environment. For data analysis, software suites like SPSS or SAS, or their free counterparts such as DAP, gretl or PSPP are often used.

DATA SECURITY

Data security means protecting digital data, such as those in a database, from destructive forces and from the unwanted actions of unauthorized users, such as a cyberattack or a data breach.

Technologies

Disk Encryption

Disk encryption refers to encryption technology that encrypts data on a hard disk drive. Disk encryption typically takes form in either software or hardware. Disk encryption is often referred to as on-the-fly encryption (OTFE) or transparent encryption.

Software vs. Hardware-based Mechanisms for Protecting Data

Software-based security solutions encrypt the data to protect it from theft. However, a malicious program or a hacker could corrupt the data in order to make it unrecoverable, making the system unusable. Hardware-based security solutions can prevent read and write access to data, hence offering very strong protection against tampering and unauthorized access.

Hardware based security or assisted computer security offers an alternative to software-only computer security. Security tokens such as those using PKCS may be more secure due to the physical access required in order to be compromised. Access is enabled only when the token is connected and correct PIN is entered. However, dongles can be used by anyone who can gain physical access to it. Newer technologies in hardware-based security solves this problem offering full proof security for data.

Working of hardware-based security: A hardware device allows a user to log in, log out and set different privilege levels through manual actions. The device uses biometric technology to prevent malicious users from logging in, logging out, and changing privilege levels. The current state of a user of the device is read by controllers in peripheral devices such as hard disks. Illegal access by a malicious user or a malicious program is interrupted based on the current state of a user by hard disk and DVD controllers making illegal access to data impossible. Hardware-based access control is more secure than protection provided by the operating systems as operating systems are vulnerable to malicious attacks by viruses and hackers. The data on hard disks can be corrupted after a malicious access is obtained. With hardware-based protection, software cannot manipulate the user privilege levels. It is impossible for a hacker or a malicious program to gain access to secure data protected by hardware or perform unauthorized privileged operations. This assumption is broken only if the hardware itself is malicious or contains a backdoor. The hardware protects the operating system image and file system privileges from being tampered. Therefore, a completely secure system can be created using a combination of hardware-based security and secure system administration policies.

Backups

Backups are used to ensure data which is lost can be recovered from another source. It is considered essential to keep a backup of any data in most industries and the process is recommended for any files of importance to a user.

Data Masking

Data masking of structured data is the process of obscuring (masking) specific data within a database table or cell to ensure that data security is maintained and sensitive information is not exposed to unauthorized personnel. This may include masking the data from users (for example so banking customer representatives can only see the last 4 digits of a customers national identity number), developers (who need real production data to test new software releases but should not be able to see sensitive financial data), outsourcing vendors, etc.

DATA ERASURE

Data erasure (sometimes referred to as data clearing, data wiping, or data destruction) is a software-based method of overwriting the data that aims to completely destroy all electronic data residing on a hard disk drive or other digital media by using zeros and ones to overwrite data onto all sectors of the device. By overwriting the data on the storage device, the data is rendered unrecoverable and achieves data sanitization.

Ideally, software designed for data erasure should:

- Allow for selection of a specific standard, based on unique needs.

- Verify the overwriting method has been successful and removed data across the entire device.

Permanent data erasure goes beyond basic file deletion commands, which only remove direct pointers to the data disk sectors and make the data recovery possible with common software tools. Unlike degaussing and physical destruction, which render the storage media unusable, data erasure removes all information while leaving the disk operable. New flash memory-based media implementations, such as solid-state drives or USB flash drives, can cause data erasure techniques to fail allowing remnant data to be recoverable.

Software-based overwriting uses a software application to write a stream of zeros, ones or meaningless pseudorandom data onto all sectors of a hard disk drive. There are key differentiators between data erasure and other overwriting methods, which can leave data intact and raise the risk of data breach, identity theft or failure to achieve regulatory compliance. Many data eradication programs also provide multiple overwrites so that they support recognized government and industry standards, though a single-pass overwrite is widely considered to be sufficient for modern hard disk drives. Good software should provide verification of data removal, which is necessary for meeting certain standards.

To protect the data on lost or stolen media, some data erasure applications remotely destroy the data if the password is incorrectly entered. Data erasure tools can also target specific data on a disk for routine erasure, providing a hacking protection method that is less time-consuming than software encryption. Hardware/firmware encryption built into the drive itself or integrated controllers is a popular solution with no degradation in performance at all.

Encryption

When encryption is in place, data erasure acts as a complement to crypto-shredding, or the practice of 'deleting' data by (only) deleting or overwriting the encryption keys. Presently, dedicated hardware/firmware encryption solutions can perform a 256-bit full AES encryption faster than the drive electronics can write the data. Drives with this capability are known as self-encrypting drives (SEDs); they are present on most modern enterprise-level laptops and are increasingly used in the enterprise to protect the data. Changing the encryption key renders inaccessible all data stored on a SED, which is an easy and very fast method for achieving a 100% data erasure. Theft of an SED results in a physical asset loss, but the stored data is inaccessible without the decryption key that is not stored on a SED, assuming there are no effective attacks against AES or its implementation in the drive hardware.

Importance

Information technology assets commonly hold large volumes of confidential data. Social security numbers, credit card numbers, bank details, medical history and classified information are often stored on computer hard drives or servers. These can inadvertently or intentionally make their way onto other media such as printers, USB, flash, Zip, Jaz, and REV drives.

Data Breach

Increased storage of sensitive data, combined with rapid technological change and the shorter lifespan of IT assets, has driven the need for permanent data erasure of electronic devices as they are retired or refurbished. Also, compromised networks and laptop theft and loss, as well as that of other portable media, are increasingly common sources of data breaches.

If data erasure does not occur when a disk is retired or lost, an organization or user faces a possibility that the data will be stolen and compromised, leading to identity theft, loss of corporate reputation, threats to regulatory compliance and financial impacts. Companies spend large amounts of money to make sure their data is erased when they discard disks. High-profile incidents of data theft include:

- CardSystems Solutions (2005-06-19): Credit card breach exposes 40 million accounts.

- Lifeblood (2008-02-13): Missing laptops contain personal information including dates of birth and some Social Security numbers of 321,000.

- Hannaford (2008-03-17): Breach exposes 4.2 million credit, debit cards.

- Compass Bank (2008-03-21): Stolen hard drive contains 1,000,000 customer records.

- University of Florida College of Medicine, Jacksonville (2008-05-20): Photographs and identifying information of 1,900 on improperly disposed computer.

- Oklahoma Corporation Commission (2008-05-21): Server sold at auction compromises more than 5,000 Social Security numbers.

- Department of Finance, the Australian Electoral Commission and National Disability Insurance Agency (2017-11-02) - 50,000 Australians and 5000 Federal Public servant records.

Regulatory Compliance

Strict industry standards and government regulations are in place that force organizations to mitigate the risk of unauthorized exposure of confidential corporate and government data. Regulations in the United States include HIPAA (Health Insurance Portability and Accountability Act); FACTA (The Fair and Accurate Credit Transactions Act of 2003); GLB (Gramm-Leach Bliley); Sarbanes-Oxley Act (SOx); and Payment Card Industry Data Security Standards (PCI DSS) and the Data Protection Act in the United Kingdom. Failure to comply can result in fines and damage to company reputation, as well as civil and criminal liability.

Preserving Assets and the Environment

Data erasure offers an alternative to physical destruction and degaussing for secure removal of all the disk data. Physical destruction and degaussing destroy the digital media, requiring disposal and contributing to electronic waste while negatively impacting the carbon footprint of individuals and companies. Hard drives are nearly 100% recyclable and can be collected at no charge from a variety of hard drive recyclers after they have been sanitized.

Limitations

Data erasure may not work completely on flash based media, such as Solid State Drives and USB Flash Drives, as these devices can store remnant data which is inaccessible to the erasure technique, and data can be retrieved from the individual flash memory chips inside the device. Data erasure through overwriting only works on hard drives that are functioning and writing to all sectors. Bad sectors cannot usually be overwritten, but may contain recoverable information. Bad sectors, however, may be invisible to the host system and thus to the erasing software. Disk encryption before use prevents this problem. Software-driven data erasure could also be compromised by malicious code.

Differentiators

Software-based data erasure uses a disk accessible application to write a combination of ones, zeroes and any other alpha numeric character also known as the "mask" onto each hard disk drive sector. The level of security when using software data destruction tools are increased dramatically by pre-testing hard drives for sector abnormalities and ensuring that the drive is 100% in working order. The number of wipes has become obsolete with the more recent inclusion of a "verify pass" which scans all sectors of the disk and checks against what character should be there i.e.; 1 Pass of AA has to fill every writable sector of the hard disk. This makes any more than 1 Pass an unnecessary and certainly a more damaging act especially as drives have passed the 1TB mark.

Full Disk Overwriting

While there are many overwriting programs, only those capable of complete data erasure offer full security by destroying the data on all areas of a hard drive. Disk overwriting programs that cannot access the entire hard drive, including hidden/locked areas like the host protected area (HPA), device configuration overlay (DCO), and remapped sectors, perform an incomplete erasure, leaving some of the data intact. By accessing the entire hard drive, data erasure eliminates the risk of data remanence.

Data erasure can also bypass the Operating System (OS). Overwriting programs that operate through the OS will not always perform a complete erasure because they cannot modify the contents of the hard drive that are actively in use by that OS. Because of this, many data erasure programs like DBAN are provided in a bootable format, where you run off of a live CD that has all of the necessary software to erase the disk.

Hardware Support

Data erasure can be deployed over a network to target multiple PCs rather than having to erase each one sequentially. In contrast with DOS-based overwriting programs that may not detect all network hardware, Linux-based data erasure software supports high-end server and storage area network (SAN) environments with hardware support for Serial ATA, Serial Attached SCSI (SAS) and Fibre Channel disks and remapped sectors. It operates directly with sector sizes such as 520, 524, and 528, removing the need to first reformat back to 512 sector size. WinPE has now overtaken Linux as the environment of choice since drivers can be added with little effort. This also helps with data destruction of tablets and other handheld devices that require pure UEFI environments without hardware NIC's installed and/or are lacking UEFI network stack support.

Standards

Many government and industry standards exist for software-based overwriting that removes the data. A key factor in meeting these standards is the number of times the data is overwritten. Also, some standards require a method to verify that all the data have been removed from the entire hard drive and to view the overwrite pattern. Complete data erasure should account for hidden areas, typically DCO, HPA and remapped sectors.

The 1995 edition of the National Industrial Security Program Operating Manual (DoD 5220.22-M) permitted the use of overwriting techniques to sanitize some types of media by writing all addressable locations with a character, its complement, and then a random character. This provision was removed in a 2001 change to the manual and was never permitted for Top Secret media, but it is still listed as a technique by many providers of the data erasure software.

Data erasure software should provide the user with a validation certificate indicating that the overwriting procedure was completed properly. Data erasure software should also comply with requirements to erase hidden areas, provide a defects log list and list bad sectors that could not be overwritten.

Overwriting Standard	Date	Overwriting Rounds	Pattern	Notes
U.S. Navy Staff Office Publication NAVSO P-5239-26	1993	3	A character, its complement, random.	Verification is mandatory.
U.S. Air Force System Security Instruction 5020	1996	3	All zeros, all ones, any character.	Verification is mandatory.
Peter Gutmann's Algorithm	1996	1 to 35	Various, including all of the other listed methods.	Originally intended for MFM and RLL disks, which are now obsolete.
Bruce Schneier's Algorithm	1996	7	All ones, all zeros, pseudo-random sequence five times.	
U.S. DoD Unclassified Computer Hard Drive Disposition	2001	3	A character, its complement, another pattern.	
German Federal Office for Information Security	2004	2–3	Non-uniform pattern, its complement.	
Communications Security Establishment Canada ITSG-06	2006	3	All ones or zeros, its complement, a pseudo-random pattern.	For unclassified media.
NIST SP-800-88	2006	1		
U.S. National Industrial Security Program Operating Manual (DoD 5220.22-M)	2006			No longer specifies any method.
NSA/CSS Storage Device Declassification Manual (SDDM)	2007	0		Degauss or destroy only.
Australian Government ICT Security Manual 2014 – Controls	2014	1	Random pattern (only for disks larger than 15 GB).	Degauss magnetic media or destroy Top Secret media.
New Zealand Government Communications Security Bureau NZSIT 402	2008	1		For data up to Confidential.

British HMG Infosec Standard 5, Baseline Standard		1	Random Pattern.	Verification is mandatory.
British HMG Infosec Standard 5, Enhanced Standard		3	All ones, all zeros, random.	Verification is mandatory.
NIST SP-800-88 Rev. 1	2014	1	All zeros.	Outlines solutions based on media type.

Data can sometimes be recovered from a broken hard drive. However, if the platters on a hard drive are damaged, such as by drilling a hole through the drive (and the platters inside), then the data can only theoretically be recovered by bit-by-bit analysis of each platter with advanced forensic technology.

Number of Overwrites Needed

Data on floppy disks can sometimes be recovered by forensic analysis even after the disks have been overwritten once with zeros (or random zeros and ones). This is not the case with modern hard drives:

- According to a publication "For storage devices containing magnetic media, a single overwrite pass with a fixed pattern such as binary zeros typically hinders recovery of data even if state of the art laboratory techniques are applied to attempt to retrieve the data." It recommends cryptographic erase as a more general mechanism.

- According to a research Secure erase does a single on-track erasure of the data on the disk drive. The U.S. National Security Agency published an Information Assurance Approval of single-pass overwrite, after technical testing at CMRR showed that multiple on-track overwrite passes gave no additional erasure." "Secure erase" is a utility built into modern ATA hard drives that overwrites all data on a disk, including remapped (error) sectors.

- Further analysis by Wright et al. seems to also indicate that one overwrite is all that is generally required.

E-waste and Information Security

E-waste presents a potential security threat to individuals and exporting countries. Hard drives that are not properly erased before the computer is disposed of can be reopened, exposing sensitive information. Credit card numbers, private financial data, account information and records of online transactions can be accessed by most willing individuals.

The e-waste centre of Agbogbloshie, Ghana. Multimillion-dollar agreements from United States security institutions such as the Defense Intelligence Agency (DIA), the Transportation Security Administration and Homeland Security have all resurfaced in Agbogbloshie.

DATA RETRIEVAL

Data retrieval, in database management, involves extracting the wanted data from a database. The two primary forms of the retrieved data are reports and queries. In order to retrieve the desired data the user present a set of criteria by a query. Reports and queries are the two primary forms of the retrieved data from a database. There are some overlaps between them, but queries generally select a relatively small portion of the database, while reports show larger amounts of data. Queries also present the data in a standard format and usually display it on the monitor; whereas reports allow formatting of the output however you like and is normally printed. Data recovery is the process of salvaging data from damaged, failed, corrupted, or inaccessible secondary storage media when it cannot be accessed normally. Often the data are being salvaged from storage media such as internal or external hard disk drives, solid-state drives (SSD), USB flash drive, storage tapes, CDs(Compact Disc), DVDs(Digital Versatile/Video Disc), RAID(Redundant array of independent disks), and other electronics. Recovery may be required due to physical damage to the storage device or logical damage to the file system that prevents it from being mounted by the host operating system.

The most common "data recovery" scenario involves an operating system (OS) failure (typically on a single-disk, single-partition, single-OS system), in which case the goal is simply to copy all wanted files to another disk. This can be easily accomplished with a Live CD, most of which provide a means to mount the system drive and backup disks or removable media, and to move the files from the system disk to the backup media with a file manager or optical disc authoring software. Such cases can often be mitigated by disk partitioning and consistently storing valuable data files (or copies of them) on a different partition from the replaceable OS system files.

Another scenario involves a disk-level failure, such as a compromised file system or disk partition, or a hard disk failure. In any of these cases, the data cannot be easily read. Depending on the situation, solutions involve repairing the file system, partition table or master boot record, or hard disk recovery techniques ranging from software-based recovery of corrupted data to hardware replacement on a physically damaged disk. If hard disk recovery is necessary, the disk itself has typically failed permanently, and the focus is rather on a one-time recovery, salvaging whatever data can be read.

In a third scenario, files have been "deleted" from a storage medium. Typically, the contents of deleted files are not removed immediately from the drive, instead, references to them in the directory structure are removed, and the space they occupy is made available for later overwriting. In the meantime, the original file contents remain, often in a number of disconnected fragments, and may be recoverable.

The term "data recovery" is also used in the context of forensic applications or espionage, where data which has been encrypted or hidden, rather than damaged, is recovered.

Recovering Data after Physical Damage

A wide variety of failures can cause physical damage to storage media. CD-ROMs can have their metallic substrate or dye layer scratched off, hard disks can suffer any of several mechanical failures, such as head crashes and failed motors, tapes can simply break. Physical damage always causes at least some data loss, and in many cases the logical structures of the file system are damaged as well. Any logical damage must be dealt with before files can be salvaged from the failed media.

Most physical damage cannot be repaired by end users. For example, opening a hard disk drive in a normal environment can allow airborne dust to settle on the platter and become caught between the platter and the read/write head, causing new head crashes that further damage the platter and thus compromise the recovery process. Furthermore, end users generally do not have the hardware or technical expertise required to make these repairs. Consequently, costly data recovery companies are often employed to salvage important data.

The Principle of Data Recovery

Data recovery is a process of finding and recovering data, in which there may be some risk, for no all situations can be anticipated or prearranged. It means maybe there will be some unexpected things happen. So you need to reduce the following:

- Danger in data recovery to the lowest.

- Backup all the data in your hard disk.

- Prevent the equipment from being damaged again.

- Don't write anything to the device on which you want to recover data.

- Try to get detailed information on how the data lost and the losing process.

- Backup the data recovered in time.

Recovery Techniques

Recovering data from physically damaged hardware can involve multiple techniques. Some damage can be repaired by replacing parts in the hard disk. This alone may make the disk usable, but there may still be logical damage. A specialized disk-imaging procedure is used to recover every readable bit from the surface. Once this image is acquired and saved on a reliable medium, the image can be safely analyzed for logical damage and will possibly allow much of the original file system to be reconstructed.

Hardware Repair

A damaged printed circuit board (PCB) may be replaced during recovery procedures by an identical PCB from a healthy drive, this does not necessarily work, as data specific to an individual drive unit may be stored on a chip, so that even boards manufactured to be identical may not work on a drive mechanism for which they are not set up.

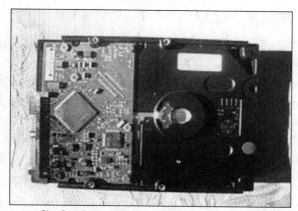

Media that has suffered a catastrophic electronic failure requires data recovery in order to salvage its contents.

Other examples of physical recovery procedures include performing a live PCB swap (in which the System Area of the HDD is damaged on the target drive which is then instead read from the donor drive, the PCB then disconnected while still under power and transferred to the target drive), read/write head assembly with matching parts from a healthy drive, removing the hard disk platters from the original damaged drive and installing them into a healthy drive, and oftentimes a combination of all of these procedures. Some procedures require training for successful use, most void manufacturers' warranties.

Recovering Data after Logical (Non-hardware) Damage

Corrupt Partitions and File Systems, Media Errors

In some cases, data on a hard drive can be unreadable due to damage to the partition table or file system, or to (intermittent) media errors. In the majority of these cases, at least a portion of the original data can be recovered by repairing the damaged partition table or filesystem using specialized data recovery software such as Testdisk; software like dd_rescue can image media despite intermittent errors, and image raw data when there is partition table or filesystem damage. This type of data recovery can be performed by people without expertise in drive hardware, as it requires no special physical equipment or access to platters. Sometimes data can be recovered using relatively simple methods and tools, more serious cases can require expert intervention, particularly if parts of files are irrecoverable. Data carving is the recovery of parts of damaged files using knowledge of their structure.

Result of a failed data recovery from a Hard disk drive.

Overwritten Data

When data has been physically overwritten on a hard disk drive it is generally assumed that the previous data is no longer possible to recover. Substantial criticism has followed, primarily dealing with the lack of any concrete examples of significant amounts of overwritten data being recovered. Although Gutmann's theory may be correct, there is no practical evidence that overwritten data can be recovered. Moreover, there are good reasons to think that it cannot. To guard against this type of data recovery, Gutmann and Colin Plumb designed a method of irreversibly scrubbing data, known as the Gutmann method and used by several disk-scrubbing software packages.

Solid-state drives (SSD) overwrite data differently than hard disk drives (HDD) which makes at least some of their data easier to recover. Most SSDs use flash memory to store data in pages and blocks, referenced by logical block addresses (LBA) which are managed by the flash translation layer (FTL). When the FTL modifies a sector it writes the new data to another location and updates the map so the new data appears at the target LBA. This leaves the pre-modification data in place, with possibly many generations, and recoverable by data recovery software.

Recovering Deleted Data

Data can be deleted from hard drive by a mistake. In this case recovery process may be similar to Recovering data after logical (non-hardware) damage. Main position of this process is to choose data recovery software (example: Recuva).

Remote Data Recovery

It is not always necessary for experts to have physical access to the damaged drive, where data can be recovered by software techniques; they can often be used remotely, with an expert using a computer at another location linked by an Internet or other connection to equipment at the fault site. Remote recovery requires a stable connection of adequate bandwidth. It is not applicable where access to the hardware is required, as for cases of physical damage.

DATABASE

Database, also called electronic database, is any collection of data, or information, that is specially organized for rapid search and retrieval by a computer. Databases are structured to facilitate the storage, retrieval, modification, and deletion of data in conjunction with various data-processing operations. A database management system (DBMS) extracts information from the database in response to queries.

A database is stored as a file or a set of files on magnetic disk or tape, optical disk, or some other secondary storage device. The information in these files may be broken down into records, each of which consists of one or more fields. Fields are the basic units of data storage, and each field typically contains information pertaining to one aspect or attribute of the entity described by the database. Records are also organized into tables that include information about relationships between its various fields. Although database is applied loosely to any collection of information in computer files, a database in the strict sense provides cross-referencing capabilities. Using keywords and various sorting commands, users can rapidly search, rearrange, group, and select the fields in many records to retrieve or create reports on particular aggregates of data.

Database records and files must be organized to allow retrieval of the information. Queries are the main way users retrieve database information. The power of a DBMS comes from its ability to define new relationships from the basic ones given by the tables and to use them to get responses to queries. Typically, the user provides a string of characters, and the computer searches the database for a corresponding sequence and provides the source materials in which those characters appear; a user can request, for example, all records in which the contents of the field for a person's last name is the word Smith.

The many users of a large database must be able to manipulate the information within it quickly at any given time. Moreover, large business and other organizations tend to build up many independent files containing related and even overlapping data, and their data-processing activities often require the linking of data from several files. Several different types of DBMS have been developed to support these requirements: flat, hierarchical, network, relational, and object-oriented.

Early systems were arranged sequentially (i.e., alphabetically, numerically, or chronologically); the development of direct-access storage devices made possible random access to data via indexes. In flat databases, records are organized according to a simple list of entities; many simple databases for personal computers are flat in structure. The records in hierarchical databases are organized in a treelike structure, with each level of records branching off into a set of smaller categories. Unlike hierarchical databases, which provide single links between sets of records at different levels, network databases create multiple linkages between sets by placing links, or pointers, to one set of records in another; the speed and versatility of network databases have led to their wide use within businesses and in e-commerce. Relational databases are used where associations between files or records cannot be expressed by links; a simple flat list becomes one row of a table, or "relation," and multiple relations can be mathematically associated to yield desired information. Various iterations of SQL (Structured Query Language) are widely employed in DBMS for relational databases. Object-oriented databases store and manipulate more complex data structures, called "objects," which are organized into hierarchical classes that may inherit properties from classes higher in the chain; this database structure is the most flexible and adaptable.

The information in many databases consists of natural-language texts of documents; number-oriented databases primarily contain information such as statistics, tables, financial data, and raw scientific and technical data. Small databases can be maintained on personal-computer systems and may be used by individuals at home. These and larger databases have become increasingly important in business life, in part because they are now commonly designed to be integrated with other office software, including spreadsheet programs.

Typical commercial database applications include airline reservations, production management functions, medical records in hospitals, and legal records of insurance companies. The largest databases are usually maintained by governmental agencies, business organizations, and universities. These databases may contain texts of such materials as abstracts, reports, legal statutes, wire services, newspapers and journals, encyclopaedias, and catalogs of various kinds. Reference databases contain bibliographies or indexes that serve as guides to the location of information in books, periodicals, and other published literature. Thousands of these publicly accessible databases now exist, covering topics ranging from law, medicine, and engineering to news and current events, games, classified advertisements, and instructional courses.

Increasingly, formerly separate databases are being combined electronically into larger collections known as data warehouses. Businesses and government agencies then employ "data mining" software to analyze multiple aspects of the data for various patterns. For example, a government agency might flag for human investigation a company or individual that purchased a suspicious quantity of certain equipment or materials, even though the purchases were spread around the country or through various subsidiaries.

DATABASE MANAGEMENT SYSTEM

A database management system (DBMS) is a software package designed to define, manipulate, retrieve and manage data in a database. A DBMS generally manipulates the data itself, the data format, field names, record structure and file structure. It also defines rules to validate and manipulate this data.

A DBMS relieves users of framing programs for data maintenance. Fourth-generation query languages, such as SQL, are used along with the DBMS package to interact with a database.

Some other DBMS examples include:

- MySQL,

- SQL Server,

- Oracle,

- dBASE,

- FoxPro.

A database management system receives instruction from a database administrator (DBA) and accordingly instructs the system to make the necessary changes. These commands can be to load, retrieve or modify existing data from the system.

A DBMS always provides data independence. Any change in storage mechanism and formats are performed without modifying the entire application. There are four main types of database organization:

- Relational Database: Data is organized as logically independent tables. Relationships among tables are shown through shared data. The data in one table may reference similar data in other tables, which maintains the integrity of the links among them. This feature is referred to as referential integrity – an important concept in a relational database system. Operations such as "select" and "join" can be performed on these tables. This is the most widely used system of database organization.

- Flat Database: Data is organized in a single kind of record with a fixed number of fields. This database type encounters more errors due to the repetitive nature of data.

- Object-Oriented Database: Data is organized with similarity to object-oriented programming concepts. An object consists of data and methods, while classes group objects having similar data and methods.

- Hierarchical Database: Data is organized with hierarchical relationships. It becomes a complex network if the one-to-many relationship is violated.

References

- Data-management, definition: techtarget.com , retrieved 29 June, 2019

- What-is-data-management: ngdata.com, retrieved 14 July, 2019

- Data-quality-management-and-metrics: datapine.com, retrieved 11 January, 2019

- steven ruggles; et al. "terra populus: integrated data on population and the environment". Terrapop.org. Retrieved 2013-01-19

- Data-quality-management-dqm, definition: techopedia.com, retrieved 18 April, 2019

- peter fleischer, jane horvath, shuman ghosemajumder (2008). "celebrating data privacy". Google blog. Archived from the original on 20 may 2011. Retrieved 12 august 2011

- Database, technology: britannica.com, retrieved 27 may, 2019

Information Technology Network

CHAPTER 5

A network in computing is a group of interconnected devices used to communicate with one another. Its major components are networking hardware, network topology, wireless network, internet protocol address, etc. All these diverse components of information technology network have been carefully analyzed in this chapter.

NETWORK

A network, in computing, is a group of two or more devices that can communicate. In practice, a network is comprised of a number of different computer systems connected by physical and/or wireless connections.

The scale can range from a single PC sharing out basic peripherals to massive data centers located around the World, to the Internet itself. Regardless of scope, all networks allow computers and/or individuals to share information and resources.

Computer networks serve a number of purposes, some of which include:

- Communications such as email, instant messaging, chat rooms, etc.

- Shared hardware such as printers and input devices.

- Shared data and information through the use of shared storage devices.

- Shared software, which is achieved by running applications on remote computers.

Early computer networks of the late 1950s included the U.S. military's Semi-Automatic Ground Environment (SAGE) and the commercial airline reservation system called the Semi-Automatic Business Research Environment (SABRE).

Based on designs developed in the 1960s, the Advanced Research Projects Agency Network (ARPANET) was created in 1969 by the U.S. Department of Defense and was based on circuit switching – the idea that a single communication line, such as a two-party telephone connection, deserves a dedicated circuit for the duration of the communication. This simple network evolved into the present day Internet.

Some of the basic hardware components that can be used in networks include:

- Interface Cards: These allow computers to communicate over the network with a low-level addressing system using media access control (MAC) addresses to distinguish one computer from another.

- Repeaters: These are electronic devices that amplify communication signals and also filter noise from interfering with the signals.

- Hubs: These contain multiple ports, allowing a packet of information/data to be copied unmodified and sent to all computers on the network.

- Bridges: These connect network segments, which allows information to flow only to specific destinations.

- Switches: These are devices that forward, make forwarding decisions and otherwise filter chunks of data communication between ports according to the MAC addresses in the packets of information.

- Routers: These are devices that forward packets between networks by processing the information in the packet.

- Firewalls: These reject network access requests from unsafe sources, but allow requests for safe ones.

There are various types of networks, which are classified according to specific characteristics such as connection types, whether they are wired or wireless, the scale of the network, and its architecture and topology.

Network types include local area networks, wide area networks, metropolitan area networks and backbone networks.

NETWORKING HARDWARE

Networking hardware, also known as network equipment or computer networking devices, are electronic devices which are required for communication and interaction between devices on a computer network. Specifically, they mediate data transmission in a computer network. Units which are the last receiver or generate data are called hosts or data terminal equipment.

Range

Networking devices may include gateways, routers, network bridges, modems, wireless access points, networking cables, line drivers, switches, hubs, and repeaters; and may also include hybrid network devices such as multilayer switches, protocol converters, bridge routers, proxy servers, firewalls, network address translators, multiplexers, network interface controllers, wireless network interface controllers, ISDN terminal adapters and other related hardware.

The most common kind of networking hardware today is a copper-based Ethernet adapter which is a standard inclusion on most modern computer systems. Wireless networking has become increasingly popular, especially for portable and handheld devices.

Other networking hardware used in computers includes data center equipment (such as file servers, database servers and storage areas), network services (such as DNS, DHCP, email, etc.) as well as devices which assure content delivery.

Taking a wider view, mobile phones, tablet computers and devices associated with the internet of things may also be considered networking hardware. As technology advances and IP-based networks are integrated into building infrastructure and household utilities, network hardware will become an ambiguous term owing to the vastly increasing number of network capable endpoints.

Specific Devices

Core

- Gateway: An interface providing a compatibility between networks by converting transmission speeds, protocols, codes, or security measures.

- Router: A networking device that forwards data packets between computer networks. Routers perform the "traffic directing" functions on the Internet. A data packet is typically forwarded from one router to another through the networks that constitute the internetwork until it reaches its destination node. It works on OSI layer 3.

- Switch: A device that connects devices together on a computer network, by using packet switching to receive, process and forward data to the destination device. Unlike less advanced network hubs, a network switch forwards data only to one or multiple devices that need to receive it, rather than broadcasting the same data out of each of its ports. It works on OSI layer 2.

- Bridge: A device that connects multiple network segments. It works on OSI layers 1 and 2.

- Repeater: An electronic device that receives a signal and retransmits it at a higher level or higher power, or onto the other side of an obstruction, so that the signal can cover longer distances.

- Repeater hub: For connecting multiple Ethernet devices together and making them act as a single network segment. It has multiple input/output (I/O) ports, in which a signal introduced at the input of any port appears at the output of every port except the original incoming. A hub works at the physical layer (layer 1) of the OSI model. Repeater hubs also participate in collision detection, forwarding a jam signal to all ports if it detects a collision. Hubs are now largely obsolete, having been replaced by network switches except in very old installations or specialized applications.

Hybrid

- Multilayer switch: A switch that, in addition to switching on OSI layer 2, provides functionality at higher protocol layers.

- Protocol converter: A hardware device that converts between two different types of transmission, for interoperation.

- Bridge router (brouter): A device that works as a bridge and as a router. The brouter routes packets for known protocols and simply forwards all other packets as a bridge would.

Border

Hardware or software components which typically sit on the connection point of different networks (for example, between an internal network and an external network) include:

- Proxy server: Computer network service which allows clients to make indirect network connections to other network services.

- Firewall: A piece of hardware or software put on the network to prevent some communications forbidden by the network policy. A firewall typically establishes a barrier between a trusted, secure internal network and another outside network, such as the Internet, that is assumed to not be secure or trusted.

- Network address translator (NAT): Network service (provided as hardware or as software) that converts internal to external network addresses and vice versa.

End Stations

Other hardware devices used for establishing networks or dial-up connections include:

- Network interface controller (NIC): A device connecting a computer to a wire-based computer network.

- Wireless network interface controller: A device connecting the attached computer to a radio-based computer network.

- Modem: Device that modulates an analog "carrier" signal (such as sound) to encode digital information, and that also demodulates such a carrier signal to decode the transmitted information. Used (for example) when a computer communicates with another computer over a telephone network.

- ISDN terminal adapter (TA): A specialized gateway for ISDN.

- Line driver: A device to increase transmission distance by amplifying the signal; used in base-band networks only.

NETWORK TOPOLOGY

Network topology is the arrangement of the elements (links, nodes, etc.) of a communication network. Network topology can be used to define or describe the arrangement of various types of telecommunication networks, including command and control radio networks, industrial fieldbusses and computer networks.

Network topology is the topological structure of a network and may be depicted physically or logically. It is an application of graph theory wherein communicating devices are modeled as nodes and the connections between the devices are modeled as links or lines between the nodes. Physical topology is the placement of the various components of a network (e.g., device location and cable installation), while logical topology illustrates how data flows within a network. Distances between nodes, physical interconnections, transmission rates, or signal types may differ between two different networks, yet their topologies may be identical. A network's physical topology is a particular concern of the physical layer of the OSI model.

Examples of network topologies are found in local area networks (LAN), a common computer network installation. Any given node in the LAN has one or more physical links to other devices in the network; graphically mapping these links results in a geometric shape that can be used to describe the physical topology of the network. A wide variety of physical topologies have been used in LANs, including ring, bus, mesh and star. Conversely, mapping the data flow between the components determines the logical topology of the network. In comparison, Controller Area Networks, common in vehicles, are primarily distributed control system networks of one or more controllers interconnected with sensors and actuators over, invariably, a physical bus topology.

Topologies

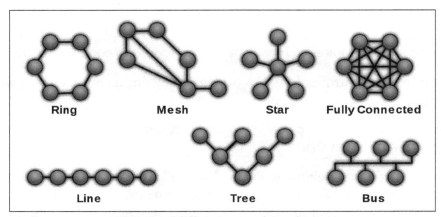

Diagram of different network topologies.

Two basic categories of network topologies exist, physical topologies and logical topologies.

The transmission medium layout used to link devices is the physical topology of the network. For conductive or fiber optical mediums, this refers to the layout of cabling, the locations of nodes, and the links between the nodes and the cabling. The physical topology of a network is determined by the capabilities of the network access devices and media, the level of control or fault tolerance desired, and the cost associated with cabling or telecommunication circuits.

In contrast, logical topology is the way that the signals act on the network media, or the way that the data passes through the network from one device to the next without regard to the physical interconnection of the devices. A network's logical topology is not necessarily the same as its physical topology. For example, the original twisted pair Ethernet using repeater hubs was a logical bus topology carried on a physical star topology. Token ring is a logical ring topology, but is wired as a physical star from the media access unit. Physically, AFDX can be a cascaded star topology of multiple dual redundant Ethernet switches; however, the AFDX Virtual links are modeled as time-switched single-transmitter bus connections, thus following the safety model of a single-transmitter bus topology previously used in aircraft. Logical topologies are often closely associated with media access control methods and protocols. Some networks are able to dynamically change their logical topology through configuration changes to their routers and switches.

Links

The transmission media (often referred to in the literature as the *physical media*) used to link devices to form a computer network include electrical cables (Ethernet, HomePNA, power line communication, G.hn), optical fiber (fiber-optic communication), and radio waves (wireless networking). In the OSI model, these are defined at layers 1 and 2 — the physical layer and the data link layer.

A widely adopted *family* of transmission media used in local area network (LAN) technology is collectively known as Ethernet. The media and protocol standards that enable communication between networked devices over Ethernet are defined by IEEE 802.3. Ethernet transmits data over both copper and fiber cables. Wireless LAN standards (e.g. those defined by IEEE 802.11) use radio waves, or others use infrared signals as a transmission medium. Power line communication uses a building's power cabling to transmit data.

Wired Technologies

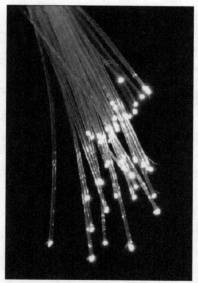

Fiber optic cables are used to transmit light from one computer/network node to another.

The orders of the following wired technologies are, roughly, from slowest to fastest transmission speed.

- Coaxial cable is widely used for cable television systems, office buildings, and other worksites for local area networks. The cables consist of copper or aluminum wire surrounded by an insulating layer (typically a flexible material with a high dielectric constant), which itself is surrounded by a conductive layer. The insulation helps minimize interference and distortion. Transmission speed ranges from 200 million bits per second to more than 500 million bits per second.

- ITU-T G.hn technology uses existing home wiring (coaxial cable, phone lines and power lines) to create a high-speed (up to 1 Gigabit/s) local area network.

- Signal traces on printed circuit boards are common for board-level serial communication, particularly between certain types integrated circuits, a common example being SPI.

- Ribbon cable (untwisted and possibly unshielded) has been a cost-effective media for serial protocols, especially within metallic enclosures or rolled within copper braid or foil, over short distances, or at lower data rates. Several serial network protocols can be deployed without shielded or twisted pair cabling, that is, with "flat" or "ribbon" cable, or a hybrid flat/twisted ribbon cable, should EMC, length, and bandwidth constraints permit: RS-232, RS-422, RS-485, CAN, GPIB, SCSI, etc.

- Twisted pair wire is the most widely used medium for all telecommunication. Twisted-pair cabling consist of copper wires that are twisted into pairs. Ordinary telephone wires consist of two insulated copper wires twisted into pairs. Computer network cabling (wired Ethernet as defined by IEEE 802.3) consists of 4 pairs of copper cabling that can be utilized for both voice and data transmission. The use of two wires twisted together helps to reduce crosstalk and electromagnetic induction. The transmission speed ranges from 2 million bits per second to 10 billion bits per second. Twisted pair cabling comes in two forms: unshielded twisted pair (UTP) and shielded twisted-pair (STP). Each form comes in several category ratings, designed for use in various scenarios.

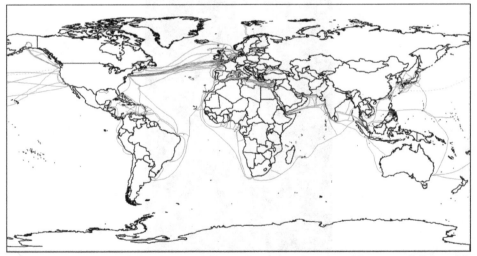

2007 map showing submarine optical fiber telecommunication cables around the world.

- An optical fiber is a glass fiber. It carries pulses of light that represent data. Some advantages of optical fibers over metal wires are very low transmission loss and immunity from electrical interference. Optical fibers can simultaneously carry multiple wavelengths of light, which greatly increases the rate that data can be sent, and helps enable data rates of up to trillions of bits per second. Optic fibers can be used for long runs of cable carrying very high data rates, and are used for undersea cables to interconnect continents.

Price is a main factor distinguishing wired- and wireless-technology options in a business. Wireless options command a price premium that can make purchasing wired computers, printers and other devices a financial benefit. Before making the decision to purchase hard-wired technology products, a review of the restrictions and limitations of the selections is necessary. Business and employee needs may override any cost considerations.

Wireless Technologies

Personal computers are very often connected to networks using wireless links.

- Terrestrial microwave: Terrestrial microwave communication uses Earth-based transmitters and receivers resembling satellite dishes. Terrestrial microwaves are in the low gigahertz range, which limits all communications to line-of-sight. Relay stations are spaced approximately 50 km (30 mi) apart.

- Communications satellites: Satellites communicate via microwave radio waves, which are not deflected by the Earth's atmosphere. The satellites are stationed in space, typically in geostationary orbit 35,786 km (22,236 mi) above the equator. These Earth-orbiting systems are capable of receiving and relaying voice, data, and TV signals.

- Cellular and PCS systems use several radio communications technologies. The systems divide the region covered into multiple geographic areas. Each area has a low-power transmitter or radio relay antenna device to relay calls from one area to the next area.

- Radio and spread spectrum technologies: Wireless local area networks use a high-frequency radio technology similar to digital cellular and a low-frequency radio technology. Wireless LANs use spread spectrum technology to enable communication between multiple devices in a limited area. IEEE 802.11 defines a common flavor of open-standards wireless radio-wave technology known as Wi-Fi.

- Free-space optical communication uses visible or invisible light for communications. In most cases, line-of-sight propagation is used, which limits the physical positioning of communicating devices.

Exotic Technologies

There have been various attempts at transporting data over exotic media:

- IP over Avian Carriers was a humorous April fool's Request for Comments, issued as RFC 1149. It was implemented in real life in 2001.

- Extending the Internet to interplanetary dimensions via radio waves, the Interplanetary Internet.

Both cases have a large round-trip delay time, which gives slow two-way communication, but doesn't prevent sending large amounts of information.

Nodes

Network nodes are the points of connection of the transmission medium to transmitters and receivers of the electrical, optical, or radio signals carried in the medium. Nodes may be associated with a computer, but certain types may have only a microcontroller at a node or possibly no programmable device at all. In the simplest of serial arrangements, one RS-232 transmitter can be connected by a pair of wires to one receiver, forming two nodes on one link, or a Point-to-Point topology. Some protocols permit a single node to only either transmit or receive (e.g., ARINC 429). Other protocols have nodes that can both transmit and receive into a single channel (e.g., CAN can have many transceivers connected to a single bus). While the conventional system building blocks of a computer network include network interface controllers (NICs), repeaters, hubs, bridges, switches, routers, modems, gateways, and firewalls, most address network concerns beyond the physical network topology and may be represented as single nodes on a particular physical network topology.

Network Interfaces

An ATM network interface in the form of an
accessory card. A lot of network interfaces are built-in.

A network interface controller (NIC) is computer hardware that provides a computer with the ability to access the transmission media, and has the ability to process low-level network information. For example, the NIC may have a connector for accepting a cable, or an aerial for wireless transmission and reception, and the associated circuitry.

The NIC responds to traffic addressed to a network address for either the NIC or the computer as a whole.

In Ethernet networks, each network interface controller has a unique Media Access Control (MAC) address—usually stored in the controller's permanent memory. To avoid address conflicts between network devices, the Institute of Electrical and Electronics Engineers (IEEE) maintains and administers MAC address uniqueness. The size of an Ethernet MAC address is six octets. The three most significant octets are reserved to identify NIC manufacturers. These manufacturers, using only their assigned prefixes, uniquely assign the three least-significant octets of every Ethernet interface they produce.

Repeaters and Hubs

A repeater is an electronic device that receives a network signal, cleans it of unnecessary noise and regenerates it. The signal may be reformed or retransmitted at a higher power level, to the other side of an obstruction possibly using a different transmission medium, so that the signal can cover longer distances without degradation. Commercial repeaters have extended RS-232 segments from 15 meters to over a kilometer. In most twisted pair Ethernet configurations, repeaters are required for cable that runs longer than 100 meters. With fiber optics, repeaters can be tens or even hundreds of kilometers apart.

Repeaters work within the physical layer of the OSI model, that is, there is no end-to-end change in the physical protocol across the repeater, or repeater pair, even if a different physical layer may be used between the ends of the repeater, or repeater pair. Repeaters require a small amount of time to regenerate the signal. This can cause a propagation delay that affects network performance and may affect proper function. As a result, many network architectures limit the number of repeaters that can be used in a row, e.g., the Ethernet 5-4-3 rule.

A repeater with multiple ports is known as hub, an Ethernet hub in Ethernet networks, a USB hub in USB networks.

- USB networks use hubs to form tiered-star topologies.

- Ethernet hubs and repeaters in LANs have been mostly obsoleted by modern switches.

Bridges

A network bridge connects and filters traffic between two network segments at the data link layer (layer 2) of the OSI model to form a single network. This breaks the network's collision domain but maintains a unified broadcast domain. Network segmentation breaks down a large, congested network into an aggregation of smaller, more efficient networks.

Bridges come in three basic types:

- Local bridges: Directly connect LANs

- Remote bridges: Can be used to create a wide area network (WAN) link between LANs. Remote bridges, where the connecting link is slower than the end networks, largely have been replaced with routers.

- Wireless bridges: Can be used to join LANs or connect remote devices to LANs.

Switches

A network switch is a device that forwards and filters OSI layer 2 datagrams (frames) between ports based on the destination MAC address in each frame. A switch is distinct from a hub in that it only forwards the frames to the physical ports involved in the communication rather than all ports connected. It can be thought of as a multi-port bridge. It learns to associate physical ports to MAC addresses by examining the source addresses of received frames. If an unknown destination is targeted, the switch broadcasts to all ports but the source. Switches normally have numerous ports, facilitating a star topology for devices, and cascading additional switches.

Multi-layer switches are capable of routing based on layer 3 addressing or additional logical levels. The term *switch* is often used loosely to include devices such as routers and bridges, as well as devices that may distribute traffic based on load or based on application content (e.g., a Web URL identifier).

Routers

A typical home or small office router showing the ADSL telephone line and Ethernet network cable connections.

A router is an internetworking device that forwards packets between networks by processing the routing information included in the packet or datagram (Internet protocol information from layer 3). The routing information is often processed in conjunction with the routing table. A router uses its routing table to determine where to forward packets. A destination in a routing table can include a "null" interface, also known as the "black hole" interface because data can go into it, however, no further processing is done for said data, i.e. the packets are dropped.

Modems

Modems (MOdulator-DEModulator) are used to connect network nodes via wire not originally designed for digital network traffic, or for wireless. To do this one or more carrier signals are modulated by the digital signal to produce an analog signal that can be tailored to give the required properties for transmission. Modems are commonly used for telephone lines, using a digital subscriber line technology.

Firewalls

A firewall is a network device for controlling network security and access rules. Firewalls are typically configured to reject access requests from unrecognized sources while allowing actions from recognized ones. The vital role firewalls play in network security grows in parallel with the constant increase in cyber attacks.

Classification

The study of network topology recognizes eight basic topologies: point-to-point, bus, star, ring or circular, mesh, tree, hybrid, or daisy chain.

Point-to-point

The simplest topology with a dedicated link between two endpoints. Easiest to understand, of the variations of point-to-point topology, is a point-to-point communication channel that appears, to the user, to be permanently associated with the two endpoints. A child's tin can telephone is one example of a *physical dedicated* channel.

Using circuit-switching or packet-switching technologies, a point-to-point circuit can be set up dynamically and dropped when no longer needed. Switched point-to-point topologies are the basic model of conventional telephony.

The value of a permanent point-to-point network is unimpeded communications between the two endpoints. The value of an on-demand point-to-point connection is proportional to the number of potential pairs of subscribers and has been expressed as Metcalfe's Law.

Daisy Chain

Daisy chaining is accomplished by connecting each computer in series to the next. If a message is intended for a computer partway down the line, each system bounces it along in sequence until it reaches the destination. A daisy-chained network can take two basic forms: linear and ring.

- A linear topology puts a two-way link between one computer and the next. However, this was expensive in the early days of computing, since each computer (except for the ones at each end) required two receivers and two transmitters.

- By connecting the computers at each end of the chain, a ring topology can be formed. When a node sends a message, the message is processed by each computer in the ring. An advantage of the ring is that the number of transmitters and receivers can be cut in half. Since a message will eventually loop all of the way around, transmission does not need to go both directions. Alternatively, the ring can be used to improve fault tolerance. If the ring breaks at a particular link then the transmission can be sent via the reverse path thereby ensuring that all nodes are always connected in the case of a single failure.

Bus

In local area networks using bus topology, each node is connected by interface connectors to a single central cable. This is the 'bus', also referred to as the backbone, or trunk) – all data transmitted between nodes in the network is transmitted over this common transmission medium and is able to be received by all nodes in the network simultaneously.

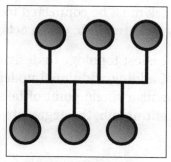

Bus network topology.

A signal containing the address of the intended receiving machine travels from a source machine in both directions to all machines connected to the bus until it finds the intended recipient, which then accepts the data. If the machine address does not match the intended address for the data, the data portion of the signal is ignored. Since the bus topology consists of only one wire it is less expensive to implement than other topologies, but the savings are offset by the higher cost of managing the network. Additionally, since the network is dependent on the single cable, it can be the single point of failure of the network. In this topology data being transferred may be accessed by any node.

Linear Bus

In a linear bus network, all of the nodes of the network are connected to a common transmission medium which has just two endpoints. When the electrical signal reaches the end of the bus, the signal is reflected back down the line, causing unwanted interference. To prevent this, the two endpoints of the bus are normally terminated with a device called a terminator.

Distributed bus

In a distributed bus network, all of the nodes of the network are connected to a common transmission medium with more than two endpoints, created by adding branches to the main section of the transmission medium – the physical distributed bus topology functions in exactly the same fashion as the physical linear bus topology because all nodes share a common transmission medium.

Star

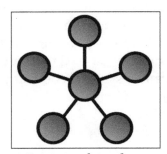

Star network topology.

In star topology, every peripheral node (computer workstation or any other peripheral) is connected to a central node called a hub or switch. The hub is the server and the peripherals are the clients. The network does not necessarily have to resemble a star to be classified as a star network, but all of the peripheral nodes on the network must be connected to one central hub. All traffic that traverses the network passes through the central hub, which acts as a signal repeater.

The star topology is considered the easiest topology to design and implement. One advantage of the star topology is the simplicity of adding additional nodes. The primary disadvantage of the star topology is that the hub represents a single point of failure. Also, since all peripheral communication must flow through the central hub, the aggregate central bandwidth forms a network bottleneck for large clusters.

Extended Star

The extended star network topology extends a physical star topology by one or more repeaters between the central node and the peripheral (or 'spoke') nodes. The repeaters are used to extend the maximum transmission distance of the physical layer, the point-to-point distance between the central node and the peripheral nodes. Repeaters allow greater transmission distance, further than would be possible using just the transmitting power of the central node. The use of repeaters can also overcome limitations from the standard upon which the physical layer is based.

A physical extended star topology in which repeaters are replaced with hubs or switches is a type of hybrid network topology and is referred to as a physical hierarchical star topology, although some texts make no distinction between the two topologies.

A physical hierarchical star topology can also be referred as a tier-star topology, this topology differs from a tree topology in the way star networks are connected together. A tier-star topology uses a central node, while a tree topology uses a central bus and can also be referred as a star-bus network.

Distributed Star

A distributed star is a network topology that is composed of individual networks that are based upon the physical star topology connected in a linear fashion – i.e., 'daisy-chained' – with no central or top level connection point (e.g., two or more 'stacked' hubs, along with their associated star connected nodes or 'spokes').

Ring

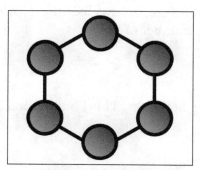
Ring network topology.

A ring topology is a bus topology in a closed loop. Data travels around the ring in one direction. When one node sends data to another, the data passes through each intermediate node on the ring until it reaches its destination. The intermediate nodes repeat (re transmit) the data to keep the signal strong. Every node is a peer; there is no hierarchical relationship of clients and servers. If one node is unable to re transmit data, it severs communication between the nodes before and after it in the bus.

Advantages:

- When the load on the network increases, its performance is better than bus topology.

- There is no need of network server to control the connectivity between workstations.

Disadvantages:

- Aggregate network bandwidth is bottlenecked by the weakest link between two nodes.

Mesh

The value of fully meshed networks is proportional to the exponent of the number of subscribers, assuming that communicating groups of any two endpoints, up to and including all the endpoints, is approximated by Reed's Law.

Fully Connected Network

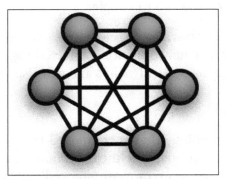

Fully connected mesh topology.

In a *fully connected network*, all nodes are interconnected. (In graph theory this is called a complete graph.) The simplest fully connected network is a two-node network. A fully connected network doesn't need to use packet switching or broadcasting. However, since the number of connections grows quadratically with the number of nodes:

$$c = \frac{n(n-1)}{2}.$$

This makes it impractical for large networks. This kind of topology does not trip and affect other nodes in the network.

Partially Connected Network

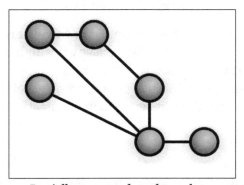

Partially connected mesh topology.

In a partially connected network, certain nodes are connected to exactly one other node; but some nodes are connected to two or more other nodes with a point-to-point link. This makes it possible to make use of some of the redundancy of mesh topology that is physically fully connected, without the expense and complexity required for a connection between every node in the network.

Hybrid

Hybrid topology is also known as hybrid network.Hybrid networks combine two or more topologies in such a way that the resulting network does not exhibit one of the standard topologies (e.g., bus, star, ring, etc.). For example, a tree network (or *star-bus network*) is a hybrid topology in which star networks are interconnected via bus networks. However, a tree network connected to another tree network is still topologically a tree network, not a distinct network type. A hybrid topology is always produced when two different basic network topologies are connected.

A *star-ring* network consists of two or more ring networks connected using a multistation access unit (MAU) as a centralized hub.

Snowflake topology is a star network of star networks.

Two other hybrid network types are *hybrid mesh* and *hierarchical star*.

Centralization

The star topology reduces the probability of a network failure by connecting all of the peripheral nodes (computers, etc.) to a central node. When the physical star topology is applied to a logical bus network such as Ethernet, this central node (traditionally a hub) rebroadcasts all transmissions received from any peripheral node to all peripheral nodes on the network, sometimes including the originating node. All peripheral nodes may thus communicate with all others by transmitting to, and receiving from, the central node only. The failure of a transmission line linking any peripheral node to the central node will result in the isolation of that peripheral node from all others, but the remaining peripheral nodes will be unaffected. However, the disadvantage is that the failure of the central node will cause the failure of all of the peripheral nodes.

If the central node is *passive*, the originating node must be able to tolerate the reception of an echo of its own transmission, delayed by the two-way round trip transmission time (i.e. to and from the central node) plus any delay generated in the central node. An *active* star network has an active central node that usually has the means to prevent echo-related problems.

A tree topology (a.k.a. hierarchical topology) can be viewed as a collection of star networks arranged in a hierarchy. This tree has individual peripheral nodes (e.g. leaves) which are required to transmit to and receive from one other node only and are not required to act as repeaters or regenerators. Unlike the star network, the functionality of the central node may be distributed.

As in the conventional star network, individual nodes may thus still be isolated from the network by a single-point failure of a transmission path to the node. If a link connecting a leaf fails, that leaf is isolated; if a connection to a non-leaf node fails, an entire section of the network becomes isolated from the rest.

To alleviate the amount of network traffic that comes from broadcasting all signals to all nodes, more advanced central nodes were developed that are able to keep track of the identities of the nodes that are connected to the network. These network switches will "learn" the layout of the network by "listening" on each port during normal data transmission, examining the data packets and recording the address/ identifier of each connected node and which port it is connected to in a lookup table held in memory. This lookup table then allows future transmissions to be forwarded to the intended destination only.

Decentralization

In a partially connected mesh topology, there are at least two nodes with two or more paths between them to provide redundant paths in case the link providing one of the paths fails. Decentralization is often used to compensate for the single-point-failure disadvantage that is present when using a single device as a central node (e.g., in star and tree networks). A special kind of mesh, limiting the number of hops between two nodes, is a hypercube. The number of arbitrary forks in mesh networks makes them more difficult to design and implement, but their decentralized nature makes them very useful. In 2012, the Institute of Electrical and Electronics Engineers (IEEE) published the Shortest Path Bridging protocol to ease configuration tasks and allows all paths to be active which increases bandwidth and redundancy between all devices.

This is similar in some ways to a grid network, where a linear or ring topology is used to connect systems in multiple directions. A multidimensional ring has a toroidal topology, for instance.

A *fully connected network*, *complete topology*, or *full mesh topology* is a network topology in which there is a direct link between all pairs of nodes. In a fully connected network with n nodes, there are n(n-1)/2 direct links. Networks designed with this topology are usually very expensive to set up, but provide a high degree of reliability due to the multiple paths for data that are provided by the large number of redundant links between nodes.

WIRELESS NETWORK

A wireless network is a computer network that uses wireless data connections between network nodes.

Wireless icon.

Wireless networking is a method by which homes, telecommunications networks and business installations avoid the costly process of introducing cables into a building, or as a connection between various equipment locations. admin telecommunications networks are generally implemented and administered using radio communication. This implementation takes place at the physical level (layer) of the OSI model network structure.

Examples of wireless networks include cell phone networks, wireless local area networks (WLANs), wireless sensor networks, satellite communication networks, and terrestrial microwave networks.

Wireless Links

Computers are very often connected to
networks using wireless links, e.g. WLANs.

- Terrestrial microwave: Terrestrial microwave communication uses Earth-based transmitters and receivers resembling satellite dishes. Terrestrial microwaves are in the low gigahertz range, which limits all communications to line-of-sight. Relay stations are spaced approximately 48 km (30 mi) apart.

- Communications satellites: Satellites communicate via microwave radio waves, which are not deflected by the Earth's atmosphere. The satellites are stationed in space, typically in geosynchronous orbit 35,400 km (22,000 mi) above the equator. These Earth-orbiting systems are capable of receiving and relaying voice, data, and TV signals.

- Cellular and PCS systems use several radio communications technologies. The systems divide the region covered into multiple geographic areas. Each area has a low-power transmitter or radio relay antenna device to relay calls from one area to the next area.

- Radio and spread spectrum technologies: Wireless local area networks use a high-frequency radio technology similar to digital cellular and a low-frequency radio technology. Wireless LANs use spread spectrum technology to enable communication between multiple devices in a limited area. IEEE 802.11 defines a common flavor of open-standards wireless radio-wave technology known as.

- Free-space optical communication uses visible or invisible light for communications. In most cases, line-of-sight propagation is used, which limits the physical positioning of communicating devices.

Types of Wireless Networks

Wireless PAN

Wireless personal area networks (WPANs) connect devices within a relatively small area, that is generally within a person's reach. For example, both Bluetooth radio and invisible infrared light provides a WPAN for interconnecting a headset to a laptop. ZigBee also supports WPAN applications. Wi-Fi PANs are becoming commonplace (2010) as equipment designers start to integrate Wi-Fi into a variety of consumer electronic devices. Intel "My WiFi" and Windows 7 "virtual Wi-Fi" capabilities have made Wi-Fi PANs simpler and easier to set up and configure.

Wireless LAN

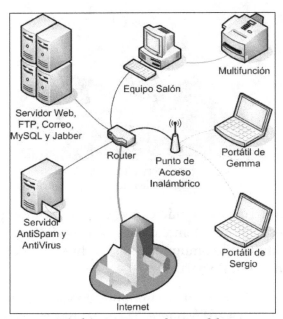

Wireless LANs are often used for
connecting to local resources and to the Internet.

A wireless local area network (WLAN) links two or more devices over a short distance using a wireless distribution method, usually providing a connection through an access point for internet access. The use of spread-spectrum or OFDM technologies may allow users to move around within a local coverage area, and still remain connected to the network.

Products using the IEEE 802.11 WLAN standards are marketed under the Wi-Fi brand name . Fixed wireless technology implements point-to-point links between computers or networks at two distant locations, often using dedicated microwave or modulated laser light beams over line of sight paths. It is often used in cities to connect networks in two or more buildings without installing a wired link. To connect to Wi-Fi, sometimes are used devices like a router or connecting HotSpot using mobile smartphones.

Wireless ad Hoc Network

A wireless ad hoc network, also known as a wireless mesh network or mobile ad hoc network (MANET), is a wireless network made up of radio nodes organized in a mesh topology. Each node forwards messages on behalf of the other nodes and each node performs routing. Ad hoc networks can "self-heal", automatically re-routing around a node that has lost power. Various network layer protocols are needed to realize ad hoc mobile networks, such as Distance Sequenced Distance Vector routing, Associativity-Based Routing, Ad hoc on-demand Distance Vector routing, and Dynamic source routing.

Wireless MAN

Wireless metropolitan area networks are a type of wireless network that connects several wireless LANs.

- WiMAX is a type of Wireless MAN and is described by the IEEE 802.16 standard.

Wireless WAN

Wireless wide area networks are wireless networks that typically cover large areas, such as between neighbouring towns and cities, or city and suburb. These networks can be used to connect branch offices of business or as a public Internet access system. The wireless connections between access points are usually point to point microwave links using parabolic dishes on the 2.4 GHz and 5.8Ghz band, rather than omnidirectional antennas used with smaller networks. A typical system contains base station gateways, access points and wireless bridging relays. Other configurations are mesh systems where each access point acts as a relay also. When combined with renewable energy systems such as photovoltaic solar panels or wind systems they can be stand alone systems.

Cellular Network

A cellular network or mobile network is a radio network distributed over land areas called cells, each served by at least one fixed-location transceiver, known as a cell site or base station. In a cellular network, each cell characteristically uses a different set of radio frequencies from all their immediate neighbouring cells to avoid any interference.

When joined together these cells provide radio coverage over a wide geographic area. This enables a large number of portable transceivers (e.g., mobile phones, pagers, etc.) to communicate with each other and with fixed transceivers and telephones anywhere in the network, via base stations, even if some of the transceivers are moving through more than one cell during transmission.

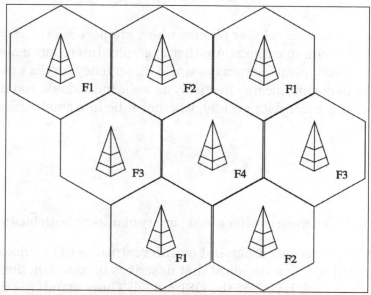

Example of frequency reuse factor or pattern 1/4.

Although originally intended for cell phones, with the development of smartphones, cellular telephone networks routinely carry data in addition to telephone conversations:

- Global System for Mobile Communications (GSM): The GSM network is divided into three major systems: the switching system, the base station system, and the operation and support system. The cell phone connects to the base system station which then connects to the operation and support station; it then connects to the switching station where the call is transferred to where it needs to go. GSM is the most common standard and is used for a majority of cell phones.

- Personal Communications Service (PCS): PCS is a radio band that can be used by mobile phones in North America and South Asia. Sprint happened to be the first service to set up a PCS.

- D-AMPS: Digital Advanced Mobile Phone Service, an upgraded version of AMPS, is being phased out due to advancement in technology. The newer GSM networks are replacing the older system.

Global area Network

A global area network (GAN) is a network used for supporting mobile across an arbitrary number of wireless LANs, satellite coverage areas, etc. The key challenge in mobile communications is handing off user communications from one local coverage area to the next. In IEEE Project 802, this involves a succession of terrestrial wireless LANs.

Space Network

Space networks are networks used for communication between spacecraft, usually in the vicinity of the Earth. The example of this is NASA's Space Network.

Uses

Some examples of usage include cellular phones which are part of everyday wireless networks, allowing easy personal communications. Another example, Intercontinental network systems, use radio satellites to communicate across the world. Emergency services such as the police utilize wireless networks to communicate effectively as well. Individuals and businesses use wireless networks to send and share data rapidly, whether it be in a small office building or across the world.

Properties

General

In a general sense, wireless networks offer a vast variety of uses by both business and home users.

"Now, the industry accepts a handful of different wireless technologies. Each wireless technology is defined by a standard that describes unique functions at both the Physical and the Data Link layers of the OSI model. These standards differ in their specified signaling methods, geographic ranges, and frequency usages, among other things.

Such differences can make certain technologies better suited to home networks and others better suited to network larger organizations."

Performance

Each standard varies in geographical range, thus making one standard more ideal than the next depending on what it is one is trying to accomplish with a wireless network. The performance of wireless networks satisfies a variety of applications such as voice and video. The use of this technology also gives room for expansions, such as from 2G to 3G and, 4G and 5G technologies, which stand for the fourth and fifth generation of cell phone mobile communications standards. As wireless networking has become commonplace, sophistication increases through configuration of network hardware and software, and greater capacity to send and receive larger amounts of data, faster, is achieved. Now the wireless network has been running on LTE, which is a 4G mobile communication standard. Users of an LTE network should have data speeds that are 10x faster than a 3G network.

Space

Space is another characteristic of wireless networking. Wireless networks offer many advantages when it comes to difficult-to-wire areas trying to communicate such as across a street or river, a warehouse on the other side of the premises or buildings that are physically separated but operate as one. Wireless networks allow for users to designate a certain space which the network will be able to communicate with other devices through that network.

Space is also created in homes as a result of eliminating clutters of wiring. This technology allows for an alternative to installing physical network mediums such as TPs, coaxes, or fiber-optics, which can also be expensive.

Home

For homeowners, wireless technology is an effective option compared to Ethernet for sharing printers, scanners, and high-speed Internet connections. WLANs help save the cost of installation of cable mediums, save time from physical installation, and also creates mobility for devices connected to the network. Wireless networks are simple and require as few as one single wireless access point connected directly to the Internet via a router.

Wireless Network Elements

The telecommunications network at the physical layer also consists of many interconnected wireline network elements (NEs). These NEs can be stand-alone systems or products that are either supplied by a single manufacturer or are assembled by the service provider (user) or system integrator with parts from several different manufacturers.

Wireless NEs are the products and devices used by a wireless carrier to provide support for the backhaul network as well as a mobile switching center (MSC).

Reliable wireless service depends on the network elements at the physical layer to be protected against all operational environments and applications.

What are especially important are the NEs that are located on the cell tower to the base station (BS) cabinet. The attachment hardware and the positioning of the antenna and associated closures and cables are required to have adequate strength, robustness, corrosion resistance, and resistance against wind, storms, icing, and other weather conditions. Requirements for individual components, such as hardware, cables, connectors, and closures, shall take into consideration the structure to which they are attached.

Difficulties

Interference

Compared to wired systems, wireless networks are frequently subject to electromagnetic interference. This can be caused by other networks or other types of equipment that generate radio waves that are within, or close, to the radio bands used for communication. Interference can degrade the signal or cause the system to fail.

Absorption and Reflection

Some materials cause absorption of electromagnetic waves, preventing it from reaching the receiver, in other cases, particularly with metallic or conductive materials reflection occurs. This can cause dead zones where no reception is available. Aluminium foiled thermal isolation in modern homes can easily reduce indoor mobile signals by 10 dB frequently leading to complaints about the bad reception of long-distance rural cell signals.

Multipath Fading

In multipath fading two or more different routes taken by the signal, due to reflections, can cause the signal to cancel out at certain locations, and to be stronger in other places (upfade).

Hidden Node Problem

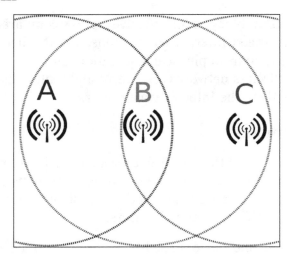

In a hidden node problem Station A can communicate with Station B. Station C can also communicate with Station B. However, Stations A and C cannot communicate with each other, but their signals can interfere at B.

The hidden node problem occurs in some types of network when a node is visible from a wireless access point (AP), but not from other nodes communicating with that AP. This leads to difficulties in media access control (collisions).

Exposed Terminal Node Problem

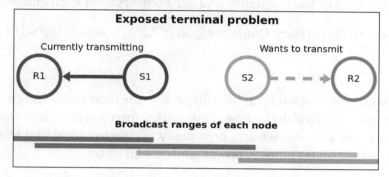

The exposed terminal problem is when a node on one network is unable to send because of co-channel interference from a node that is on a different network.

Shared Resource Problem

The wireless spectrum is a limited resource and shared by all nodes in the range of its transmitters. Bandwidth allocation becomes complex with multiple participating users. Often users are not aware that advertised numbers (e.g., for IEEE 802.11 equipment or LTE networks) are not their increasing demand, the capacity crunch is more and more likely to happen. User-in-the-loop (UIL) may be an alternative solution to ever upgrading to newer technologies for over-provisioning. Capacity, but shared with all other users and thus the individual user rate is far lower.

Capacity

Channel

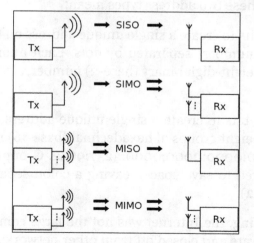

Understanding of SISO, SIMO, MISO and MIMO. Using multiple antennas and transmitting in different frequency channels can reduce fading, and can greatly increase the system capacity.

Shannon's theorem can describe the maximum data rate of any single wireless link, which relates to the bandwidth in hertz and to the noise on the channel.

One can greatly increase channel capacity by using MIMO techniques, where multiple aerials or multiple frequencies can exploit multiple paths to the receiver to achieve much higher throughput – by a factor of the product of the frequency and aerial diversity at each end.

Under Linux, the Central Regulatory Domain Agent (CRDA) controls the setting of channels.

Network

The total network bandwidth depends on how dispersive the medium is (more dispersive medium generally has better total bandwidth because it minimises interference), how many frequencies are available, how noisy those frequencies are, how many aerials are used and whether a directional antenna is in use, whether nodes employ power control and so on.

Cellular wireless networks generally have good capacity, due to their use of directional aerials, and their ability to reuse radio channels in non-adjacent cells. Additionally, cells can be made very small using low power transmitters this is used in cities to give network capacity that scales linearly with population density.

INTERNET PROTOCOL ADDRESS

Most networks today, including all computers on the Internet, use the TCP/IP protocol as the standard for how to communicate on the network. In the TCP/IP protocol, the unique identifier for a computer is called its IP address.

There are two standards for IP addresses: IP Version 4 (IPv4) and IP Version 6 (IPv6). All computers with IP addresses have an IPv4 address, and many are starting to use the new IPv6 address system as well. Here's what these two address types mean:

- IPv4 uses 32 binary bits to create a single unique address on the network. An IPv4 address is expressed by four numbers separated by dots. Each number is the decimal (base-10) representation for an eight-digit binary (base-2) number, also called an octet. For example: 216.27.61.137.

- IPv6 uses 128 binary bits to create a single unique address on the network. An IPv6 address is expressed by eight groups of hexadecimal (base-16) numbers separated by colons, as in 2001:cdba:0000:0000:0000:0000:3257:9652. Groups of numbers that contain all zeros are often omitted to save space, leaving a colon separator to mark the gap (as in 2001:cdba::3257:9652).

At the dawn of IPv4 addressing, the Internet was not the large commercial sensation it is today, and most networks were private and closed off from other networks around the world. When the Internet exploded, having only 32 bits to identify a unique Internet address caused people to panic that we'd run out of IP addresses. Under IPv4, there are 232 possible combinations, which offers just under 4.3 billion unique addresses. IPv6 raised that to a panic-relieving 2128 possible addresses.

How does your computer get its IP address? An IP address can be either dynamic or static. A static address is one that you configure yourself by editing your computer's network settings. This type of address is rare, and it can create network issues if you use it without a good understanding of TCP/IP. Dynamic addresses are the most common. They're assigned by the Dynamic Host Configuration Protocol (DHCP), a service running on the network. DHCP typically runs on network hardware such as routers or dedicated DHCP servers.

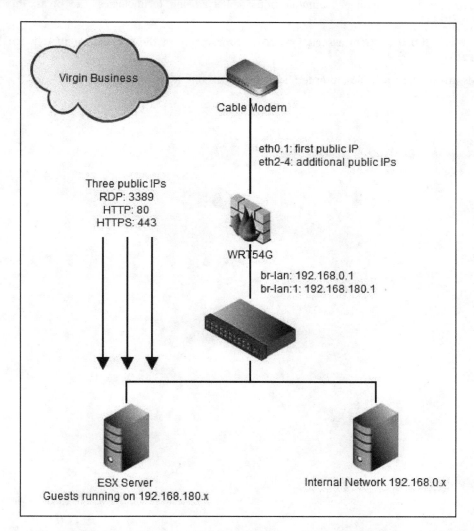

Dynamic IP addresses are issued using a leasing system, meaning that the IP address is only active for a limited time. If the lease expires, the computer will automatically request a new lease. Sometimes, this means the computer will get a new IP address, too, especially if the computer was unplugged from the network between leases. This process is usually transparent to the user unless the computer warns about an IP address conflict on the network (two computers with the same IP address). An address conflict is rare, and today's technology typically fixes the problem automatically.

References

- Network, definition: techopedia.com, retrieved 21 July, 2019

- "The tcp/ip guide - overview of key routing protocol concepts: architectures, protocol types, algorithms and metrics". Www.tcpipguide.com. Retrieved 2016-02-12

- Bicsi, b. (2002). Network design basics for cabling professionals. Mcgraw-hill professional. Isbn 9780071782968

- D. Fedyk, ed.,; p. Ashwood-smith, ed.,; d. Allan, a. Bragg,; p. Unbehagen (april 2012). "is-is extensions supporting ieee 802.1aq". Ietf. Retrieved 12 may 2012

- Asif, saad (2018). 5g mobile communications: concepts and technologies. Crc press. Pp. 128–134. Isbn 9780429881343

- "Gsm world statistics". Gsm association. 2010. Archived from the original on 19 july 2011. Retrieved 16 march 2011

- What-is-an-ip-address, basics, internet: howstuffworks.com, Retrieved 13 July, 2019

Information Technology Infrastructure

Information technology infrastructure is an element of information technology which deals with hardware, software and networking components. It can be categorized as converged infrastructure, hyper-converged infrastructure, dynamic infrastructure, information infrastructure, software-defined infrastructure, etc. This chapter has been carefully written to provide an easy understanding of the various infrastructures of information technology.

IT infrastructure refers to the composite hardware, software, network resources and services required for the existence, operation and management of an enterprise IT environment. It allows an organization to deliver IT solutions and services to its employees, partners and/or customers and is usually internal to an organization and deployed within owned facilities.

IT infrastructure consists of all components that somehow play a role in overall IT and IT-enabled operations. It can be used for internal business operations or developing customer IT or business solutions.

Typically, a standard IT infrastructure consists of the following components:

- Hardware: Servers, computers, data centers, switches, hubs and routers, and other equipment.

- Software: Enterprise resource planning (ERP), customer relationship management (CRM), productivity applications.

- Network: Network enablement, internet connectivity, firewall and security.

- Meatware: Human users, such as network administrators (NA), developers, designers and end users with access to any IT appliance or service are also part of an IT infrastructure, specifically with the advent of user-centric IT service development.

Information Technology Infrastructure Components

Switching

A network switch is the device that provides connectivity between network devices on a Local Area Network (LAN). A switch contains several ports that physically connect to other network devices – including other switches, routers and servers. Early networks used bridges, in which each device "saw" the traffic of all other devices on the network. Switches allow two devices on the network to talk to each other without having to forward that traffic to all devices on the network.

Routers

Routers move packets between networks. Routing allows devices separated on different LANs to talk to each other by determining the next "hop" that will allow the network packet to eventually get to its destination.

If you have ever manually configured your IP address on a workstation, the default gateway value that you keyed in was the IP address of your router.

Firewalls

Firewalls are security devices at the edge of the network. The firewall can be thought of as the guardian or gatekeeper.

A set of rules defines what types of network traffic will be allowed through the firewall and what will be blocked.

In the simplest version of a firewall, rules can be created which allow a specific port and /or protocol for traffic from one device (or a group of devices) to a device or group of devices. For example: if you want to host your own web server and limit it to only web traffic, you would typically have two firewall rules that look something like this:

Source	Destination	Port / Protocol	Description
any	10.1.1.100	80 / http	Web traffic in
any	10.1.1.100	443/ https	Secure web traffic in

The source is the originating device. In this case, any means 'allow any computer to communicate'. Destination is the specific IP address of your internal web server. Port/Protocol defines what type of traffic is allowed from the source to the destination. Most firewall devices allow for a description for each rule that have no effect on the rule itself. It is used only for notes.

Firewall devices can get complicated quickly. There are many different types of firewalls which approach managing traffic in different ways.

Servers

A network server is simply another computer, but usually larger in terms of resources than what most people think of. A server allows multiple users to access and share its resources. There are several types of servers, with the following being among the most common:

- A file server provides end users with a centralized location to store files. When configured correctly, file servers can allow or prevent specific users to access files.

- A directory server provides a central database of user accounts that can be used by several computers. This allows centralized management of user accounts which are used to access server resources.

- Web servers use HTTP (Hyper Text Transfer Protocol) to provide files to users through a web browser.

- There are also application servers, database servers, print servers, etc.

Physical Plant

The physical plant is all of the network cabling in your office buildings and server room/data center. This all too often neglected part of your infrastructure usually is the weakest link and is the cause of most system outages when not managed properly. There are two main types of cabling in the infrastructure: CAT 5/6/7 and fiber optic. Each type of cabling has several different subtypes, depending on the speed and distance required to connect devices.

People

By the strict ITIL definition, people are not considered part of the network infrastructure. However, without competent, well-qualified people in charge of running and maintaining your infrastructure, you will artificially limit the capabilities of your organization. In larger organizations, there are specialty positions for each of the areas. In smaller organizations, you will find that the general systems administrator handles many of the roles.

Server Rooms / Data Center

The server room, or data center (in large organizations), can be thought of as the central core of your network. It is the location in which you place all of your servers, and it usually acts as the center of most networks.

Infrastructure Software

This is perhaps the most "gray" of all infrastructure components. However, server operating systems and directory services (like MS Active Directory) should be considered to be part of the infrastructure. Without multi-user operating systems, the hardware can't perform its infrastructure functions.

Infrastructure as a Service

Infrastructure as a service (IaaS) are online services that provide high-level APIs used to dereference various low-level details of underlying network infrastructure like physical computing resources, location, data partitioning, scaling, security, backup etc. A hypervisor, such as Xen, Oracle VirtualBox, Oracle VM, KVM, VMware ESX/ESXi, or Hyper-V, LXD, runs the virtual machines as guests. Pools of hypervisors within the cloud operational system can support large numbers of virtual machines and the ability to scale services up and down according to customers' varying requirements.

Typically IaaS involves the use of a cloud orchestration technology like Open Stack, Apache Cloudstack or Open Nebula. This manages the creation of a virtual machine and decides on which hypervisor (i.e. physical host) to start it, enables VM migration features between hosts, allocates storage volumes and attaches them to VMs, usage information for billing and lots more.

An alternative to hypervisors are Linux containers, which run in isolated partitions of a single Linux kernel running directly on the physical hardware. Linux cgroups and namespaces are the underlying Linux kernel technologies used to isolate, secure and manage the containers. Containerisation offers higher performance than virtualization, because there is no hypervisor overhead. Also, container capacity auto-scales dynamically with computing load, which eliminates the problem of over-provisioning and enables usage-based billing.

IaaS clouds often offer additional resources such as a virtual-machine disk-image library, raw block storage, file or object storage, firewalls, load balancers, IP addresses, virtual local area networks (VLANs), and software bundles.

The NIST's definition of cloud computing defines Infrastructure as a Service as:

The capability provided to the consumer is to provision processing, storage, networks, and other fundamental computing resources where the consumer is able to deploy and run arbitrary software, which can include operating systems and applications. The consumer does not manage or control the underlying cloud infrastructure but has control over operating systems, storage, and deployed applications; and possibly limited control of select networking components (e.g., host firewalls).

According to the Internet Engineering Task Force (IETF), the most basic cloud-service model is that of providers offering IT infrastructure — virtual machines and other resources — as a service to subscribers.

IaaS-cloud providers supply these resources on-demand from their large pools of equipment installed in data centers. For wide-area connectivity, customers can use either the Internet or carrier clouds (dedicated virtual private networks). To deploy their applications, cloud users install operating-system images and their application software on the cloud infrastructure. In this model, the cloud user patches and maintains the operating systems and the application software. Cloud providers typically bill IaaS services on a utility computing basis: cost reflects the amount of resources allocated and consumed.

Infrastructure as Code

Infrastructure as code (IaC) is the process of managing and provisioning computer data centers through machine-readable definition files, rather than physical hardware configuration or interactive configuration tools. The IT infrastructure managed by this comprises both physical equipment such as bare-metal servers as well as virtual machines and associated configuration resources. The definitions may be in a version control system. It can use either scripts or declarative definitions, rather than manual processes, but the term is more often used to promote declarative approaches.

IaC approaches are promoted for cloud computing, which is sometimes marketed as infrastructure as a service (IaaS). IaC supports IaaS, but should not be confused with it.

IaC grew as a response to the difficulty posed from two pieces of technology – utility computing and second-generation web frameworks. In 2006, the launch of Amazon Web Services' Elastic Compute Cloud and the 1.0 version of Ruby on Rails just months before brought about widespread scaling problems for many enterprises, problems that were previously only witnessed by huge companies. With new tools emerging to handle this ever growing field, the idea of IaC was born. The thought of modelling infrastructure with code, and then having the ability to design, implement, and deploy applications infrastructure with known software best practices appealed to software developers and IT infrastructure administrators. The ability to treat it like code and use the same tools as any other software project would allow developers to rapidly deploy applications.

Added Value and Advantages

The value of IaC can be broken down into three measurable categories: cost (reduction), speed (faster execution) and risk (remove errors and security violations). Cost reduction aims at helping not only the enterprise financially, but also in terms of people and effort, meaning that by removing the manual component, people are able to refocus their efforts towards other enterprise tasks. Infrastructure automation enables speed through faster execution when configuring your infrastructure and aims at providing visibility to help other teams across the enterprise work quickly and more efficiently. Automation removes the risk associated with human error, like manual misconfiguration; removing this can decrease downtime and increase reliability. These outcomes and attributes help the enterprise move towards implementing a culture of DevOps, the combined working of development and operations.

Types of Approaches

There are generally three approaches to IaC: declarative (functional) vs. imperative (procedural) vs. intelligent (environment aware). The difference between the declarative, the imperative and the intelligent approach is essentially *'what'* versus *'how'* versus *'why'*. The declarative approach focuses on what the eventual target configuration should be; the imperative focuses on how the infrastructure is to be changed to meet this; the intelligent approach focuses on why the configuration should be a certain way in consideration of all the co-relationships and co-dependencies of multiple applications running on the same infrastructure typically found in production. The declarative approach defines the desired state and the system executes what needs to happen to achieve that desired state. Imperative defines specific commands that need to be executed in the appropriate order to end with the desired conclusion. The intelligent determines the correct desired state before the system executes what needs to happen to achieve a desired state that does not impact co-dependent applications. Environment aware desired state is the next generation of IaC.

Methods

There are two methods of IaC: *'push'* and *'pull'*. The main difference is the manner in which the servers are told how to be configured. In the pull method the server to be configured will pull its configuration from the controlling server. In the push method the controlling server pushes the configuration to the destination system.

Tools

There are m1any tools that fulfill infrastructure automation capabilities and use IaC. Broadly speaking, any framework or tool that performs changes or configures infrastructure declaratively or imperatively based on a programmatic approach can be considered IaC. Traditionally, server (lifecycle) automation and configuration management tools were used to accomplish IaC. Now enterprises are also using continuous configuration automation tools or stand-alone IaC frameworks, such as Microsoft's PowerShell DSC or AWS CloudFormation.

Continuous Configuration Automation

All continuous configuration automation (CCA) tools can be thought of as an extension of traditional IaC frameworks. They leverage IaC to change, configure, and automate infrastructure, and they also provide visibility, efficiency and flexibility in how infrastructure is managed. These additional attributes provide enterprise-level security and compliance - making companies keen on implementing these types of tools.

Community Content

An important aspect when considering CCA tools, if they are open source, is the community content. As Gartner states, the value of CCA tools is "as dependent on user-community-contributed content and support as it is on the commercial maturity and performance of the automation tooling." Vendors like Puppet and Chef, those that have been around a significant amount of time, have created their own communities. Chef has Chef Community Repository and Puppet has PuppetForge. Other vendors rely on adjacent communities and leverage other IaC frameworks such as PowerShell DSC. New vendors are emerging that are not content driven, but model driven with the intelligence in the product to deliver content. These visual, object-oriented systems work well for developers, but they are especially useful to production oriented DevOps and operations constituents that value models versus scripting for content. As the field continues to develop and change, the community based content will become ever important to how IaC tools are used, unless they are model driven and object oriented.

Notable CCA tools include:

Tool	Released by	Method	Approach	Written in	Comments
Pulumi	Pulumi	Push	Declarative	Typescript, Python, Go	
Chef	Chef (2009)	Pull	Declarative and imperative	Ruby	
Otter	Inedo	Push	Declarative and imperative	-	Windows oriented
Puppet	Puppet (2005)	Pull	Declarative	C++ & Clojure from 4.0, Ruby	
SaltStack	SaltStack	Push and Pull	Declarative and imperative	Python	
CFEngine	CFEngine	Pull	Declarative	-	
Terraform	HashiCorp (2014)	Push	Declarative	Go	
DSC	Microsoft	Push/Pull	Declarative/Imperative	PowerShell	
Ansible / Ansible Tower	RedHat (2012)	Push	Declarative and imperative	Python	

Other tools include AWS CloudFormation, cdist, StackStorm and Juju (software).

Relationship to DevOps

IaC can be a key attribute of enabling best practices in DevOps – Developers become more involved in defining configuration and Ops teams get involved earlier in the development process.

Tools that utilize IaC bring visibility to the state and configuration of servers and ultimately provide the visibility to users within the enterprise, aiming to bring teams together to maximize their efforts. Automation in general aims to take the confusion and error-prone aspect of manual processes and make it more efficient, and productive. Allowing for better software and applications to be created with flexibility, less downtime, and an overall cost effective way for the company. IaC is intended to reduce the complexity that kills efficiency out of manual configuration. Automation and collaboration are considered central points in DevOps; Infrastructure automation tools are often included as components of a DevOps toolchain.

CONVERGED INFRASTRUCTURE

Converged infrastructure, sometimes known as converged architecture, is an approach to data center management that packages compute, networking, servers, storage and virtualization tools on a prequalified turnkey appliance. Converged systems include a toolkit of management software.

Converged infrastructure is gaining momentum as IT organizations shift away from owning and managing hardware to a flexible self-service model in which resources are consumed on demand. Rather than multiple IT assets existing in independent silos, converged infrastructure bundles hardware components with management software to orchestrate and provision the resources as a single integrated system.

The goal of converged infrastructure is to reduce complexity in data center management. The principle design factor is to eliminate issues of hardware incompatibility. Ease of deployment of converged infrastructure is appealing to enterprises that write cloud-native applications or host an internal hybrid or private cloud.

Gartner classifies converged infrastructure, along with hyper-converged infrastructure (HCI), within the category of integrated infrastructure systems or integrated stack systems.

Comparing Converged Infrastructure to Traditional Data Center Design

Traditional data center design requires that application servers, backup appliances, hypervisors, network cards and file storage systems be individually configured and linked together. Typically, each component is managed separately by a dedicated IT team. This arrangement serves organizations that have petabytes of data across thousands of applications, but management challenges can arise when trying to rationalize the costs or undertake a refresh cycle.

For example, the storage you buy comes from a different vendor than the one who supplies your servers and network cards, with each hardware device having different warranty periods and service-level agreements.

By contrast, converged infrastructure vendors offer branded and supported products in which all the components -- servers, software, storage and switches -- reside natively on a qualified hardware appliance. Owing to its smaller physical footprint in the data center, converged infrastructure helps to reduce the costs associated with cabling, cooling and power.

Table: Key Features of converged infrastructure products.

Feature	Your Choices	What to Evaluate
Data Protection	Raid (dedication storage)	Rebuild Time
	Replication	Performance during Rebuild
	Erasure Coding	Erasure Coding
Solid- state Storage	Flash In Server	Data locality
	Flash in shared array	Tiering
		Quality of Service
Flexibility	Turnkey (no choice)	Install on bare- metal system
	Software only	Ability to add only capacity or performance nodes
Data efficiency	Deduplication	Level or rate of optimization
	Compression	Performance impact of optimization
	Writable snapshots (clones)	Scalability of optimization

Converged Infrastructure Cloud use Cases: Benefits and Drawbacks

Converged architecture is based on a modular design that presents resources as pooled capacity. Each preconfigured module added to the system provides a predictable unit of compute, memory or storage. This visibility into resource consumption enables organizations to rapidly scale private cloud infrastructure to support cloud computing, virtualization and IT management at remote branch offices.

One advantage to buying a converged system is the peace of mind that comes with purchasing a vendor's validated platform. A typical converged infrastructure stack is preconfigured to address the needs of a specific workload, such as virtual desktop infrastructure or database applications.

Converged infrastructure products enable users to independently tune the individual components that comprise the architecture. This flexibility offers improved management flexibility over other IT architectures. The vendor supplying the converged system provides a single point of contact for maintenance and service issues.

However, there are limitations as to what you can do with converged technology. A user has little latitude to alter the basic converged infrastructure configuration. Separately adding components following the initial installation increases cost and complexity, negating the advantages that make converged infrastructure attractive in the first place.

Deploying a Converged Infrastructure

There are various ways to implement converged infrastructure. You could use a vendor-tested hardware reference architecture, install a cluster of stand-alone appliances or take a software-driven, hyper-converged approach.

A converged infrastructure reference architecture refers to a set of preconfigured and validated hardware recommendations that pinpoint specific data center workloads. A vendor's reference architecture helps guide enterprises on the optimal deployment and use of the converged infrastructure components.

Users may opt to purchase a dedicated appliance as the platform on which to run a converged infrastructure. Using this approach, a vendor will provide a single hardware appliance that consolidates compute, storage, networking and virtualization resources, either sourced directly from the vendor or its partners. Customers can expand the converged cluster by purchasing additional appliances to achieve horizontal scalability.

Hyper-converged architecture abstracts compute, networking and storage from the underlying physical hardware, while adding virtualization software features. Hyper-converged products offer additional functionality for cloud bursting or disaster recovery. Administrators are able to manage both physical and virtual infrastructures -- whether on site or in the cloud -- in a federated manner using a single pane of glass.

Converged vs. Hyper-converged Infrastructure vs. Composable Infrastructure

Although converged infrastructure and hyper-converged infrastructure are sometimes used interchangeably, the technologies differ slightly in the implementation and range of features.

The converged infrastructure market sprang from the concept of HCI. In a converged infrastructure, the discrete hardware components may be separated and used independently. This component separation is not supported by HCI platforms.

Table: Differences distinguish integration, convergence, and hyper-convergence in data IT systems.

Technology	What is It	Benefit of Data Centres	Limitations	Examples
Integration	Integration is making disparate things work together, including servers, network gear, storage systems and other devices purchased from a variety of vendors.	Solves traditional enterprise computing dilemma where IT architects and administrators assemble, connect, configure and optimize IT equipment and software	Equipment and software do not natively work together, so the integration process can be costly or time consuming-or both Each New addition to data centre requires additional work	Integration is performed by consultants- value added integrators
Converged infrastructure	A vendor preassembles and integrates essential compute, storage and network gear into a single product offering with a common physical enclosure.	Accelerates and simplifies data centre deployment with fewer errors. Can boost performance and resource utilization. A common management interface and no trial and error tuning Single vendor service and support	While the vendor handles integration, users still pay for proprietary hardware and management. Vendors may update the CI box's feature sets to a slower rate than their other products	Dell Active System Manager Hitachi Unified Compute Platform HP Converged System IBM pure Flex Net App Flex Pod Oracle Private Cloud Appliance

Hyper-Converged infrastructure	A converged infra-structure with a software- based and driven architecture that vendors run with white box serv-ers and other generic hardware	Users Experience seamless manage-ment and expansion of various compute, storage and network devices. Mumerous services integrated, such as backup, data dedu-plication, WAN ac-celeration, and SSD storage and cache	Capacity is expanded simply by adding more boxes, but data centres lose the choice of different vendors manage-ment software or hardware that might best suit and appli-cation.	VMware EVO.RAIL SimpliVity Omni-Cube and OmniStack Nutanix NX with Acropolis and Prism Maxta MxSP and Max Deploy Scale Computing HC# and HC appli-ance

Hyper-converged infrastructure enables other components to be added by implementing software-defined storage features. For example, hyper-converged infrastructure supports such data center necessities as backup software, inline data deduplication and compression, replication, snapshots, and WAN optimization. A good way to think of the distinction is that converged infrastructure is based mainly around the supported hardware, whereas HCI combines the hardware with granular data services.

In general, converged infrastructure products are customized to support the particular application workloads of large-scale enterprises. Hyper-converged infrastructure is geared for small and mid-range enterprises that don't require as much customization.

A related term, composable infrastructure, bears similarities to converged and hyper-converged infrastructure systems. The distinction of composable infrastructure is that users are able to re-configure the infrastructure as workloads evolve within a data center. In composable infrastructure, an IT administrator does not need to be concerned with the physical location of the IT components. Instead, objects expose information via management APIs to enable automated discovery and delivery of services on demand.

HYPER-CONVERGED INFRASTRUCTURE

Hyper-converged is an IT framework that combines storage, computing and networking into a single system in an effort to reduce data center complexity and increase scalability. Hyper-converged plat-forms include a hypervisor for virtualized computing, software-defined storage, and virtualized net-working, and they typically run on standard, off-the-shelf servers. Multiple nodes can be clustered to-gether to create pools of shared compute and storage resources, designed for convenient consumption.

The use of commodity hardware, supported by a single vendor, yields an infrastructure that's designed to be more flexible and simpler to manage than traditional enterprise storage infrastructure. For IT leaders who are embarking on data center modernization projects, Hyper-converged can provide the agility of public cloud infrastructure without relinquishing control of hardware on their own premises.

Difference between Hyper-converged and Converged Infrastructure

Hyper-converged adds deeper levels of abstraction and greater levels of automation.

Converged infrastructure involves a preconfigured package of software and hardware in a single system for simplified management. But with a converged infrastructure, the compute, storage, and networking components are discrete and can be separated. In a Hyper-converged environment, the components can't be separated; the software-defined elements are implemented virtually, with seamless integration into the hypervisor environment. This allows organizations to easily expand capacity by deploying additional modules.

Benefits of Hyper-converged Infrastructure Solutions

Hyper-converged infrastructure promises to deliver simplicity and flexibility when compared with legacy solutions. The integrated storage systems, servers and networking switches are designed to be managed as a single system, across all instances of a Hyper-converged infrastructure. The inherent management capabilities enable ease of use, and software-defined storage is expected to yield greater scalability and resource efficiency. Companies can start small and grow resources as needed. HCI vendors also tout potential cost savings in areas including data center power and space; IT labor; and avoidance of licensed software such as backup or disaster recovery tools.

DYNAMIC INFRASTRUCTURE

Dynamic Infrastructure is an information technology concept related to the design of data centers, whereby the underlying hardware and software can respond dynamically and more efficiently to changing levels of demand. In other words, data center assets such as storage and processing power can be provisioned (made available) to meet surges in user's needs. The concept has also been referred to as *Infrastructure 2.0* and *Next Generation Data Center*.

Concept

The basic premise of dynamic infrastructures is to leverage pooled IT resources to provide flexible IT capacity, enabling the allocation of resources in line with demand from business processes. This is achieved by using server virtualization technology to pool computing resources wherever possible, and allocating these resources on-demand using automated tools. This allows for load balancing and is a more efficient approach than keeping massive computing resources in reserve to run tasks that take place, for example, once a month, but are otherwise under-utilized.

Dynamic Infrastructures may also be used to provide security and data protection when workloads are moved during migrations, provisioning, enhancing performance or building co-location facilities.

Dynamic infrastructures were promoted to enhance performance, scalability, system availability and uptime, increasing server utilization and the ability to perform routine maintenance on either physical or virtual systems all while minimizing interruption to business operations and reducing cost for IT. Dynamic infrastructures also provide the fundamental business continuity and high availability requirements to facilitate cloud or grid computing.

For networking companies, infrastructure 2.0 refers to the ability of networks to keep up with the movement and scale requirements of new enterprise IT initiatives, especially virtualization and cloud computing. According to companies like Cisco, F5 Networks and Infoblox, network automation and connectivity intelligence between networks, applications and endpoints will be required to reap the full benefits of virtualization and many types of cloud computing. This will require network management and infrastructure to be consolidated, enabling higher levels of dynamic control and connectivity between networks, systems and endpoints.

Early examples of server-level dynamic infrastructures are the FlexFrame for SAP and FlexFrame for Oracle introduced by Fujitsu Siemens Computers (now Fujitsu) in 2003. The FlexFrame approach was to dynamically assign servers to applications on demand, leveling peaks and enabling organizations to maximize the benefit from their IT investments.

Benefits

Dynamic infrastructures take advantage of intelligence gained across the network. By design, every dynamic infrastructure is service-oriented and focused on supporting and enabling the end users in a highly responsive way. It can utilize alternative sourcing approaches, like cloud computing to deliver new services with agility and speed.

Global organizations already have the foundation for a dynamic infrastructure that will bring together the business and IT infrastructure to create new possibilities. For example:

- Transportation companies can optimize their vehicles' routes leveraging GPS and traffic information.

- Facilities organizations can secure access to locations and track the movement of assets by leveraging RFID technology.

- Production environments can monitor and manage presses, valves and assembly equipment through embedded electronics.

- Technology systems can be optimized for energy efficiency, managing spikes in demand, and ensuring disaster recovery readiness.

- Communications companies can better monitor usage by location, user or function, and optimize routing to enhance user experience.

- Utility companies can reduce energy usage with a "smart grid."

INFORMATION INFRASTRUCTURE

An information infrastructure is defined by Ole Hanseth as "a shared, evolving, open, standardized, and heterogeneous installed base" and by Pironti as all of the people, processes, procedures, tools, facilities, and technology which supports the creation, use, transport, storage, and destruction of information.

The notion of information infrastructures, introduced in the 1990s and refined during the following decade, has proven quite fruitful to the information systems (IS) field. It changed the perspective from organizations to networks and from systems to infrastructure, allowing for a global and emergent perspective on information systems. Information infrastructure is a technical structure of an organizational form, an analytical perspective or a semantic network.

The concept of information infrastructure (II) was introduced in the early 1990s, first as a political initiative, later as a more specific concept in IS research. For the IS research community an important inspiration was Hughes' accounts of large technical systems, analyzed as socio-technical power structures.

Information infrastructure, as a theory, has been used to frame a number of extensive case studies, and in particular to develop an alternative approach to IS design: "Infrastructures should rather be built by establishing working local solutions supporting local practices which subsequently are linked together rather than by defining universal standards and subsequently implementing them". It has later been developed into a full design theory, focusing on the growth of an installed base.

Information infrastructures include the Internet, health systems and corporate systems. It is also consistent to include innovations such as Facebook, LinkedIn and MySpace as excellent examples. Bowker has described several key terms and concepts that are enormously helpful for analyzing information infrastructure: imbrication, bootstrapping, figure/ground, and a short discussion of infrastructural inversion. "Imbrication" is an analytic concept that helps to ask questions about historical data. "Bootstrapping" is the idea that infrastructure must already exist in order to exist.

"Technological and non-technological elements that are linked".

"Information infrastructures can, as formative contexts, shape not only the work routines, but also the ways people look at practices, consider them 'natural' and give them their overarching character of necessity. Infrastructure becomes an essential factor shaping the taken-for-grantedness of organizational practices".

"The technological and human components, networks, systems, and processes that contribute to the functioning of the health information system".

The set of organizational practices, technical infrastructure and social norms that collectively provide for the smooth operation of scientific work at a distance.

"A shared, evolving, heterogeneous installed base of IT capabilities developed on open and standardized interfaces".

Theories of Information Infrastructure

Dimensions of Infrastructure

According to Star and Ruhleder, there are 8 dimensions of information infrastructures:

- Embeddedness,
- Transparency,
- Reach or scope,

- Learned as part of membership,

- Links with conventions of practice,

- Embodiment of standards,

- Built on an installed base,

- Becomes visible upon breakdown.

Information Infrastructure as Public Policy

Presidential Chair and Professor of Information Studies at the University of California, Los Angeles, Christine L. Borgman argues information infrastructures, like all infrastructures, are "subject to public policy". In the United States, public policy defines information infrastructures as the "physical and cyber-based systems essential to the minimum operations of the economy and government" and connected by information technologies.

Global Information Infrastructure (GII)

Borgman says governments, businesses, communities, and individuals can work together to create a global information infrastructure which links "the world's telecommunication and computer networks together" and would enable the transmission of "every conceivable information and communication application."

Currently, the Internet is the default global information infrastructure."

SOFTWARE-DEFINED INFRASTRUCTURE

Software-defined infrastructure (SDI) is defined as a system where software controls computing hardware without significant human intervention. In a software-defined infrastructure system, some level of automation enables systems to be provisioned and work to some extent without human guidance.

Although software-defined infrastructure has become an industry buzzword, many IT experts have been able to poke holes in it, arguing that the definition of software-defined infrastructure is exceedingly vague. For example, one subset of software-defined infrastructure is software-defined storage, and in evaluating how storage has changed in the last 40 years or so, one see that almost any modern storage system has some element of software-defined infrastructure involved.

Someone who is critiquing the idea of software-defined infrastructure as groundbreaking technology would argue that ever since people did away with punch cards and other physical hardware controls, software-defined infrastructure has been technically universal. The same case could be made for other flavors of software-defined infrastructure – the result is that understanding the extent of software-defined infrastructure involves assessing exactly how much automation is put into any system and how well software can control hardware and what it can do without human help in terms of specific functionality.

Software-Defined Infrastructure (SDI) has emerged as a promising approach to address the extensive demands on maximizing the value potential of infrastructure deployments. SDI refers to the operation and control of IT infrastructure entirely using software technologies and without involvement of the human element. Processes including infrastructure control, management, provisioning, configuration and other architectural operations are performed automatically via software as per application requirements and the defined operational policies. Since the changes are not dependent or limited to the human involvement, SDI enables intelligent infrastructure processes based on the changing IT operation requirements in real-time. The IT infrastructure therefore becomes intelligent, taking smart decisions on its own in order to meet the defined goals on SLAs, performance, security and other considerations. SDI allows the infrastructure to operate as a self-aware, self-healing, self-scaling and self-optimizing IT environment to enable truly agile business processes.

The Software-Defined Infrastructure stack typically comprises of the following components:

- Physical Infrastructure: At the machine level, SDI comprises of the hardware resources such as servers and networking devices, as well as firmware, hypervisors and other endpoint terminals. The infrastructure components may be scaled on an ongoing basis to address changing IT needs, while the SDI functionality can encompass the expanding infrastructure.

- Virtualization Layers: Virtualization is applied to the infrastructure resources such as storage and network components. A heterogeneous architecture of computing resources is maintained. This component sits directly above the physical infrastructure level within an SDI architecture.

- Software-Defined Capabilities: Capabilities such as Software-Defined Networking (SDN), Software-Defined Compute and Software Defined Storage are applied to the virtualized layer of computing resources. Intelligent monitoring and control systems are deployed to automatically transform the network, compute and storage resources as per the architecture policies. End-users may define their requirements pertaining to resource provisioning and server deployment, while the intelligent control systems will take on the responsibility of configuring the underlying infrastructure and managing the virtualized resources.

- Management Services: At the infrastructure management level, SDI may involve the user-interface to define parameters such as SLA performance, availability, scalability and elasticity. IT admins or internal IT users may also request provisioning of resources. The management services layer will take care of all infrastructure operations necessary to ensure that desired standards of SLA and performance are maintained.

The SDI approach goes beyond the deployment of core SDI components and should be designed to realize the key attributes of a successful SDI strategy. These attributes may vary based on organizational requirements regarding the infrastructure scalability, agility, security, performance, reliability and compliance. Common attributes may include the following:

Intelligent Virtualization: SDI should aim to enhance the portability of IT workloads and remove dependencies from the underlying infrastructure. While virtualization and layers of abstraction are necessary, an effective SDI infrastructure comprises of strong intelligence capabilities to orchestrate the infrastructure resources and architecture for maximum performance and reliability.

Software-Driven Innovation: Software-centric SDI strategy focuses on using commercial off the shelf hardware instead of investing in proprietary and customized hardware solutions. Software is used to fill the gap in transforming commercial hardware platforms into a flexible and scalable infrastructure backend. Open source hardware designs can further help remove the barriers in scaling the infrastructure to meet the desired standards of an SDI architecture.

Modular Design: Adaptability is a key attribute of an effective SDI strategy and enabled by introducing modularity in the design of the software architecture. The roles of different infrastructure resources are distributed across different technical functionality as defined by the software. Techniques such as Software Orient Architecture (SOA) design or microservices may be used for modularity.

Context Awareness: Legacy infrastructure architecture may not be designed to collect information on context such as incidents, triggers, warning, events or other parameters from related infrastructure components. An effective SDI strategy should involve selective identification, access and analysis of relevant metrics to accurately determine and manage performance, security and compliance of the IT infrastructure.

Performance Focused: Organizations may assess the performance in terms of availability, security and compliance posture of the wider infrastructure. The SDI approach should be designed to achieve high standards of performance by introducing capabilities such as strong encryption and access controls, redundancy in architecture, monitoring, visibility and control over the infrastructure.

Policy Based Systems: The SDI should be designed to meet the purpose and goals of the organization's infrastructure operations. A policy-driven approach should be established to continuously monitor infrastructure performance and enforce the changes necessary to comply with the IT, operational and business policies. Instead of introducing manual automation scripts every time a change is needed, SDI can automatically identify the requirements and issues appropriate commands to infrastructure components.

Open Source Driven: Open source technologies remove the barriers that prevent elastic and flexible operations of the infrastructure. An SDI architecture requires multiple interfaces and components to operate as integrated, interoperable, elastic and flexible pool of infrastructure resources. By following the open standards, organizations can build an open and agile IT environment that allows the software to manage, configure, provision and operate the infrastructure autonomously while meeting intended SLA performance standards.

Software Defined Infrastructure allows organizations to control how IT workloads are distributed and optimized to maximize the value potential of infrastructure deployments. Early movers in the SDI journey can take advantage of the technology and deliver optimum levels of service delivery for customers in terms of low latency and high performance of apps as their key competitive differentiation. The ability to realize the true potential of infrastructure deployments and operate agile software-driven architecture empowers organizations to test new business models and offer improved customer experiences in response to changing market trends. For progressive organizations, SDI continues to prevail as a key business enabler with its expanding scope of automation, intelligence and virtualization applied to cloud-based data center technologies.

References

- It-infrastructure, definition: techopedia.com, Retrieved 24 March, 2019

- Alex amies; harm sluiman; qiang guo tong; guo ning liu (2 july 2012). Developing and hosting applications on the cloud: develop hosting applica cloud. Pearson education. Isbn 978-0-13-306685-2

- What-is-it-infrastructure-and-what-are-its-components: bmc.com, Retrieved 1 June, 2019

- Venezia, paul (21 november 2013). "puppet vs. Chef vs. Ansible vs. Salt". Networkworld.com. Network world. Retrieved 14 december 2015

- Converged-infrastructure, definition: techtarget.com, Retrieved 21 March, 2019

- What-is-hyperconvergence: networkworld.com, Retrieved 12 April, 2019

- Software-defined-infrastructure-sdi, definition: techopedia.com, Retrieved 23 June, 2019

- Software-defined-infrastructure: bmc.com, Retrieved 3 August, 2019

Diverse Aspects of Information Technology

Information technology has a wide range of applications which include information retrieval, data mining, information extraction, data storage, ontology, strategic management, content management, information architecture, etc. These diverse applications of information technology have been thoroughly discussed in this chapter.

INFORMATION RETRIEVAL

Information retrieval (IR) may be defined as a software program that deals with the organization, storage, retrieval and evaluation of information from document repositories particularly textual information. The system assists users in finding the information they require but it does not explicitly return the answers of the questions. It informs the existence and location of documents that might consist of the required information. The documents that satisfy user's requirement are called relevant documents. A perfect IR system will retrieve only relevant documents.

With the help of the following diagram, we can understand the process of information retrieval (IR) –

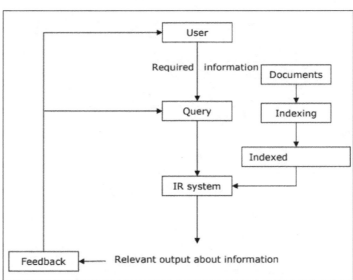

It is clear from the above diagram that a user who needs information will have to formulate a request in the form of query in natural language. Then the IR system will respond by retrieving the relevant output, in the form of documents, about the required information.

Classical Problem in Information Retrieval (IR) System

The main goal of IR research is to develop a model for retrieving information from the repositories of documents. Here, we are going to discuss a classical problem, named ad-hoc retrieval problem, related to the IR system.

In ad-hoc retrieval, the user must enter a query in natural language that describes the required information. Then the IR system will return the required documents related to the desired information. For example, suppose we are searching something on the Internet and it gives some exact pages that are relevant as per our requirement but there can be some non-relevant pages too. This is due to the ad-hoc retrieval problem.

Aspects of Ad-hoc Retrieval

Followings are some aspects of ad-hoc retrieval that are addressed in IR research:

- How users with the help of relevance feedback can improve original formulation of a query?

- How to implement database merging, i.e., how results from different text databases can be merged into one result set?

- How to handle partly corrupted data? Which models are appropriate for the same?

Information Retrieval (IR) Model

Mathematically, models are used in many scientific areas having objective to understand some phenomenon in the real world. A model of information retrieval predicts and explains what a user will find in relevance to the given query. IR model is basically a pattern that defines the above-mentioned aspects of retrieval procedure and consists of the following:

- A model for documents.

- A model for queries.

- A matching function that compares queries to documents.

Mathematically, a retrieval model consists of:

D – Representation for documents.

R – Representation for queries.

F – The modeling framework for D, Q along with relationship between them.

$R(q, d_i)$ – A similarity function which orders the documents with respect to the query. It is also called ranking.

Types of Information Retrieval (IR) Model

An information model (IR) model can be classified into three basic models.

Classical IR Model

It is the simplest and easy to implement IR model. This model is based on mathematical knowledge that was easily recognized and understood as well. Boolean, Vector and Probabilistic are the three classical IR models.

Non-Classical IR Model

It is completely opposite to classical IR model. Such kind of IR models are based on principles other than similarity, probability, Boolean operations. Information logic model, situation theory model and interaction models are the examples of non-classical IR model.

Alternative IR Model

It is the enhancement of classical IR model making use of some specific techniques from some other fields. Cluster model, fuzzy model and latent semantic indexing (LSI) models are the example of alternative IR model.

Design Features of Information Retrieval (IR) Systems

Let us now learn about the design features of IR systems –

Inverted Index

The primary data structure of most of the IR systems is in the form of inverted index. We can define an inverted index as a data structure that list, for every word, all documents that contain it and frequency of the occurrences in document. It makes it easy to search for 'hits' of a query word.

Stop Word Elimination

Stop words are those high frequency words that are deemed unlikely to be useful for searching. They have less semantic weights. All such kind of words are in a list called stop list. For example, articles "a", "an", "the" and prepositions like "in", "of", "for", "at" etc. are the examples of stop words. The size of the inverted index can be significantly reduced by stop list. As per Zipf's law, a stop list covering a few dozen words reduces the size of inverted index by almost half. On the other hand, sometimes the elimination of stop word may cause elimination of the term that is useful for searching. For example, if we eliminate the alphabet "A" from "Vitamin A" then it would have no significance.

Stemming

Stemming, the simplified form of morphological analysis, is the heuristic process of extracting the base form of words by chopping off the ends of words. For example, the words laughing, laughs, laughed would be stemmed to the root word laugh.

The Boolean Model

It is the oldest information retrieval (IR) model. The model is based on set theory and the Boolean algebra, where documents are sets of terms and queries are Boolean expressions on terms. The Boolean Model can be defined as –

- D – A set of words, i.e., the indexing terms present in a document. Here, each term is either present (1) or absent (0).

- Q – A Boolean expression, where terms are the index terms and operators are logical products – AND, logical sum – OR and logical difference – NOT

- F – Boolean algebra over sets of terms as well as over sets of documents

- If we talk about the relevance feedback, then in Boolean IR model the Relevance prediction can be defined as follows –

- R – A document is predicted as relevant to the query expression if and only if it satisfies the query expression as –

    $$((text \lor information) \land rerieval \land \sim theory)$$

We can explain this model by a query term as an unambiguous definition of a set of documents.

For example, the query term "economic" defines the set of documents that are indexed with the term "economic".

Now, what would be the result after combining terms with Boolean AND Operator? It will define a document set that is smaller than or equal to the document sets of any of the single terms. For example, the query with terms "social" and "economic" will produce the documents set of documents that are indexed with both the terms. In other words, document set with the intersection of both the sets.

Now, what would be the result after combining terms with Boolean OR operator? It will define a document set that is bigger than or equal to the document sets of any of the single terms. For example, the query with terms "social" or "economic" will produce the documents set of documents that are indexed with either the term "social" or "economic". In other words, document set with the union of both the sets.

Advantages of the Boolean Model

The advantages of the Boolean Model are as follows –

- The simplest model, which is based on sets.

- Easy to understand and implement.

- It only retrieves exact matches

- It gives the user, a sense of control over the system.

Disadvantages of the Boolean Model

The disadvantages of the Boolean Model are as follows –

- The model's similarity function is Boolean. Hence, there would be no partial matches. This can be annoying for the users.

- In this model, the Boolean operator usage has much more influence than a critical word.

- The query language is expressive, but it is complicated too.

- No ranking for retrieved documents.

Vector Space Model

Due to the above disadvantages of the Boolean Model, Gerard Salton and his colleagues suggested a model, which is based on Luhn's similarity criterion. The similarity criterion formulated by Luhn states, "the more two representations agreed in given elements and their distribution, the higher would be the probability of their representing similar information."

Consider the following important points to understand more about the Vector Space Model –

- The index representations (documents) and the queries are considered as vectors embedded in a high dimensional Euclidean space.

- The similarity measure of a document vector to a query vector is usually the cosine of the angle between them.

Cosine Similarity Measure Formula

Cosine is a normalized dot product, which can be calculated with the help of the following formula –

$$Score\left(\vec{d}\vec{q}\right) = \frac{\sum_{k=1}^{m} d_k \cdot q_k}{\sqrt{\sum_{k=1}^{m}\left(d_k\right)^2} \cdot \sqrt{\sum_{k=1}^{m} m\left(q_k\right)^2}}$$

$$Score\left(\vec{d}\vec{q}\right) = 1 \ when \ d = q$$

$$Score\left(\vec{d}\vec{q}\right) = 0 \ when \ d \ and \ q \ share \ no \ items$$

Vector Space Representation with Query and Document

The query and documents are represented by a two-dimensional vector space. The terms are car and insurance. There is one query and three documents in the vector space.

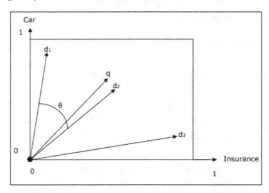

The top ranked document in response to the terms car and insurance will be the document d_2 because the angle between q and d_2 is the smallest. The reason behind this is that both the concepts car and insurance are salient in d_2 and hence have the high weights. On the other side, d_1 and d_3 also mention both the terms but in each case, one of them is not a centrally important term in the document.

Term Weighting

Term weighting means the weights on the terms in vector space. Higher the weight of the term, greater would be the impact of the term on cosine. More weights should be assigned to the more important terms in the model. Now the question that arises here is how can we model this.

One way to do this is to count the words in a document as its term weight. However, do you think it would be effective method?

Another method, which is more effective, is to use term frequency (tf_{ij}), document frequency (df_i) and collection frequency (cf_i).

Term Frequency (tf_{ij})

It may be defined as the number of occurrences of w_i in d_j. The information that is captured by term frequency is how salient a word is within the given document or in other words we can say that the higher the term frequency the more that word is a good description of the content of that document.

Document Frequency (df_i)

It may be defined as the total number of documents in the collection in which w_i occurs. It is an indicator of informativeness. Semantically focused words will occur several times in the document unlike the semantically unfocused words.

Collection Frequency (cf_i)

It may be defined as the total number of occurrences of w_i in the collection.

Mathematically, $df_i \leq cf_i$ and $\sum_j tf_{ij} = cf_i$

Forms of Document Frequency Weighting

Let us now learn about the different forms of document frequency weighting. The forms are described below:

Term Frequency Factor

This is also classified as the term frequency factor, which means that if a term t appears often in a document then a query containing t should retrieve that document. We can combine word's term frequency (tf_{ij}) and document frequency (df_i) into a single weight as follows:

$$weight(i,j) = \begin{cases} \left(1 + log\left(tf_{ij}\right)\right) log \dfrac{N}{df_i} & if\ tf_{i,j} \geq 1 \\ 0 & if\ tf_{i,j} = 0 \end{cases}$$

Here N is the total number of documents.

Inverse Document Frequency (idf)

This is another form of document frequency weighting and often called idf weighting or inverse document frequency weighting. The important point of idf weighting is that the term's scarcity across the collection is a measure of its importance and importance is inversely proportional to frequency of occurrence.

Mathematically,

$$idf_t = log\left(1 + \frac{N}{n_t}\right)$$

$$idf_t = log\left(1 + \frac{N - n_t}{n_t}\right)$$

Here,

N = documents in the collection

n_t = documents containing term t

User Query Improvement

The primary goal of any information retrieval system must be accuracy – to produce relevant documents as per the user's requirement. However, the question that arises here is how can we improve the output by improving user's query formation style. Certainly, the output of any IR system is dependent on the user's query and a well-formatted query will produce more accurate results. The user can improve his/her query with the help of relevance feedback, an important aspect of any IR model.

Relevance Feedback

Relevance feedback takes the output that is initially returned from the given query. This initial output can be used to gather user information and to know whether that output is relevant to perform a new query or not. The feedbacks can be classified as follows –

Explicit Feedback

It may be defined as the feedback that is obtained from the assessors of relevance. These assessors will also indicate the relevance of a document retrieved from the query. In order to improve query retrieval performance, the relevance feedback information needs to be interpolated with the original query.

Assessors or other users of the system may indicate the relevance explicitly by using the following relevance systems –

- Binary relevance system – This relevance feedback system indicates that a document is either relevant (1) or irrelevant (0) for a given query.

- Graded relevance system – The graded relevance feedback system indicates the relevance of a document, for a given query, on the basis of grading by using numbers, letters or descriptions. The description can be like "not relevant", "somewhat relevant", "very relevant" or "relevant".

Implicit Feedback

It is the feedback that is inferred from user behavior. The behavior includes the duration of time user spent viewing a document, which document is selected for viewing and which is not, page browsing and scrolling actions, etc. One of the best examples of implicit feedback is dwell time, which is a measure of how much time a user spends viewing the page linked to in a search result.

Pseudo Feedback

It is also called Blind feedback. It provides a method for automatic local analysis. The manual part of relevance feedback is automated with the help of Pseudo relevance feedback so that the user gets improved retrieval performance without an extended interaction. The main advantage of this feedback system is that it does not require assessors like in explicit relevance feedback system.

Consider the following steps to implement this feedback –

- Step 1 – First, the result returned by initial query must be taken as relevant result. The range of relevant result must be in top 10-50 results.

- Step 2 – Now, select the top 20-30 terms from the documents using for instance term frequency(tf)-inverse document frequency(idf) weight.

- Step 3 – Add these terms to the query and match the returned documents. Then return the most relevant documents.

DATA MINING

Data mining is the process of discovering patterns in large data sets involving methods at the intersection of machine learning, statistics, and database systems. Data mining is an interdisciplinary subfield of computer science and statistics with an overall goal to extract information (with intelligent methods) from a data set and transform the information into a comprehensible structure for further use. Data mining is the analysis step of the "knowledge discovery in databases" process or KDD. Aside from the raw analysis step, it also involves database and data management aspects, data pre-processing, model and inference considerations, interestingness metrics, complexity considerations, post-processing of discovered structures, visualization, and online updating.

The term "data mining" is a misnomer, because the goal is the extraction of patterns and knowledge from large amounts of data, not the extraction (*mining*) of data itself. It also is a buzzword and is frequently applied to any form of large-scale data or information processing (collection, extraction, warehousing, analysis, and statistics) as well as any application of computer decision support system, including artificial intelligence (e.g., machine learning) and business intelligence.

The actual data mining task is the semi-automatic or automatic analysis of large quantities of data to extract previously unknown, interesting patterns such as groups of data records (cluster analysis), unusual records (anomaly detection), and dependencies (association rule mining, sequential pattern mining). This usually involves using database techniques such as spatial indices. These patterns can then be seen as a kind of summary of the input data, and may be used in further analysis or, for example, in machine learning and predictive analytics. For example, the data mining step might identify multiple groups in the data, which can then be used to obtain more accurate prediction results by a decision support system. Neither the data collection, data preparation, nor result interpretation and reporting is part of the data mining step, but do belong to the overall KDD process as additional steps.

The difference between data analysis and data mining is that data analysis is used to test models and hypotheses on the dataset, e.g., analyzing the effectiveness of a marketing campaign, regardless of the amount of data; in contrast, data mining uses machine-learning and statistical models to uncover clandestine or hidden patterns in a large volume of data.

The related terms *data dredging*, *data fishing*, and *data snooping* refer to the use of data mining methods to sample parts of a larger population data set that are (or may be) too small for reliable statistical inferences to be made about the validity of any patterns discovered. These methods can, however, be used in creating new hypotheses to test against the larger data populations.

The manual extraction of patterns from data has occurred for centuries. Early methods of identifying patterns in data include Bayes' theorem and regression analysis. The proliferation, ubiquity and increasing power of computer technology has dramatically increased data collection, storage, and manipulation ability. As data sets have grown in size and complexity, direct "hands-on" data analysis has increasingly been augmented with indirect, automated data processing, aided by other discoveries in computer science, such as neural networks, cluster analysis, genetic algorithms, decision trees and decision rules, and support vector machines. Data mining is the process of applying these methods with the intention of uncovering hidden patterns in large data sets. It bridges the gap from applied statistics and artificial intelligence (which usually provide the mathematical background) to database management by exploiting the way data is stored and indexed in databases to execute the actual learning and discovery algorithms more efficiently, allowing such methods to be applied to ever larger data sets.

Process

The knowledge discovery in databases (KDD) process is commonly defined with the stages:

- Selection,
- Pre-processing,
- Transformation,
- Data mining,
- Interpretation/evaluation.

It exists, however, in many variations on this theme, such as the Cross-industry standard process for data mining (CRISP-DM) which defines six phases:

- Business understanding,
- Data understanding,
- Data preparation,
- Modeling,
- Evaluation,
- Deployment.

or a simplified process such as (1) Pre-processing, (2) Data Mining, and (3) Results Validation.

Polls conducted in 2002, 2004, 2007 and 2014 show that the CRISP-DM methodology is the leading methodology used by data miners. The only other data mining standard named in these polls was SEMMA. However, 3–4 times as many people reported using CRISP-DM. Several teams of researchers have published reviews of data mining process models, and Azevedo and Santos conducted a comparison of CRISP-DM and SEMMA in 2008.

Pre-processing

Before data mining algorithms can be used, a target data set must be assembled. As data mining can only uncover patterns actually present in the data, the target data set must be large enough to contain these patterns while remaining concise enough to be mined within an acceptable time limit. A common source for data is a data mart or data warehouse. Pre-processing is essential to analyze the multivariate data sets before data mining. The target set is then cleaned. Data cleaning removes the observations containing noise and those with missing data.

Classes of Data Mining

Data mining involves six common classes of tasks:

- Anomaly detection (outlier/change/deviation detection): The identification of unusual data records, that might be interesting or data errors that require further investigation.

- Association rule learning (dependency modeling): Searches for relationships between variables. For example, a supermarket might gather data on customer purchasing habits. Using association rule learning, the supermarket can determine which products are frequently bought together and use this information for marketing purposes. This is sometimes referred to as market basket analysis.

- Clustering: Is the task of discovering groups and structures in the data that are in some way or another "similar", without using known structures in the data.

- Classification: Is the task of generalizing known structure to apply to new data. For example, an e-mail program might attempt to classify an e-mail as "legitimate" or as "spam".

- Regression: Attempts to find a function which models the data with the least error that is, for estimating the relationships among data or datasets.

- Summarization: Providing a more compact representation of the data set, including visualization and report generation.

Results Validation

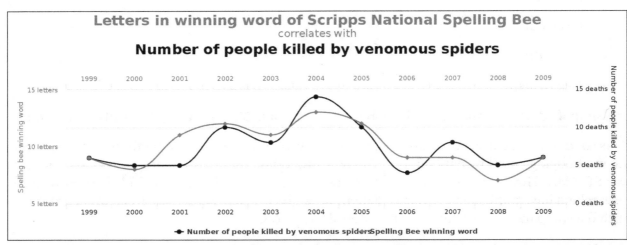

An example of data produced by data dredging through a bot operated by statistician Tyler Vigen, apparently showing a close link between the best word winning a spelling bee competition and the number of people in the United States killed by venomous spiders. The similarity in trends is obviously a coincidence.

Data mining can unintentionally be misused, and can then produce results which appear to be significant; but which do not actually predict future behavior and cannot be reproduced on a new sample of data and bear little use. Often this results from investigating too many hypotheses and not performing proper statistical hypothesis testing. A simple version of this problem in machine learning is known as overfitting, but the same problem can arise at different phases of the process and thus a train/test split - when applicable at all - may not be sufficient to prevent this from happening.

The final step of knowledge discovery from data is to verify that the patterns produced by the data mining algorithms occur in the wider data set. Not all patterns found by data mining algorithms are necessarily valid. It is common for data mining algorithms to find patterns in the training set which are not present in the general data set. This is called overfitting. To overcome this, the evaluation uses a test set of data on which the data mining algorithm was not trained. The learned patterns are applied to this test set, and the resulting output is compared to the desired output. For example, a data mining algorithm trying to distinguish "spam" from "legitimate" emails would be trained on a training set of sample e-mails. Once trained, the learned patterns would be applied to the test set of e-mails on which it had *not* been trained. The accuracy of the patterns can then be measured from how many e-mails they correctly classify. A number of statistical methods may be used to evaluate the algorithm, such as ROC curves.

If the learned patterns do not meet the desired standards, subsequently it is necessary to re-evaluate and change the pre-processing and data mining steps. If the learned patterns do meet the desired standards, then the final step is to interpret the learned patterns and turn them into knowledge.

Research

The premier professional body in the field is the Association for Computing Machinery's (ACM) Special Interest Group (SIG) on Knowledge Discovery and Data Mining (SIGKDD). Since 1989, this ACM SIG has hosted an annual international conference and published its proceedings, and since 1999 it has published a biannual academic journal titled "SIGKDD Explorations".

Computer science conferences on data mining include:

- CIKM Conference: ACM Conference on Information and Knowledge Management.

- European Conference on Machine Learning and Principles and Practice of Knowledge Discovery in Databases

- KDD Conference: ACM SIGKDD Conference on Knowledge Discovery and Data Mining.

Data mining topics are also present on many data management/database conferences such as the ICDE Conference, SIGMOD Conference and International Conference on Very Large Data Bases.

Standards

There have been some efforts to define standards for the data mining process, for example the 1999 European Cross Industry Standard Process for Data Mining (CRISP-DM 1.0) and the 2004 Java Data Mining standard (JDM 1.0). Development on successors to these processes (CRISP-DM 2.0 and JDM 2.0) was active in 2006, but has stalled since. JDM 2.0 was withdrawn without reaching a final draft.

For exchanging the extracted models – in particular for use in predictive analytics – the key standard is the Predictive Model Markup Language (PMML), which is an XML-based language developed by the Data Mining Group (DMG) and supported as exchange format by many data mining applications. As the name suggests, it only covers prediction models, a particular data mining task of high importance to business applications. However, extensions to cover (for example) subspace clustering have been proposed independently of the DMG.

Privacy Concerns and Ethics

While the term "data mining" itself may have no ethical implications, it is often associated with the mining of information in relation to peoples' behavior (ethical and otherwise).

The ways in which data mining can be used can in some cases and contexts raise questions regarding privacy, legality, and ethics. In particular, data mining government or commercial data sets for national security or law enforcement purposes, such as in the Total Information Awareness Program or in ADVISE, has raised privacy concerns.

Data mining requires data preparation which uncovers information or patterns which compromises confidentiality and privacy obligations. A common way for this to occur is through data aggregation. Data aggregation involves combining data together in a way that facilitates analysis (but that also might make identification of private, individual-level data deducible or otherwise apparent). This is not data mining *per se*, but a result of the preparation of data before – and for the purposes of – the analysis. The threat to an individual's privacy comes into play when the data, once compiled, cause the data miner, or anyone who has access to the newly compiled data set, to be able to identify specific individuals, especially when the data were originally anonymous.

It is recommended to be aware of the following before data are collected:

- The purpose of the data collection and any (known) data mining projects;
- How the data will be used;
- Who will be able to mine the data and use the data and their derivatives;
- The status of security surrounding access to the data;
- How collected data can be updated.

Data may also be modified so as to *become* anonymous, so that individuals may not readily be identified. However, even "anonymized" data sets can potentially contain enough information to allow identification of individuals, as occurred when journalists were able to find several individuals based on a set of search histories that were inadvertently released by AOL.

The inadvertent revelation of personally identifiable information leading to the provider violates Fair Information Practices. This indiscretion can cause financial, emotional, or bodily harm to the indicated individual. In one instance of privacy violation, the patrons of Walgreens filed a lawsuit against the company in 2011 for selling prescription information to data mining companies who in turn provided the data to pharmaceutical companies.

Situation in Europe

Europe has rather strong privacy laws, and efforts are underway to further strengthen the rights of the consumers. However, the U.S.-E.U. Safe Harbor Principles currently effectively expose European users to privacy exploitation by U.S. companies. As a consequence of Edward Snowden's global surveillance disclosure, there has been increased discussion to revoke this agreement, as in particular the data will be fully exposed to the National Security Agency, and attempts to reach an agreement have failed.

Situation in the United States

In the United States, privacy concerns have been addressed by the US Congress via the passage of regulatory controls such as the Health Insurance Portability and Accountability Act (HIPAA). The HIPAA requires individuals to give their "informed consent" regarding information they provide and its intended present and future uses. According to an article in *Biotech Business Week*, "in practice, HIPAA may not offer any greater protection than the longstanding regulations in the research arena,' says the AAHC. More importantly, the rule's goal of protection through informed consent is approach a level of incomprehensibility to average individuals." This underscores the necessity for data anonymity in data aggregation and mining practices.

U.S. information privacy legislation such as HIPAA and the Family Educational Rights and Privacy Act (FERPA) applies only to the specific areas that each such law addresses. Use of data mining by the majority of businesses in the U.S. is not controlled by any legislation.

Copyright Law

Situation in Europe

Under European copyright and database laws, the mining of in-copyright works (such as by web mining) without the permission of the copyright owner is not legal. Where a database is pure data in Europe, it may be that there is no copyright – but database rights may exist so data mining becomes subject to intellectual property owners' rights that are protected by the Database Directive. On the recommendation of the Hargreaves review, this led to the UK government to amend its copyright law in 2014 to allow content mining as a limitation and exception. The UK was the second country in the world to do so after Japan, which introduced an exception in 2009 for data mining. However, due to the restriction of the Information Society Directive (2001), the UK exception only allows content mining for non-commercial purposes. UK copyright law also does not allow this provision to be overridden by contractual terms and conditions.

The European Commission facilitated stakeholder discussion on text and data mining in 2013, under the title of Licences for Europe. The focus on the solution to this legal issue, such as licensing rather than limitations and exceptions, led to representatives of universities, researchers, libraries, civil society groups and open access publishers to leave the stakeholder dialogue in May 2013.

Situation in the United States

US copyright law, and in particular its provision for fair use, means that content mining in America, as well as other fair use countries such as Israel, Taiwan and South Korea is viewed as being legal. As content mining is transformative, that is it does not supplant the original work, it is viewed as being lawful under fair use. For example, as part of the Google Book settlement the presiding judge on the case ruled that Google's digitisation project of in-copyright books was lawful, in part because of the transformative uses that the digitization project displayed - one being text and data mining.

Software

Free Open-source Data Mining Software and Applications

The following applications are available under free/open source licenses. Public access to application source code is also available.

- Carrot: Text and search results clustering framework.

- Chemicalize.org: A chemical structure miner and web search engine.

- ELKI: A university research project with advanced cluster analysis and outlier detection methods written in the Java language.

- GATE: A natural language processing and language engineering tool.

- KNIME: The Konstanz Information Miner, a user friendly and comprehensive data analytics framework.

- Massive Online Analysis (MOA): A real-time big data stream mining with concept drift tool in the Java programming language.

- MEPX: Cross platform tool for regression and classification problems based on a Genetic Programming variant.

- ML-Flex: A software package that enables users to integrate with third-party machine-learning packages written in any programming language, execute classification analyses in parallel across multiple computing nodes, and produce HTML reports of classification results.

- mlpack: A collection of ready-to-use machine learning algorithms written in the C++ language.

- NLTK (Natural Language Toolkit): A suite of libraries and programs for symbolic and statistical natural language processing (NLP) for the Python language.

- OpenNN: Open neural networks library.

- Orange: A component-based data mining and machine learning software suite written in the Python language.

- R: A programming language and software environment for statistical computing, data mining, and graphics. It is part of the GNU Project.

- scikit-learn is an open source machine learning library for the Python programming language

- Torch: An open-source deep learning library for the Lua programming language and scientific computing framework with wide support for machine learning algorithms.

- UIMA: The UIMA (Unstructured Information Management Architecture) is a component framework for analyzing unstructured content such as text, audio and video – originally developed by IBM.

- Weka: A suite of machine learning software applications written in the Java programming language.

Proprietary Data-mining Software and Applications

The following applications are available under proprietary licenses.

- Angoss Knowledge Studio: Data mining tool.

- Clarabridge: Text analytics product.

- LIONsolver: An integrated software application for data mining, business intelligence, and modeling that implements the Learning and Intelligent Optimization (LION) approach.

- Megaputer Intelligence: Data and text mining software is called PolyAnalyst.

- Microsoft Analysis Services: Data mining software provided by Microsoft.

- NetOwl: Suite of multilingual text and entity analytics products that enable data mining.

- Oracle Data Mining: Data mining software by Oracle Corporation.

- PSeven: Platform for automation of engineering simulation and analysis, multidisciplinary optimization and data mining provided by DATADVANCE.

- Qlucore Omics Explorer: Data mining software.

- RapidMiner: An environment for machine learning and data mining experiments.

- SAS Enterprise Miner: Data mining software provided by the SAS Institute.

- SPSS Modeler: Data mining software provided by IBM.

- STATISTICA Data Miner: Data mining software provided by StatSoft.

- Tanagra: Visualisation-oriented data mining software, also for teaching.

- Vertica: Data mining software provided by Hewlett-Packard.

INFORMATION EXTRACTION

Information extraction (IE) is the task of automatically extracting structured information from unstructured and/or semi-structured machine-readable documents. In most of the cases this activity concerns processing human language texts by means of natural language processing (NLP). Recent activities in multimedia document processing like automatic annotation and content extraction out of images/audio/video/documents could be seen as information extraction

Due to the difficulty of the problem, current approaches to IE focus on narrowly restricted domains. An example is the extraction from newswire reports of corporate mergers, such as denoted by the formal relation:

$$MergerBetween(company_1, company_2, date),,$$

from an online news sentence such as:

"Yesterday, New York based Foo Inc. announced their acquisition of Bar Corp."

A broad goal of IE is to allow computation to be done on the previously unstructured data. A more specific goal is to allow logical reasoning to draw inferences based on the logical content of the input data. Structured data is semantically well-defined data from a chosen target domain, interpreted with respect to category and context.

Information Extraction is the part of a greater puzzle which deals with the problem of devising automatic methods for text management, beyond its transmission, storage and display. The discipline of information retrieval (IR) has developed automatic methods, typically of a statistical flavor, for indexing large document collections and classifying documents. Another complementary approach is that of natural language processing (NLP) which has solved the problem of modelling human language processing with considerable success when taking into account the magnitude of the task. In terms of both difficulty and emphasis, IE deals with tasks in between both IR and NLP. In terms of input, IE assumes the existence of a set of documents in which each document follows a template, i.e. describes one or more entities or events in a manner that is similar to those in other documents but differing in the details. An example, consider a group of newswire articles on Latin American terrorism with each article presumed to be based upon one or more terroristic acts. We also define for any given IE task a template, which is a(or a set of) case frame(s) to hold the information contained in a single document. For the terrorism example, a template would have slots corresponding to the perpetrator, victim, and weapon of the terroristic act, and the date on which the event happened. An IE system for this problem is required to "understand" an attack article only enough to find data corresponding to the slots in this template.

The present significance of IE pertains to the growing amount of information available in unstructured form. Tim Berners-Lee, inventor of the world wide web, refers to the existing Internet as the web of *documents* and advocates that more of the content be made available as a web of *data*. Until this transpires, the web largely consists of unstructured documents lacking semantic metadata. Knowledge contained within these documents can be made more accessible for machine processing by means of transformation into relational form, or by marking-up with XML tags. An intelligent agent monitoring a news data feed requires IE to transform unstructured data into something that can be reasoned with. A typical application of IE is to scan a set of documents written in a natural language and populate a database with the information extracted.

Tasks and Subtasks

Applying information extraction to text is linked to the problem of text simplification in order to create a structured view of the information present in free text. The overall goal being to create a more easily machine-readable text to process the sentences. Typical IE tasks and subtasks include:

- Template filling: Extracting a fixed set of fields from a document, e.g. extract perpetrators, victims, time, etc. from a newspaper article about a terrorist attack.

  - Event extraction: Given an input document, output zero or more event templates. For instance, a newspaper article might describe multiple terrorist attacks.

- Knowledge Base Population: Fill a database of facts given a set of documents. Typically the database is in the form of triplets, (entity 1, relation, entity 2), e.g. (Barack Obama, Spouse, Michelle Obama).

  - Named entity recognition: Recognition of known entity names (for people and organizations), place names, temporal expressions, and certain types of numerical expressions, by employing existing knowledge of the domain or information extracted from other sentences. Typically the recognition task involves assigning a unique identifier to the extracted entity. A simpler task is named entity detection, which aims at detecting entities without having any existing knowledge about the entity instances. For example, in processing the sentence "M. Smith likes fishing", named entity detection would denote detecting that the phrase "M. Smith" does refer to a person, but without necessarily having (or using) any knowledge about a certain *M. Smith* who is (or, "might be") the specific person whom that sentence is talking about.

  - Coreference resolution: Detection of coreference and anaphoric links between text entities. In IE tasks, this is typically restricted to finding links between previously-extracted named entities. For example, "International Business Machines" and "IBM" refer to the same real-world entity. If we take the two sentences "M. Smith likes fishing. But he doesn't like biking", it would be beneficial to detect that "he" is referring to the previously detected person "M. Smith".

- ○ Relationship extraction: Identification of relations between entities, such as-

  - □ PERSON works for ORGANIZATION (extracted from the sentence "Bill works for IBM.")

  - □ PERSON located in LOCATION (extracted from the sentence "Bill is in France.")

- • Semi-structured information extraction which may refer to any IE that tries to restore some kind of information structure that has been lost through publication, such as:

  - ○ Table extraction: Finding and extracting tables from documents .

  - ○ Table information extraction: Extracting information in structured manner from the tables. This is more complex task than table extraction, as table extraction is only the first step, while understanding the roles of the cells, rows, columns, linking the information inside the table and understanding the information presented in the table are additional tasks necessary for table information extraction.

  - ○ Comments extraction: Extracting comments from actual content of article in order to restore the link between author of each sentence

- • Language and vocabulary analysis:

  - ○ Terminology extraction: Finding the relevant terms for a given corpus

- • Audio extraction:

  - ○ Template-based music extraction: Finding relevant characteristic in an audio signal taken from a given repertoire; for instance time indexes of occurrences of percussive sounds can be extracted in order to represent the essential rhythmic component of a music piece.

Note that this list is not exhaustive and that the exact meaning of IE activities is not commonly accepted and that many approaches combine multiple sub-tasks of IE in order to achieve a wider goal. Machine learning, statistical analysis and/or natural language processing are often used in IE.

IE on non-text documents is becoming an increasingly interesting topic in research, and information extracted from multimedia documents can now be expressed in a high level structure as it is done on text. This naturally leads to the fusion of extracted information from multiple kinds of documents and sources.

World Wide Web Applications

IE has been the focus of the MUC conferences. The proliferation of the Web, however, intensified the need for developing IE systems that help people to cope with the enormous amount of data that is available online. Systems that perform IE from online text should meet the requirements of low cost, flexibility in development and easy adaptation to new domains. MUC systems fail to meet those criteria. Moreover, linguistic analysis performed for unstructured text does not exploit the HTML/XML tags and the layout formats that are available in online texts. As a result, less linguistically intensive approaches have been developed for IE on the Web using wrappers, which are sets of highly accurate rules that extract a particular page's content. Manually developing wrappers has proved to be a time-consuming task, requiring a high level of expertise. Machine learning techniques, either supervised or unsupervised, have been used to induce such rules automatically.

Wrappers typically handle highly structured collections of web pages, such as product catalogs and telephone directories. They fail, however, when the text type is less structured, which is also common on the Web. Recent effort on *adaptive information extraction* motivates the development of IE systems that can handle different types of text, from well-structured to almost free text -where common wrappers fail- including mixed types. Such systems can exploit shallow natural language knowledge and thus can be also applied to less structured texts.

A recent development is Visual Information Extraction, that relies on rendering a webpage in a browser and creating rules based on the proximity of regions in the rendered web page. This helps in extracting entities from complex web pages that may exhibit a visual pattern, but lack a discernible pattern in the HTML source code.

Approaches

The following standard approaches are now widely accepted:

- Hand-written regular expressions (or nested group of regular expressions)
- Using classifiers:
  - Generative: Naïve Bayes classifier.
  - Discriminative: Maximum entropy models such as Multinomial logistic regression.
- Sequence models:
  - Recurrent neural network.
  - Hidden Markov model.
  - Conditional Markov model (CMM) / Maximum-entropy Markov model (MEMM).
  - Conditional random fields (CRF) are commonly used in conjunction with IE for tasks as varied as extracting information from research papers to extracting navigation instructions.

Numerous other approaches exist for IE including hybrid approaches that combine some of the standard approaches previously listed.

Free or Open Source Software and Services

- General Architecture for Text Engineering (GATE) is bundled with a free Information Extraction system.

- Apache OpenNLP is a Java machine learning toolkit for natural language processing.

- OpenCalais is an automated information extraction web service from Thomson Reuters (Free limited version).

- Machine Learning for Language Toolkit (Mallet) is a Java-based package for a variety of natural language processing tasks, including information extraction.

- DBpedia Spotlight is an open source tool in Java/Scala (and free web service) that can be used for named entity recognition and name resolution.

- Natural Language Toolkit is a suite of libraries and programs for symbolic and statistical natural language processing (NLP) for the Python programming language.

Commercial Software and Services

- SAS Text Analytics.

- IBM Watson.

- Wolfram Natural Language Understanding.

DATA STORAGE

Data storage is the collective methods and technologies that capture and retain digital information on electromagnetic, optical or silicon-based storage media. Storage is a key component of digital devices, as consumers and businesses have come to rely on it to preserve information ranging from personal photos to business-critical information.

Storage is frequently used to describe the devices and data connected to the computer through input/output (I/O) operations, including hard disks, flash devices, tape systems and other media types.

Importance of Data Storage

Underscoring the importance of storage is a steady climb in the generation of new data, which is attributable to big data and the profusion of internet of things (IoT) devices. Modern storage systems require enhanced capabilities to allow enterprises to apply machine learning-enabled artificial intelligence (AI) to capture this data, analyze it and wring maximum value from it.

Larger application scripts and real-time database analytics have contributed to the advent of highly dense and scalable storage systems, including high-performance computing storage, converged infrastructure, composable storage systems, hyper-converged storage infrastructure, scale-out and scale-up network-attached storage (NAS) and object storage platforms.

By 2025, it is expected that 163 zettabytes (ZB) of new data will be generated, according to a report by IT analyst firm IDC. That estimate represents a potential tenfold increase from the 16 ZB produced through 2016.

Working of Data Storage

The term storage may refer both to a user's data generally and, more specifically, to the integrated hardware and software systems used to capture, manage and prioritize the data. This includes information in applications, databases, data warehouses, archiving, backup appliances and cloud storage.

Digital information is written to target storage media through the use of software commands. The smallest unit of measure in a computer memory is a bit, described with a binary value of 0 or 1, according to the level of electrical voltage contained in a single capacitor. Eight bits make up one byte.

Other capacity measurements to know are:

- Kilobit (Kb)

- Megabit (Mb)

- Gigabit (Gb)

- Terabit (Tb)

- Petabit (Pb)

- Exabit (Eb)

Larger measures include:

- Kilobyte (KB) equal to 1,024 bytes.

- Megabyte (MB) equal to 1,024 KB.

- Gigabyte (GB) equal to 1,024 MB.

- Terabyte (TB) equal to 1,024 GB.

- Petabyte (PB) equal to 1,024 TB.

- Exabyte (EB) equal to 1,024 PB.

Few organizations require a single storage system or connected system that can reach an exabyte of data, but there are storage systems that scale to multiple petabytes.

Data storage capacity requirements define how much storage is needed to run an application, a set of applications or data sets. Capacity requirements take into account the types of data. For instance, simple documents may only require kilobytes of capacity, while graphic-intensive files, such as digital photographs, may take up megabytes, and a video file can require gigabytes of storage. Computer applications commonly list the minimum and recommended capacity requirements needed to run them.

On an electromechanical disk, bytes store blocks of data within sectors. A hard disk is a circular platter coated with a thin layer of magnetic material. The disk is inserted on a spindle and spins at speeds of up to 15,000 revolutions per minute (rpm). As it rotates, data is written on the disk surface using magnetic recording heads. A high-speed actuator arm positions the recording head to the first available space on the disk, allowing data to be written in a circular fashion.

A sector on a standard disk is 512 bytes. Recent advances in disk include shingled magnetic recording, in which data writes occur in overlapping fashion to boost the platter's areal density.

On solid-state drives (SSDs), data is written to pooled NAND flash, designed with floating gate transistors that enable the cell to retain an electrical charge. An SSD is not technically a drive, but it exhibits design characteristics similar to an integrated circuit, featuring potentially millions of nanotransistors placed on millimeter-sized silicon chips.

Backup data copies are written to disk appliances with the aid of a hierarchical storage management system. And although less commonly practiced than in years past, the tactic of some organizations remains to write disk-based backup data to magnetic tape as a tertiary storage tier. This is a best practice in organizations subject to legal regulations.

A virtual tape library (VTL) uses no tape at all. It is a system in which data is written sequentially to disks, but retains the characteristics and properties of tape. The value of a VTL is its quick recovery and scalability.

Evaluating the Storage Hierarchy

Organizations increasingly use tiered storage to automate data placement on different storage media, based on an application's capacity, compliance and performance requirements.

Enterprise data storage is often classified as primary and secondary storage, depending on how the data is used and the type of media it requires. Primary storage handles application workloads central to a company's day-to-day production and main lines of business.

Primary storage is occasionally referred to as main storage or primary memory. Data is held in random access memory (RAM) and other built-in devices, such as the processor's L1 cache. Secondary storage encompasses data on flash, hard disk, tape and other devices requiring I/O operations. Secondary storage media is often used in backup and cloud storage.

Primary storage generally provides faster access than secondary storage due to the proximity of storage to the computer processor. On the other hand, secondary storage can hold much more data than primary storage. Secondary storage also replicates inactive data to a backup storage device, yet keeps it highly available in case it is needed again.

Digital transformation of business has prompted more and more companies to deploy multiple hybrid clouds, adding a remote tier to buttress local storage.

Types of Data Storage Devices/Mediums

Data storage media have varying levels of capacity and speed. These include cache memory, dynamic RAM (DRAM) or main memory; magnetic tape and magnetic disk; optical disc, such as CDs, DVDs and Blu-ray disks; flash memory and various iterations of in-memory storage; and cache memory.

Along with main memory, computers contain nonvolatile read-only memory (ROM), meaning data cannot be written to it.

The main types of storage media in use today include hard disk drives (HDDs), solid-state storage, optical storage and tape. Spinning HDDs use platters stacked on top of each other coated in magnetic media with disk heads that read and write data to the media. HDDs are widely used storage in personal computers, servers and enterprise storage systems, but SSDs are starting to reach performance and price parity with disk.

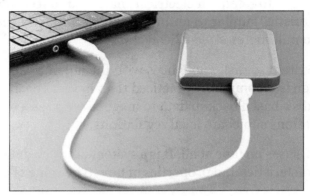

SSDs store data on nonvolatile flash memory chips. Unlike spinning disk drives, SSDs have no moving parts. They are increasingly found in all types of computers, although they remain more expensive than HDDs. Although they haven't gone mainstream yet, some manufacturers are shipping storage devices that combine a hybrid of RAM and flash.

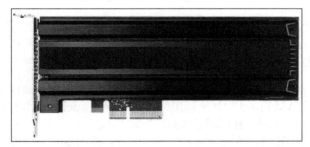

Optical data storage is popular in consumer products, such as computer games and movies, and is also used in high-capacity data archiving systems.

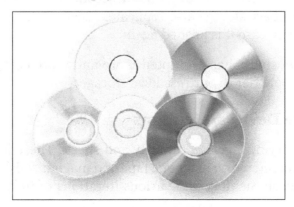

Flash memory cards are integrated in digital cameras and mobile devices, such as smartphones, tablets, audio recorders and media players. Flash memory is found on Secure Digital cards, CompactFlash cards, MultiMediaCards and USB memory sticks.

Physical magnetic floppy disks are rarely used in the era of flash. Unlike older models, newer computer systems are not equipped with slots to insert floppy disks, which emerged as an alternative to magnetic disk. Use of floppy disks started in the 1970s but was phased out in the late 1990s. Virtual floppy disks are sometimes used in place of the 3.5-inch physical diskette, allowing users to mount an image file mapped to the A: drive on a computer.

Enterprise Storage Networks and Server-side Flash

Enterprise storage vendors provide integrated NAS systems to help organizations collect and manage large volumes of data. The hardware includes storage arrays or storage servers equipped with hard drives, flash drives or a hybrid combination, and storage OS software to deliver array-based data services.

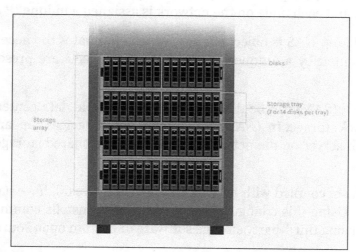

The storage management software offers data protection tools for archiving, clones, copy data management, replication and snapshots. Data reduction features, including compression, data deduplication and thin provisioning, are becoming standard features of most storage arrays. The software also provides policy-based management to govern data placement for tiering to secondary data storage or a hybrid cloud to support a disaster recovery plan or long-term retention.

Since 2011, an increasing number of enterprises have implemented all-flash arrays outfitted only with NAND flash-based SSDs, either as an adjunct or replacement to disk arrays.

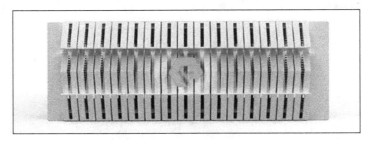

Unlike disk, flash storage devices do not rely on moving mechanical parts to store data, thus offering faster access to data and lower latency than HDDs. Flash is nonvolatile, allowing data to persist in memory even if the storage system loses power. Disk-based storage systems require onboard battery backup or capacitors to keep data persistent. However, flash has not yet achieved an endurance equivalent to disk, leading to hybrid arrays that integrate both types of media.

There are three basic designs of networked storage systems. In its simplest configuration, direct-attached storage (DAS) involves the internal hard drive in an individual computer. In the enterprise, DAS can be a cluster of drives in a server or a group of external drives that attach directly to the server though the Small Computer System Interface (SCSI), Serial Attached SCSI (SAS), Fibre Channel (FC) or internet SCSI (iSCSI).

NAS is a file-based architecture in which multiple file nodes are shared by users, typically across an Ethernet-based local area network (LAN) connection. The advantage of NAS is that filers do not require a full-featured enterprise storage operating system. NAS devices are managed with a browser-based utility, and each node on the network is assigned a unique IP address.

Closely related to scale-out NAS is object storage, which eliminates the necessity of a file system. Each object is represented by a unique identifier. All the objects are presented in a single flat namespace.

A storage area network (SAN) can be designed to span multiple data center locations that need high-performance block storage. In a SAN environment, block devices appear to the host as locally attached storage. Each server on the network is able to access shared storage as though it were a direct-attached drive.

Advances in NAND flash, coupled with falling prices in recent years, have paved the way for software-defined storage. Using this configuration, an enterprise installs commodity-priced SSDs in an x86-based server, using third-party storage software or custom open source code to apply storage management.

Nonvolatile memory express (NVMe) is a developing industry protocol for flash. Industry observers expect NVMe to emerge as the de facto standard for flash storage. NVMe flash will allow applications to communicate directly with a central processing unit (CPU) via Peripheral Component Interconnect Express (PCIe) links, bypassing SCSI command sets transported to a network host bus adapter. NVMe over Fabrics (NVMe-oF) is intended to speed the transfer of data between a host computer and flash target, using established Ethernet, FC or InfiniBand network connectivity.

A nonvolatile dual inline memory module (NVDIMM) is hybrid NAND and DRAM with integrated backup power that plugs into a standard DIMM slot on a memory bus. NVDIMMs only use flash for backup, processing normal calculations in the DRAM. An NVDIMM puts flash closer to the motherboard, presuming the computer's manufacturer has modified the server and developed basic input-output system (BIOS) drivers to recognize the device. NVDIMMs are a way to extend system memory or add a jolt of high-performance storage, rather than to add capacity. Current NVDIMMs on the market top out at 32 GB, but the form factor has seen density increases from 8 GB to 16 GB in just a few years.

Computer Data Storage

1 GiB of SDRAM mounted in a personal computer. An example of *primary* storage.

15 GiB PATA hard disk drive (HDD) from 1999; when connected to a computer it serves as *secondary* storage.

160 GB SDLT tape cartridge, an example of *off-line* storage. When used within a robotic tape library, it is classified as *tertiary* storage instead.

A spindle of DVD-RW's.

Computer data storage, often called storage, is a technology consisting of computer components and recording media that are used to retain digital data. It is a core function and fundamental component of computers.

The central processing unit (CPU) of a computer is what manipulates data by performing computations. In practice, almost all computers use a storage hierarchy, which puts fast but expensive and small storage options close to the CPU and slower but larger and cheaper options farther away. Generally the fast volatile technologies (which lose data when off power) are referred to as "memory", while slower persistent technologies are referred to as "storage".

Even the very first computer designs, Charles Babbage's Analytical Engine and Percy Ludgate's Analytical Machine, clearly distinguished between processing and memory (Babbage stored numbers as rotations of gears, while Ludgate stored numbers as displacements of rods in shuttles). This distinction was extended in the Von Neumann architecture, where the CPU consists of two main parts: The control unit and the arithmetic logic unit (ALU). The former controls the flow of data between the CPU and memory, while the latter performs arithmetic and logical operations on data.

Functionality

Without a significant amount of memory, a computer would merely be able to perform fixed operations and immediately output the result. It would have to be reconfigured to change its behavior. This is acceptable for devices such as desk calculators, digital signal processors, and other specialized devices. Von Neumann machines differ in having a memory in which they store their operating instructions and data. Such computers are more versatile in that they do not need to have their hardware reconfigured for each new program, but can simply be reprogrammed with new in-memory instructions; they also tend to be simpler to design, in that a relatively simple processor may keep state between successive computations to build up complex procedural results. Most modern computers are von Neumann machines.

Data Organization and Representation

A modern digital computer represents data using the binary numeral system. Text, numbers, pictures, audio, and nearly any other form of information can be converted into a string of bits, or binary digits, each of which has a value of 1 or 0. The most common unit of storage is the byte, equal to 8 bits. A piece of information can be handled by any computer or device whose storage space is large enough to accommodate *the binary representation of the piece of information*, or simply data. For example, the complete works of Shakespeare, about 1250 pages in print, can be stored in about five megabytes (40 million bits) with one byte per character.

Data are encoded by assigning a bit pattern to each character, digit, or multimedia object. Many standards exist for encoding (e.g., character encodings like ASCII, image encodings like JPEG, video encodings like MPEG-4).

By adding bits to each encoded unit, redundancy allows the computer to both detect errors in coded data and correct them based on mathematical algorithms. Errors generally occur in low probabilities due to random bit value flipping, or "physical bit fatigue", loss of the physical bit in storage of its ability to maintain a distinguishable value (0 or 1), or due to errors in inter or intra-computer communication. A random bit flip (e.g., due to random radiation) is typically corrected upon detection. A bit, or a group of malfunctioning physical bits (not always the specific defective bit is known; group definition depends on specific storage device) is typically automatically fenced-out, taken out of use by the device, and replaced with another functioning equivalent group in the device, where the corrected bit values are restored (if possible). The cyclic redundancy check (CRC) method is typically used in communications and storage for error detection. A detected error is then retried.

Data compression methods allow in many cases (such as a database) to represent a string of bits by a shorter bit string ("compress") and reconstruct the original string ("decompress") when needed. This utilizes substantially less storage (tens of percents) for many types of data at the cost of more computation (compress and decompress when needed). Analysis of trade-off between storage cost saving and costs of related computations and possible delays in data availability is done before deciding whether to keep certain data compressed or not.

For security reasons certain types of data (e.g., credit-card information) may be kept encrypted in storage to prevent the possibility of unauthorized information reconstruction from chunks of storage snapshots.

Hierarchy of Storage

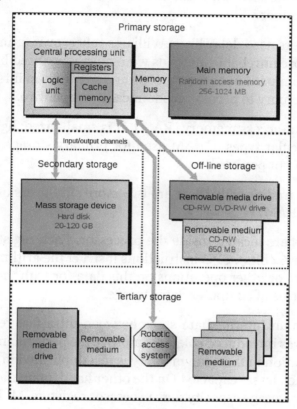

Various forms of storage, divided according to their distance from the central processing unit. The fundamental components of a general-purpose computer are arithmetic and logic unit, control circuitry, storage space, and input/output devices. Technology and capacity as in common home computers around 2005.

Generally, the lower a storage is in the hierarchy, the lesser its bandwidth and the greater its access latency is from the CPU. This traditional division of storage to primary, secondary, tertiary and off-line storage is also guided by cost per bit.

In contemporary usage, "memory" is usually semiconductor storage read-write random-access memory, typically DRAM (dynamic RAM) or other forms of fast but temporary storage. "Storage" consists of storage devices and their media not directly accessible by the CPU (secondary or tertiary storage), typically hard disk drives, optical disc drives, and other devices slower than RAM but non-volatile (retaining contents when powered down).

Historically, memory has been called core memory, main memory, real storage or internal memory. Meanwhile, non-volatile storage devices have been referred to as secondary storage, external memory or auxiliary/peripheral storage.

Primary Storage

Primary storage (also known as main memory, internal memory or prime memory), often referred to simply as memory, is the only one directly accessible to the CPU. The CPU continuously reads instructions stored there and executes them as required. Any data actively operated on is also stored there in uniform manner.

Historically, early computers used delay lines, Williams tubes, or rotating magnetic drums as primary storage. By 1954, those unreliable methods were mostly replaced by magnetic core memory. Core memory remained dominant until the 1970s, when advances in integrated circuit technology allowed semiconductor memory to become economically competitive.

This led to modern random-access memory (RAM). It is small-sized, light, but quite expensive at the same time. (The particular types of RAM used for primary storage are also volatile, i.e. they lose the information when not powered).

As shown in the diagram, traditionally there are two more sub-layers of the primary storage, besides main large-capacity RAM:

- Processor registers are located inside the processor. Each register typically holds a word of data (often 32 or 64 bits). CPU instructions instruct the arithmetic logic unit to perform various calculations or other operations on this data (or with the help of it). Registers are the fastest of all forms of computer data storage.

- Processor cache is an intermediate stage between ultra-fast registers and much slower main memory. It was introduced solely to improve the performance of computers. Most actively used information in the main memory is just duplicated in the cache memory, which is faster, but of much lesser capacity. On the other hand, main memory is much slower, but has a much greater storage capacity than processor registers. Multi-level hierarchical cache setup is also commonly used—*primary cache* being smallest, fastest and located inside the processor; *secondary cache* being somewhat larger and slower.

Main memory is directly or indirectly connected to the central processing unit via a *memory bus*. It is actually two buses: an address bus and a data bus. The CPU firstly sends a number through an address bus, a number called memory address, that indicates the desired location of data. Then it reads or writes the data in the memory cells using the data bus. Additionally, a memory management unit (MMU) is a small device between CPU and RAM recalculating the actual memory address, for example to provide an abstraction of virtual memory or other tasks.

As the RAM types used for primary storage are volatile (uninitialized at start up), a computer containing only such storage would not have a source to read instructions from, in order to start the computer. Hence, non-volatile primary storage containing a small startup program (BIOS) is used to bootstrap the computer, that is, to read a larger program from non-volatile *secondary* storage to RAM and start to execute it. A non-volatile technology used for this purpose is called ROM, for read-only memory (the terminology may be somewhat confusing as most ROM types are also capable of *random access*).

Many types of "ROM" are not literally *read only*, as updates to them are possible; however it is slow and memory must be erased in large portions before it can be re-written. Some embedded systems run programs directly from ROM (or similar), because such programs are rarely changed. Standard computers do not store non-rudimentary programs in ROM, and rather, use large capacities of secondary storage, which is non-volatile as well, and not as costly.

Recently, primary storage and secondary storage in some uses refer to what was historically called, respectively, secondary storage and tertiary storage.

Secondary Storage

A hard disk drive with protective cover removed.

Secondary storage (also known as external memory or auxiliary storage), differs from primary storage in that it is not directly accessible by the CPU. The computer usually uses its input/output channels to access secondary storage and transfer the desired data to primary storage. Secondary storage is non-volatile (retaining data when power is shut off). Modern computer systems typically have two orders of magnitude more secondary storage than primary storage because secondary storage is less expensive.

In modern computers, hard disk drives (HDDs) or solid-state drives (SSDs) are usually used as secondary storage. The access time per byte for HDDs or SSDs is typically measured in milliseconds (one thousandth seconds), while the access time per byte for primary storage is measured in nanoseconds (one billionth seconds). Thus, secondary storage is significantly slower than primary storage. Rotating optical storage devices, such as CD and DVD drives, have even longer access times. Other examples of secondary storage technologies include USB flash drives, floppy disks, magnetic tape, paper tape, punched cards, and RAM disks.

Once the disk read/write head on HDDs reaches the proper placement and the data, subsequent data on the track are very fast to access. To reduce the seek time and rotational latency, data are transferred to and from disks in large contiguous blocks. Sequential or block access on disks is orders of magnitude faster than random access, and many sophisticated paradigms have been developed to design efficient algorithms based upon sequential and block access. Another way to reduce the I/O bottleneck is to use multiple disks in parallel in order to increase the bandwidth between primary and secondary memory.

Secondary storage is often formatted according to a file system format, which provides the abstraction necessary to organize data into files and directories, while also providing metadata describing the owner of a certain file, the access time, the access permissions, and other information.

Most computer operating systems use the concept of virtual memory, allowing utilization of more primary storage capacity than is physically available in the system. As the primary memory fills up, the system moves the least-used chunks (pages) to a swap file or page file on secondary storage, retrieving them later when needed. If a lot of pages are moved to slower secondary storage, the system performance is degraded.

Tertiary Storage

A large tape library, with tape cartridges placed on shelves in the front, and a robotic arm moving in the back. Visible height of the library is about 180 cm.

Tertiary storage or *tertiary memory* is a level below secondary storage. Typically, it involves a robotic mechanism which will *mount* (insert) and *dismount* removable mass storage media into a storage device according to the system's demands; such data are often copied to secondary storage before use. It is primarily used for archiving rarely accessed information since it is much slower than secondary storage (e.g. 5–60 seconds vs. 1–10 milliseconds). This is primarily useful for extraordinarily large data stores, accessed without human operators. Typical examples include tape libraries and optical jukeboxes.

When a computer needs to read information from the tertiary storage, it will first consult a catalog database to determine which tape or disc contains the information. Next, the computer will instruct a robotic arm to fetch the medium and place it in a drive. When the computer has finished reading the information, the robotic arm will return the medium to its place in the library.

Tertiary storage is also known as *nearline storage* because it is "near to online". The formal distinction between online, nearline, and offline storage is:

- Online storage is immediately available for I/O.

- Nearline storage is not immediately available, but can be made online quickly without human intervention.

- Offline storage is not immediately available, and requires some human intervention to become online.

For example, always-on spinning hard disk drives are online storage, while spinning drives that spin down automatically, such as in massive arrays of idle disks (MAID), are nearline storage. Removable media such as tape cartridges that can be automatically loaded, as in tape libraries, are nearline storage, while tape cartridges that must be manually loaded are offline storage.

Off-line Storage

Off-line storage is a computer data storage on a medium or a device that is not under the control of a processing unit. The medium is recorded, usually in a secondary or tertiary storage device, and then physically removed or disconnected. It must be inserted or connected by a human operator before a computer can access it again. Unlike tertiary storage, it cannot be accessed without human interaction.

Off-line storage is used to transfer information, since the detached medium can be easily physically transported. Additionally, in case a disaster, for example a fire, destroys the original data, a medium in a remote location will probably be unaffected, enabling disaster recovery. Off-line storage increases general information security, since it is physically inaccessible from a computer, and data confidentiality or integrity cannot be affected by computer-based attack techniques. Also, if the information stored for archival purposes is rarely accessed, off-line storage is less expensive than tertiary storage.

In modern personal computers, most secondary and tertiary storage media are also used for off-line storage. Optical discs and flash memory devices are most popular, and to much lesser extent removable hard disk drives. In enterprise uses, magnetic tape is predominant. Older examples are floppy disks, Zip disks, or punched cards.

Characteristics of Storage

A 1 GB module of laptop DDR2 RAM.

Storage technologies at all levels of the storage hierarchy can be differentiated by evaluating certain core characteristics as well as measuring characteristics specific to a particular implementation.

These core characteristics are volatility, mutability, accessibility, and addressability. For any particular implementation of any storage technology, the characteristics worth measuring are capacity and performance.

Volatility

Non-volatile memory retains the stored information even if not constantly supplied with electric power. It is suitable for long-term storage of information. Volatile memory requires constant power to maintain the stored information. The fastest memory technologies are volatile ones, although that is not a universal rule. Since the primary storage is required to be very fast, it predominantly uses volatile memory.

Dynamic random-access memory is a form of volatile memory that also requires the stored information to be periodically reread and rewritten, or refreshed, otherwise it would vanish. Static random-access memory is a form of volatile memory similar to DRAM with the exception that it never needs to be refreshed as long as power is applied; it loses its content when the power supply is lost.

An uninterruptible power supply (UPS) can be used to give a computer a brief window of time to move information from primary volatile storage into non-volatile storage before the batteries are exhausted. Some systems, for example EMC Symmetrix, have integrated batteries that maintain volatile storage for several minutes.

Mutability

- Read/write storage or mutable storage: Allows information to be overwritten at any time. A computer without some amount of read/write storage for primary storage purposes would be useless for many tasks. Modern computers typically use read/write storage also for secondary storage.

- Slow write, fast read storage: Read/write storage which allows information to be overwritten multiple times, but with the write operation being much slower than the read operation. Examples include CD-RW and SSD.

- Write once storage: Write Once Read Many (WORM) allows the information to be written only once at some point after manufacture. Examples include semiconductor programmable read-only memory and CD-R.

- Read only storage: Retains the information stored at the time of manufacture. Examples include mask ROM ICs and CD-ROM.

Accessibility

- Random access: Any location in storage can be accessed at any moment in approximately the same amount of time. Such characteristic is well suited for primary and secondary storage. Most semiconductor memories and disk drives provide random access.

- Sequential access: The accessing of pieces of information will be in a serial order, one after the other; therefore the time to access a particular piece of information depends upon which piece of information was last accessed. Such characteristic is typical of off-line storage.

Addressability

- Location-addressable: Each individually accessible unit of information in storage is selected with its numerical memory address. In modern computers, location-addressable storage usually limits to primary storage, accessed internally by computer programs, since location-addressability is very efficient, but burdensome for humans.

- File addressable: Information is divided into *files* of variable length, and a particular file is selected with human-readable directory and file names. The underlying device is still location-addressable, but the operating system of a computer provides the file system abstraction to make the operation more understandable. In modern computers, secondary, tertiary and off-line storage use file systems.

- Content-addressable: Each individually accessible unit of information is selected based on the basis of (part of) the contents stored there. Content-addressable storage can be implemented using software (computer program) or hardware (computer device), with hardware being faster but more expensive option. Hardware content addressable memory is often used in a computer's CPU cache.

Capacity

- Raw capacity: The total amount of stored information that a storage device or medium can hold. It is expressed as a quantity of bits or bytes (e.g. 10.4 megabytes).

- Memory storage density: The compactness of stored information. It is the storage capacity of a medium divided with a unit of length, area or volume (e.g. 1.2 megabytes per square inch).

Performance

- Latency: The time it takes to access a particular location in storage. The relevant unit of measurement is typically nanosecond for primary storage, millisecond for secondary storage, and second for tertiary storage. It may make sense to separate read latency and write latency (especially for non-volatile memory) and in case of sequential access storage, minimum, maximum and average latency.

- Throughput: The rate at which information can be read from or written to the storage. In computer data storage, throughput is usually expressed in terms of megabytes per second (MB/s), though bit rate may also be used. As with latency, read rate and write rate may need to be differentiated. Also accessing media sequentially, as opposed to randomly, typically yields maximum throughput.

- Granularity: The size of the largest "chunk" of data that can be efficiently accessed as a single unit, e.g. without introducing additional latency.

- Reliability: The probability of spontaneous bit value change under various conditions, or overall failure rate.

Utilities such as hdparm and sar can be used to measure IO performance in Linux.

Energy use

- Storage devices that reduce fan usage, automatically shut-down during inactivity, and low power hard drives can reduce energy consumption by 90 percent.

- 2.5-inch hard disk drives often consume less power than larger ones. Low capacity solid-state drives have no moving parts and consume less power than hard disks. Also, memory may use more power than hard disks. Large caches, which are used to avoid hitting the memory wall, may also consume a large amount of power.

Security

Full disk encryption, volume and virtual disk encryption, andor file/folder encryption is readily available for most storage devices.

Hardware memory encryption is available in Intel Architecture, supporting Total Memory Encryption (TME) and page granular memory encryption with multiple keys (MKTME). and in SPARC M7 generation since October 2015.

Storage Media

As of 2011, the most commonly used data storage media are semiconductor, magnetic, and optical, while paper still sees some limited usage. Some other fundamental storage technologies, such as all-flash arrays (AFAs) are proposed for development.

Semiconductor

Semiconductor memory uses semiconductor-based integrated circuits to store information. A semiconductor memory chip may contain millions of tiny transistors or capacitors. Both *volatile* and *non-volatile* forms of semiconductor memory exist. In modern computers, primary storage almost exclusively consists of dynamic volatile semiconductor memory or dynamic random-access memory. Since the turn of the century, a type of non-volatile semiconductor memory known as flash memory has steadily gained share as off-line storage for home computers. Non-volatile semiconductor memory is also used for secondary storage in various advanced electronic devices and specialized computers that are designed for them.

As early as 2006, notebook and desktop computer manufacturers started using flash-based solid-state drives (SSDs) as default configuration options for the secondary storage either in addition to or instead of the more traditional HDD.

Magnetic

Magnetic storage uses different patterns of magnetization on a magnetically coated surface to store information. Magnetic storage is *non-volatile*. The information is accessed using one or more read/write heads which may contain one or more recording transducers. A read/write head only covers a part of the surface so that the head or medium or both must be moved relative to another in order to access data. In modern computers, magnetic storage will take these forms:

- Magnetic disk:

  ○ Floppy disk, used for off-line storage.

- ◦ Hard disk drive, used for secondary storage.
- Magnetic tape, used for tertiary and off-line storage.
- Carousel memory (magnetic rolls).

In early computers, magnetic storage was also used as:

- Primary storage in a form of magnetic memory, or core memory, core rope memory, thin-film memory and/or twistor memory.
- Tertiary (e.g. NCR CRAM) or off line storage in the form of magnetic cards.
- Magnetic tape was then often used for secondary storage.

Optical

Optical storage, the typical optical disc, stores information in deformities on the surface of a circular disc and reads this information by illuminating the surface with a laser diode and observing the reflection. Optical disc storage is *non-volatile*. The deformities may be permanent (read only media), formed once (write once media) or reversible (recordable or read/write media). The following forms are currently in common use:

- CD, CD-ROM, DVD, BD-ROM: Read only storage, used for mass distribution of digital information (music, video, computer programs).
- CD-R, DVD-R, DVD+R, BD-R: Write once storage, used for tertiary and off-line storage.
- CD-RW, DVD-RW, DVD+RW, DVD-RAM, BD-RE: Slow write, fast read storage, used for tertiary and off-line storage.
- Ultra Density Optical or UDO is similar in capacity to BD-R or BD-RE and is slow write, fast read storage used for tertiary and off-line storage.

Magneto-optical disc storage is optical disc storage where the magnetic state on a ferromagnetic surface stores information. The information is read optically and written by combining magnetic and optical methods. Magneto-optical disc storage is *non-volatile*, *sequential access*, slow write, fast read storage used for tertiary and off-line storage.

3D optical data storage has also been proposed.

Light induced magnetization melting in magnetic photoconductors has also been proposed for high-speed low-energy consumption magneto-optical storage.

Paper

Paper data storage, typically in the form of paper tape or punched cards, has long been used to store information for automatic processing, particularly before general-purpose computers existed. Information was recorded by punching holes into the paper or cardboard medium and was read mechanically (or later optically) to determine whether a particular location on the medium was solid or contained a hole. A few technologies allow people to make marks on paper that are easily read by machine—these are widely used for tabulating votes and grading standardized tests. Barcodes made it possible for any object that was to be sold or transported to have some computer readable information securely attached to it.

Other Storage Media or Substrates

- Vacuum tube memory: A Williams tube used a cathode ray tube, and a Selectron tube used a large vacuum tube to store information. These primary storage devices were short-lived in the market, since the Williams tube was unreliable and the Selectron tube was expensive.

- Electro-acoustic memory: Delay line memory used sound waves in a substance such as mercury to store information. Delay line memory was dynamic volatile, cycle sequential read/write storage, and was used for primary storage.

- Optical tape: Is a medium for optical storage generally consisting of a long and narrow strip of plastic onto which patterns can be written and from which the patterns can be read back. It shares some technologies with cinema film stock and optical discs, but is compatible with neither. The motivation behind developing this technology was the possibility of far greater storage capacities than either magnetic tape or optical discs.

- Phase-change memory: Uses different mechanical phases of phase-change material to store information in an X-Y addressable matrix, and reads the information by observing the varying electrical resistance of the material. Phase-change memory would be non-volatile, random-access read/write storage, and might be used for primary, secondary and off-line storage. Most rewritable and many write once optical disks already use phase change material to store information.

- Holographic data storage: Stores information optically inside crystals or photopolymers. Holographic storage can utilize the whole volume of the storage medium, unlike optical disc storage which is limited to a small number of surface layers. Holographic storage would be non-volatile, sequential access, and either write once or read/write storage. It might be used for secondary and off-line storage.

- Molecular memory: Stores information in polymer that can store electric charge. Molecular memory might be especially suited for primary storage. The theoretical storage capacity of molecular memory is 10 terabits per square inch.

- Magnetic photoconductors: Store magnetic information which can be modified by low-light illumination.

- DNA: Stores information in DNA nucleotides. It was first done in 2012 when researchers achieved a rate of 1.28 petabytes per gram of DNA. In March 2017 scientists reported that a new algorithm called a DNA fountain achieved 85% of the theoretical limit, at 215 petabytes per gram of DNA.

Related Technologies

Redundancy

While a group of bits malfunction may be resolved by error detection and correction mechanisms, storage device malfunction requires different solutions. The following solutions are commonly used and valid for most storage devices:

- Device mirroring (replication): A common solution to the problem is constantly maintaining an identical copy of device content on another device (typically of a same type). The downside is that this doubles the storage, and both devices (copies) need to be updated simultaneously with some overhead and possibly some delays. The upside is possible concurrent read of a same data group by two independent processes, which increases performance. When one of the replicated devices is detected to be defective, the other copy is still operational, and is being utilized to generate a new copy on another device (usually available operational in a pool of stand-by devices for this purpose).

- Redundant array of independent disks (RAID): This method generalizes the device mirroring above by allowing one device in a group of N devices to fail and be replaced with the content restored (Device mirroring is RAID with N=2). RAID groups of N=5 or N=6 are common. N>2 saves storage, when comparing with N=2, at the cost of more processing during both regular operation (with often reduced performance) and defective device replacement.

Device mirroring and typical RAID are designed to handle a single device failure in the RAID group of devices. However, if a second failure occurs before the RAID group is completely repaired from the first failure, then data can be lost. The probability of a single failure is typically small. Thus the probability of two failures in a same RAID group in time proximity is much smaller (approximately the probability squared, i.e., multiplied by itself). If a database cannot tolerate even such smaller probability of data loss, then the RAID group itself is replicated (mirrored). In many cases such mirroring is done geographically remotely, in a different storage array, to handle also recovery from disasters.

Network Connectivity

A secondary or tertiary storage may connect to a computer utilizing computer networks. This concept does not pertain to the primary storage, which is shared between multiple processors to a lesser degree.

- Direct-attached storage (DAS) is a traditional mass storage, that does not use any network. This is still a most popular approach. This retronym was coined recently, together with NAS and SAN.

- Network-attached storage (NAS) is mass storage attached to a computer which another computer can access at file level over a local area network, a private wide area network, or in the case of online file storage, over the Internet. NAS is commonly associated with the NFS and CIFS/SMB protocols.

- Storage area network (SAN) is a specialized network, that provides other computers with storage capacity. The crucial difference between NAS and SAN, is that NAS presents and manages file systems to client computers, while SAN provides access at block-addressing (raw) level, leaving it to attaching systems to manage data or file systems within the provided capacity. SAN is commonly associated with Fibre Channel networks.

Robotic Storage

Large quantities of individual magnetic tapes, and optical or magneto-optical discs may be stored in robotic tertiary storage devices. In tape storage field they are known as tape libraries, and in optical storage field optical jukeboxes, or optical disk libraries per analogy. The smallest forms of either technology containing just one drive device are referred to as autoloaders or autochangers.

Robotic-access storage devices may have a number of slots, each holding individual media, and usually one or more picking robots that traverse the slots and load media to built-in drives. The arrangement of the slots and picking devices affects performance. Important characteristics of such storage are possible expansion options: adding slots, modules, drives, robots. Tape libraries may have from 10 to more than 100,000 slots, and provide terabytes or petabytes of near-line information. Optical jukeboxes are somewhat smaller solutions, up to 1,000 slots.

Robotic storage is used for backups, and for high-capacity archives in imaging, medical, and video industries. Hierarchical storage management is a most known archiving strategy of automatically *migrating* long-unused files from fast hard disk storage to libraries or jukeboxes. If the files are needed, they are *retrieved* back to disk.

ONTOLOGY

In computer science and information science, an ontology encompasses a representation, formal naming and definition of the categories, properties and relations between the concepts, data and entities that substantiate one, many or all domains of discourse.

Every field creates ontologies to limit complexity and organize information into data and knowledge. As new ontologies are made, their use hopefully improves problem solving within that domain. Translating research papers within every field is a problem made easier when experts from different countries maintain a controlled vocabulary of jargon between each of their languages.

Since Google started an initiative called Knowledge Graph in 2012, a substantial amount of research has used the phrase knowledge graph as a generalized term. Although there is no clear definition for the term knowledge graph, it is sometimes used as synonym for ontology. One common interpretation is that a knowledge graph represents a collection of interlinked descriptions of entities – real-world objects, events, situations or abstract concepts. Unlike ontologies, knowledge graphs, such as Google's Knowledge Graph, often contain large volumes of factual information with less formal semantics. In some contexts, the term *knowledge graph* is used to refer to any knowledge base that is represented as a graph.

What ontologies in both information science and philosophy have in common is the attempt to represent entities, ideas and events, with all their interdependent properties and relations, according to a system of categories. In both fields, there is considerable work on problems of ontology engineering (e.g., Quine and Kripke in philosophy, Sowa and Guarino in computer science), and debates concerning to what extent normative ontology is possible (e.g., foundationalism and coherentism in philosophy, BFO and Cyc in artificial intelligence). Applied ontology is considered a spiritual successor to prior work in philosophy, however many current efforts are more concerned with establishing controlled vocabularies of narrow domains than first principles, the existence of fixed essences or whether enduring objects (e.g., perdurantism and endurantism) may be ontologically more primary than processes.

Every field uses ontological assumptions to frame explicit theories, research and applications. For instance, the definition and ontology of economics is a primacy concern in Marxist economics, but also in other subfields of economics. An example of economics relying on information science occurs in cases where a simulation or model is intended to enable economic decisions, such as determining what capital assets are at risk and by how much.

Artificial intelligence has retained the most attention regarding applied ontology in subfields like natural language processing within machine translation and knowledge representation, but ontology editors are being used often in a range of fields like education without the intent to contribute to AI.

Ontologies arise out of the branch of philosophy known as metaphysics, which deals with questions like "what exists?" and "what is the nature of reality?". One of five traditional branches of philosophy, metaphysics is concerned with exploring existence through properties, entities and relations such as those between particulars and universals, intrinsic and extrinsic properties, or essence and existence. Metaphysics has been an ongoing topic of discussion since recorded history.

Since the mid-1970s, researchers in the field of artificial intelligence (AI) have recognized that knowledge engineering is the key to building large and powerful AI systems. AI researchers argued that they could create new ontologies as computational models that enable certain kinds of automated reasoning, which was only marginally successful. In the 1980s, the AI community began to use the term *ontology* to refer to both a theory of a modeled world and a component of knowledge-based systems. In particular, David Powers introduced the word *ontology* to AI to refer to real world or robotic grounding, publishing in 1990 literature reviews emphasizing grounded ontology in association with the call for papers for a AAAI Summer Symposium Machine Learning of Natural Language and Ontology, with an expanded version published in SIGART Bulletin and included as a preface to the proceedings. Some researchers, drawing inspiration from philosophical ontologies, viewed computational ontology as a kind of applied philosophy.

In 1993, the widely cited web page and paper "Toward Principles for the Design of Ontologies Used for Knowledge Sharing" by Tom Gruber used *ontology* as a technical term in computer science closely related to earlier idea of semantic networks and taxonomies. Gruber introduced the term as *a specification of a conceptualization*:

> An ontology is a description (like a formal specification of a program) of the concepts and relationships that can formally exist for an agent or a community of agents. This definition is consistent with the usage of ontology as set of concept definitions, but more general. And it is a different sense of the word than its use in philosophy.

Attempting to distance ontologies from taxonomies and similar efforts in knowledge modeling that rely on classes and inheritance, Gruber stated:

> Ontologies are often equated with taxonomic hierarchies of classes, class definitions, and the subsumption relation, but ontologies need not be limited to these forms. Ontologies are also not limited to conservative definitions — that is, definitions in the traditional logic sense that only introduce terminology and do not add any knowledge about the world. To specify a conceptualization, one needs to state axioms that do constrain the possible interpretations for the defined terms.

As refinement of Gruber's definition Feilmayr and Wöß (2016) stated: "An ontology is a formal, explicit specification of a shared conceptualization that is characterized by high semantic expressiveness required for increased complexity."

Components

Contemporary ontologies share many structural similarities, regardless of the language in which they are expressed. Most ontologies describe individuals (instances), classes (concepts), attributes and relations. In this section each of these components is discussed in turn.

Common components of ontologies include:

- Individuals: Instances or objects (the basic or "ground level" objects).

- Classes: Sets, collections, concepts, classes in programming, types of objects or kinds of things.

- Attributes: Aspects, properties, features, characteristics or parameters that objects (and classes) can have.

- Relations: Ways in which classes and individuals can be related to one another.

- Function terms: Complex structures formed from certain relations that can be used in place of an individual term in a statement.

- Restrictions: Formally stated descriptions of what must be true in order for some assertion to be accepted as input.

- Rules: Statements in the form of an if-then (antecedent-consequent) sentence that describe the logical inferences that can be drawn from an assertion in a particular form.

- Axioms: Assertions (including rules) in a logical form that together comprise the overall theory that the ontology describes in its domain of application. This definition differs from that of "axioms" in generative grammar and formal logic. In those disciplines, axioms include only statements asserted as *a priori* knowledge. As used here, "axioms" also include the theory derived from axiomatic statements.

- Events: The changing of attributes or relations.

Ontologies are commonly encoded using ontology languages.

Types

Domain Ontology

A domain ontology (or domain-specific ontology) represents concepts which belong to a part of the world, such as biology or politics. Each domain ontology typically models domain-specific definitions of terms. For example, the word *card* has many different meanings. An ontology about the domain of poker would model the "playing card" meaning of the word, while an ontology about the domain of computer hardware would model the "punched card" and "video card" meanings.

Since domain ontologies are written by different people, they represent concepts in very specific and unique ways, and are often incompatible within the same project. As systems that rely on domain ontologies expand, they often need to merge domain ontologies by hand-tuning each entity or using a combination of software merging and hand-tuning. This presents a challenge to the ontology designer. Different ontologies in the same domain arise due to different languages, different intended usage of the ontologies, and different perceptions of the domain (based on cultural background, education, ideology, etc.).

At present, merging ontologies that are not developed from a common upper ontology is a largely manual process and therefore time-consuming and expensive. Domain ontologies that use the same upper ontology to provide a set of basic elements with which to specify the meanings of the domain ontology entities can be merged with less effort. There are studies on generalized techniques for merging ontologies, but this area of research is still ongoing, and it's a recent event to see the issue sidestepped by having multiple domain ontologies using the same upper ontology like the OBO Foundry.

Upper Ontology

An upper ontology (or foundation ontology) is a model of the common relations and objects that are generally applicable across a wide range of domain ontologies. It usually employs a core glossary that contains the terms and associated object descriptions as they are used in various relevant domain ontologies.

Standardized upper ontologies available for use include BFO, BORO method, Dublin Core, GFO, Cyc, SUMO, UMBEL, the Unified Foundational Ontology (UFO), and DOLCE. WordNet has been considered an upper ontology by some and has been used as a linguistic tool for learning domain ontologies.

Hybrid Ontology

The Gellish ontology is an example of a combination of an upper and a domain ontology.

Visualization

A survey of ontology visualization methods is presented by Katifori et al. An updated survey of ontology visualization methods and tools was published by Dudás et al. The most established ontology visualization methods, namely indented tree and graph visualization are evaluated by Fu et al. A visual language for ontologies represented in OWL is specified by the Visual Notation for OWL Ontologies (VOWL).

Engineering

Ontology engineering (also called ontology building) is a set of tasks related to the development of ontologies for a particular domain. It is a subfield of knowledge engineering that studies the ontology development process, the ontology life cycle, the methods and methodologies for building ontologies, and the tools and languages that support them.

Ontology engineering aims to make explicit the knowledge contained in software applications, and organizational procedures for a particular domain. Ontology engineering offers a direction for overcoming semantic obstacles, such as those related to the definitions of business terms and software classes. Known challenges with ontology engineering include:

- Ensuring the ontology is *current* with domain knowledge and term use.

- Providing *sufficient specificity and concept coverage* for the domain of interest, thus minimizing the content completeness problem.

- Ensuring the ontology can support its use cases.

Editors

Ontology editors are applications designed to assist in the creation or manipulation of ontologies. It is common for ontology editors to use one or more ontology languages.

Aspects of ontology editors include: visual navigation possibilities within the knowledge model, inference engines and information extraction; support for modules; the import and export of foreign knowledge representation languages for ontology matching; and the support of meta-ontologies such as OWL-S, Dublin Core, etc.

Name	Written in	License	Features	Publisher/Creator
a.k.a. software			Ontology, taxonomy and thesaurus management software.	The Synercon Group.
Anzo for Excel			Includes an RDFS and OWL ontology editor within Excel; generates ontologies from Excel spreadsheets.	Cambridge Semantics.
Be Informed Suite		Commercial	Tool for building large ontology based applications. Includes visual editors, inference engines, export to standard formats.	
Chimaera			Other web service	Stanford University
CmapTools	Java based		Ontology Editor (COE) ontology editor Supports numerous formats.	Florida Institute for Human and Machine Cognition.
dot15926 Editor	Python	Open source	Ontology editor for data compliant to engineering ontology standard ISO 15926. Allows Python scripting and pattern-based data analysis. Supports extensions.	

EMFText OWL2 Manchester Editor	Eclipse-based	open-source	Pellet integration.	
Enterprise Architect			Along with UML modeling, supports OMG's Ontology Definition MetaModel which includes OWL and RDF.	Sparx Systems
Fluent Editor			Ontology editor for OWL and SWRL with Controlled Natural Language (Controlled English). Supports OWL, RDF, DL and Functional rendering, unlimited imports and built-in reasoning services.	
TODE	.Net		Tool for Ontology Development and Editing.	
VocBench			Collaborative Web Platform for Management of SKOS thesauri, OWL ontologies and OntoLex lexicons, now in its third incarnation supported by the ISA2 program of the EU.	Originally developed on a joint effort between University of Rome Tor Vergata and the Food and the Agriculture Organization of the United Nations.

Learning

Ontology learning is the automatic or semi-automatic creation of ontologies, including extracting a domain's terms from natural language text. As building ontologies manually is extremely labor-intensive and time consuming, there is great motivation to automate the process. Information extraction and text mining have been explored to automatically link ontologies to documents, for example in the context of the BioCreative challenges.

Languages

An ontology language is a formal language used to encode an ontology. There are a number of such languages for ontologies, both proprietary and standards-based:

- Common Algebraic Specification Language is a general logic-based specification language developed within the IFIP working group 1.3 "Foundations of System Specifications" and is a *de facto* standard language for software specifications. It is now being applied to ontology specifications in order to provide modularity and structuring mechanisms.

- Common logic is ISO standard 24707, a specification of a family of ontology languages that can be accurately translated into each other.

- The Cyc project has its own ontology language called CycL, based on first-order predicate calculus with some higher-order extensions.

- DOGMA (Developing Ontology-Grounded Methods and Applications) adopts the fact-oriented modeling approach to provide a higher level of semantic stability.

- The Gellish language includes rules for its own extension and thus integrates an ontology with an ontology language.

- IDEF5 is a software engineering method to develop and maintain usable, accurate, domain ontologies.

- KIF is a syntax for first-order logic that is based on S-expressions. SUO-KIF is a derivative version supporting the Suggested Upper Merged Ontology.

- MOF and UML are standards of the OMG.

- Olog is a category theoretic approach to ontologies, emphasizing translations between ontologies using functors.

- OBO, a language used for biological and biomedical ontologies.

- OntoUML is an ontologically well-founded profile of UML for conceptual modeling of domain ontologies.

- OWL is a language for making ontological statements, developed as a follow-on from RDF and RDFS, as well as earlier ontology language projects including OIL, DAML, and DAML+OIL. OWL is intended to be used over the World Wide Web, and all its elements (classes, properties and individuals) are defined as RDF resources, and identified by URIs.

- Rule Interchange Format (RIF) and F-Logic combine ontologies and rules.

- Semantic Application Design Language (SADL) captures a subset of the expressiveness of OWL, using an English-like language entered via an Eclipse Plug-in.

- SBVR (Semantics of Business Vocabularies and Rules) is an OMG standard adopted in industry to build ontologies.

- TOVE Project, TOronto Virtual Enterprise project.

INFORMATION TECHNOLOGY IN STRATEGIC MANAGEMENT

Information technology focuses on processing of information which is the basic part of strategic management process, called Strategic analysis.

In this regard, Information technology is used to as an essential input to the process of strategic decisions.

The word Information System in this context describes a usage of a computer system to process data and produce business information. For processing of data Hardware, software, peoples, procedures are considered.i.e.they constitute information system.Here, Hardware is referred as part of a computer system that can be touched and seen by our sense organs. Keyboard, Mouse, Monitor, printer etc are grouped under Hardware. However, Software is part of a computer system that cannot be touched with our necked eyes. This include operating system software, and the applications software, hence, computer becomes nothing by itself without software.

Using information systems import a number of impacts on an organization success. These impacts can benefit the organization, users of the information system, and any individual or group who will interact with the information system.

Some of the specific benefits are,adding value to products (goods and services),better safety,better service,competitive advantage,fewer errors,greater accuracy,higher quality products,improve communications,increase efficiency,increase productivity,more efficient administration,more opportunities,reduce labor required,reduce costs,helps in decision making,superior control over operations etc.

All the above benefits come from the capability of the computer system in relation to speed, consistency, precision and reliability. Here after, some of the benefits are illustrated.

In relation to time related benefits, classical idiom appears to be relevant, "time is money". This is to mean that every minute of second has value for a person who utilizes the time effectively.

Accordingly, business organization has to treat their customers by providing appropriate services accurately and timely. However, Most of the time, we could not achieve or delay in delivering information, service, and products on time due to limited usage of information technology. But, with the help of information technology more work can be done timely by individuals, businesses, services and government organizations with high speed and accuracy. Hence, computer systems can process and helps to convert a bulk of data to meaningful information within a fraction of seconds; faster than people. These results in minimization of information gap among organizational units and enhance business efficiency.

The other use of Information technology is consistency. It is one of the qualities of computer system to retrieve repeated actions every time precisely.

In addition to the benefits stated under speed and consistency, Information technology also provide a benefit of precision.

Furthermore, due to speed, consistency and precision the computer system provides reliability. It is to mean that information technology gives the same result again and again unless and otherwise the input raw data is changed.

Therefore, emphasis has to be given for the Management information systems outputs as it is always based on the input we provide and the instructions. (That is, the internal programming codes initiated by our input).

Recognizing the above described benefits currently, most business organizations are using information technology by allocating huge investment so as to equip the management information system for the attainment of the business objectives. On the other hand, as capital investment on information and communication technology within business organization continues to increase, it is also necessary to optimize the benefits from such investment. That is to say, there is an expectation that business organizations not only maximize the benefits of adopting information and communication technology but also expected to minimize possible drawbacks and risks that are associated with rapid technological change and offer competitive advantage.

Generally, information technology system helps in effective utilization of resources. Like efficient utilization of manpower in the business not only to concentrate on routine manual works but to go beyond and spend time on "what-if analysis scenarios".

Information Technology and Strategy

Some managers did not give more attention about the benefits of information systems on the business strategy process. Such lack of attention is related to a number of factors. First, there appears to be some gaps as how information technology could be used in their Strategic management process.

Second, there was a great misunderstanding on the usefulness of the information technology on business strategy. But nowadays, most of the business entities understood the benefits of the information technology systems as an enabler of their strategic management system process.

Besides, there is more awareness where and when to implement it and use information technology in the process of crafting different strategies that lead them to the road of stakeholders satisfaction.

Some of the application areas like transaction processing systems and decision support systems (DSS) have been used as the main information system so as to enhance business performances.

In addition to the above advantages large computer network that shares different information with reliable and easy internet systems has been used by the organization for the purpose of communication, distribution of information, to offer goods and services online to customer, to interact with other business organization either for business transaction or information exchanges etc.

Such internet usage leads to live in a global village in which computers and peoples are linked within companies, countries, and continents resulting easy communications in reducing the time and geographical barriers.

In this regard Mr. Kodama, asserts the importance of Information Technology in this competitive business world as crucial for business sector to consider and emphasis on the significance and role of information and communication technology for setting up competitive businesses, managing global corporations, adding business value, and providing valued products and/or services to their potential markets.

The main points on the above statement intended to address the capability of information technology to transform corporate data into meaningful and actionable information that helps the strategic management process of a business.

Gerald V., also confirm that, information technology systems enable workers to process more items, and allowing the firm to expand without increasing labor costs beyond the ability of reducing errors in the data which leads to improved decision making. The stated findings also indicate the importance of information technology in business strategy.

Consistent with the above justification, in the developed country, almost all transaction has been undergoing electronically through internet infrastructure called electronic commerce (e-commerce). Such transaction decreases the intermediaries between the business and the end users. It reduces costs like labor, document preparation, telephoning, and mail preparation etc. and IT become part of the daily life activity.

On the other hand, in developing country there are some gaps in using Information technology in their business strategy as well as day to day activity as compared to the developed country. Therefore more efforts are expected in the future to get competitive advantages from application of information technology.

Management Information System

Management information system (MIS) is a computer system designed to help managers in planning and directing business and organizational operations. There are two main purposes of management information system. First: it helps to generate reports like financial statements mainly Balance sheet, Income statement, and cash flow statement, and other reports that help managers for planning and decision making purposes.Similarly,inventory status reports and performance reports needed for routine or non-routine purposes, can be generated using MIS and more others.

The second purpose of management information system is to generate other tailored reports as per the managers and customers requirements. Here, it is very important to emphasize on the role of experienced computer programmers and system analysts in developing Management information systems to meet the business objectives. The Managers role on designing phase of management information system is very important to provide his business objectives i.e. to cite problems that needs to be solved by the new system and to provide information about the existing non automated system strength and weakness and to let know the analyst the main points that the new system should encompasses and the required alignment with the company strategy. Hence, the General functional requirements expected from the final delivery of the software are expected from the business owner. Then after the system analyst will prepare a detailed document that can be changed into a programming language by the programmer.

During the final delivery of the system, care has to be taken whether the required functionality has properly incorporated or not, because this is the base that helps managers get information for decision making purpose.

Similarly, on using management information system in the business organization again care has to be taken on the amount of information generated from the system for the management purpose. Only the relevant report at the right time, in the right place, in the right format must be generated. Otherwise the managers may face the problem of information overload. The main purpose of the above descriptions is just to mention some of the most important precaution in implementing MIS.

To sum up, information technology system is a vital tool for proper management of the business if and only if it is properly used.

Strategic Management

Gregory G. and etal define Strategic management is a process of the analysis, decision, and actions an organization undertakes in order to create and sustain competitive advantages.

Strategic management focuses on building a solid underlying structure of a business and through combining all efforts in the business.

Thus, Strategic management answers as to how the identified business objectives are achieved with what resource a company needs to adapt so as to quickly response to the new challenges.

Hence, an organization must have clear strategy that is developed carefully in order to meet the organizational goal. This responsibility lies on management's shoulder. Besides, management decision in every strategic issue should be based on tangible evidences and information and such decisions must be taken on time.

In order to make proper decisions on time all necessary information must be available too. Therefore, the strategic management processes need to be supported by information technology systems in order not to miss the open advantage of information technology, mainly efficiency and accuracy.

Understanding the organization

The key to gaining strategic advantages from information technology systems lies in understanding the process of functional requirement gathering, and as to how the functional requirement changes to management information system, installing, implementing, adapting and managing a strategic information system.

A thoroughly understanding of the business requirements are firstly needed before any activities of implementation. Furthermore, being participation is another element of strategic management hence participation is required from all groups of the organization starting from the bottom level employee to top level executives. This helps in understanding business requirement and core issues to include in the development of the management information system. Moreover the commitment of the top level of management is outweigh more as in any other management systems, like Total Quality management.

Therefore, it is very important to have good strategic leader that by no means assures the use of information technology in the strategic process for the company.

Consequently, the leader will set the overall directions and the key criteria for the acquisitions of information systems and information technology. Then after, the next top senior experts should decide on the specific objectives of the intended systems preferably with the consultation of the management information systems professionals either inside or outside the company. In addition, the management of the implementation of information systems should be managed by the information system professionals with key other personnel's in the business.

To facilitate the implementation process constant support to the system users should be provided. In addition, awareness creation method has to be established in order to provide information to all employees regarding on the usage and benefits of information technology and information system. If not, one can be challenging occurrences and change resistances will soon come early on implementing the system.

Consistently to the above fact Eliezer G. advices on the need to strategically manage Information technology by senior mangers particularly on understanding of the diffusion of the technology and its role in information gathering, processing, and transferring at all levels through the services of IS/MIS. Furthermore he emphasized on the need that information technology is to be left to the sole discretion of information professionals.

From the above, it may be inferred that, strategy management process success depends on information, the process of managing information system which is a crucial task that needs continuous consideration and follow-up. Therefore, leaders in the business area have to understand the value of information technology. However most of the time the cause of difficulties in using information technology in strategy management process may not solely the failure of the Managers, but the way how to manage the information technology systems also contribute greatly.

Moreover, information technology systems are a tool for executives that must be aligned with the organizational setup in order to eliminate the barriers to use the system effectively.

Strategic Leaders and IT Implementation

In a business organization, three types of strategic leaders might be cited; the first one is the leader that advocates the use of information technology in using in their strategy management process. Such type of Strategic leader has enough knowledge of usage of information technology. Besides such leaders may have some form of formal or informal awareness on the benefit and on the use of information technology. Hence such managers are committed to invest considerable investment on Management information system projects to supplement strategic process using information technology.

The second type of leaders are leaders who also have a good understanding of the benefits of information technology systems but thinks that the investment cost in implementing management information systems will negatively impact on the profitability of the business. They luck full confidence in using of Information technology systems.

The third types of leaders are those who do not have awareness on the benefits of the use of information technology systems and misunderstand information technology and its strategic significance. Such leaders do not want to use information technology systems mainly due to a fear of new technologies and the outputs in using it. Such types of leaders appear to be more deficient in modernization concepts or just think using the technology as fashion.

In my opinion, the basic differences of the three strategic leaders lie on the understanding of the benefits of information technology, on understanding of the organization long term plan (strategic vision) and, the current competitive world situations.

Consistently with the above idea, Linda L. & Susan B. describe two basic impacts in using electronics support. The First one is, if one is confident with the technology he will explore every e-avenue and fully utilize all of the facilities available. Conversely, if one is a more novice user he may look blankly at the computer screen and panic.

Therefore, to continually compete in this competitive market, business should continually support by the information technology systems and also continual update and usage of the latest systems makes to win in the market.

Role of Information Technology in Strategy Management

As previously discussed, Management information system relates on processing of raw data and outputs in such a way that managers and customers' need. Hence Management information system helps business in analyzing data accurately and quickly. This information flow helps managers to use the outputs of the management information system for different quality decision by adding value to the product and service that the organization provide.

As a result, information technology has becoming an integral part of business strategy.

Therefore, investing in information systems can pay off the company mainly by supporting the core business. For example, firms that interact with its customer frequently may develop online systems using internet. Hence, using internet minimizes the time needed.

On the other hand, some large companies may have more than two core departments. Then as far as they are the heart of the business, information technology can such support that core departments. For example, in Beverage industry, the core department is the production section. Therefore, the strategic leader has to equip the section with a modern technological device that uses information technology and every data in relation to production to captured, analyse and report in the predefined format to the manager. Hence such system helps in getting necessary information for managing large production data. Besides Automated systems are the most cost efficient way to organize large scale production. These can produce economies of scale in promotion, purchasing, and production; economies of scope in distribution and promotion; reduced overhead allocation per unit; and shorter break-even times more easily. This absolute cost advantage can mean greater profits and revenue.

The same is true for the service giving organization; it has to equip with proper information system to satisfy their customer by providing the services required accurately on time.

Therefore, it is possible to suggest that information technology can support any part of the core system of any business organizations and can be used as strategic tool .But this does not mean that information technology alone makes the business strategy of the company to be succeed; but while factors like human resource can also contribute to the long term goal of the business.

CONTENT MANAGEMENT

Content management (CM) is a set of processes and technologies that supports the collection, managing, and publishing of information in any form or medium. When stored and accessed via computers, this information may be more specifically referred to as digital content, or simply as content.

- Digital content may take the form of text (such as electronic documents), multimedia files (such as audio or video files), or any other file type that follows a content lifecycle requiring management.

- The process is complex enough to manage that several large and small commercial software vendors such as Interwoven and Microsoft offer content management software to control and automate significant aspects of the content lifecycle.

Content Management System

A content management system (CMS) is a software application or set of related programs that are used to create and manage digital content. CMSes are typically used for enterprise content management (ECM) and web content management (WCM). An ECM facilitates collaboration in the workplace by integrating document management, digital asset management and records retention functionalities, and providing end users with role-based access to the organization's digital assets. A WCM facilitates collaborative authoring for websites. ECM software often includes a WCM publishing functionality, but ECM webpages typically remain behind the organization's firewall.

Both enterprise content management and web content management systems have two components: a content management application (CMA) and a content delivery application (CDA). The CMA is a graphical user interface (GUI) that allows the user to control the design, creation, modification and removal of content from a website without needing to know anything about HTML. The CDA component provides the back-end services that support management and delivery of the content once it has been created in the CMA.

Features of CMSes

Features can vary amongst the various CMS offerings, but the core functions are often considered to be indexing, search and retrieval, format management, revision control and publishing.

- Intuitive indexing, search and retrieval features index all data for easy access through search functions and allow users to search by attributes such as publication dates, keywords or author.

- Format management facilitates turn scanned paper documents and legacy electronic documents into HTML or PDF documents.

- Revision features allow content to be updated and edited after initial publication. Revision control also tracks any changes made to files by individuals.

- Publishing functionality allows individuals to use a template or a set of templates approved by the organization, as well as wizards and other tools to create or modify content.

A CMS may also provide tools for one-to-one marketing. One-to-one marketing is the ability of a website to tailor its content and advertising to a user's specific characteristics using information provided by the user or gathered by the site -- for instance, a particular user's page sequence pattern. For example, if the user visited a search engine and searched for digital camera, the advertising banners would feature businesses that sell digital cameras instead of businesses that sell garden products.

Other popular features of CMSes include:

- SEO-friendly URLs.

- Integrated and online help, including discussion boards.

- Group-based permission systems.

- Full template support and customizable templates.

- Easy wizard-based install and versioning procedures.

- Admin panel with multiple language support.

- Content hierarchy with unlimited depth and size.

- Minimal server requirements.

- Integrated file managers.

- Integrated audit logs.

Choosing a CMS

There is almost no limit to the factors that must be considered before an organization decides to invest in a CMS. There are a few basic functionalities to always look for, such as an easy-to-use editor interface and intelligent search capabilities. However, for some organizations, the software they use depends on certain requirements.

For example, consider the organization's size and geographic dispersion. The CMS administrator must know how many people will be utilizing the application, whether the CMS will require multilanguage support and what size support team will be needed to maintain operations. It's also important to consider the level of control both administrators and end users will have when using the CMS. The diversity of the electronic data forms used within an organization must also be considered. All types of digital content should be indexed easily.

INFORMATION ARCHITECTURE

Information architecture (IA) is a science of organizing and structuring content of the websites, web and mobile applications, and social media software. An American architect and graphic designer, Richard Saul Wurman, is considered to be a founder of the IA field. Today, there are many specialists working on IA development who have established the Information Architecture Institute. According to the IAI experts, information architecture is the practice of deciding how to arrange the parts of something to be understandable.

Information architecture aims at organizing content so that users would easily adjust to the functionality of the product and could find everything they need without big effort. The content structure depends on various factors. First of all, IA experts consider the specifics of the target audience needs because IA puts user satisfaction as a priority. Also, the structure depends on the type of the product and the offers companies have. For example, if we compare a retail website and a blog, we'll see two absolutely different structures both efficient for accomplishing certain objectives. Information architecture has become the fundamental study in many spheres including design and software development.

The Role of Information Architecture in Design

Nowadays, when the user-centered approach in design is a top trend, many designers learn the principles of information architecture science which they believe is a foundation of efficient design. IA forms a skeleton of any design project. Visual elements, functionality, interaction, and navigation are built according to the information architecture principles. The thing is that even compelling content elements and powerful UI design can fail without appropriate IA. Unorganized content makes navigation difficult and inexplicit, so the users can easily get lost and feel annoyed. If the users face first bad interaction, they may not give the second chance to your product.

Many companies don't see the importance of information architecture because they think it's impractical. It's hard to argue that IA takes some time to create it and requires specific skills to do it efficiently. However, powerful IA is a guarantee of the high-quality product since it reduces the possibility of the usability and navigation problems. This way, well-thought information architecture can save both time and money of the company which otherwise they would have spent on fixing and improvement.

IA System Components

If you want to build strong information architecture for the product, you need to understand what it consists of. Pioneers of the IA field, Lou Rosenfeld and Peter Morville in their book "Information Architecture for the World Wide Web" have distinguished four main components: organization systems, labeling systems, navigation systems and searching systems.

Organization Systems

These are the groups or the categories in which the information is divided. Such system helps users to predict where they can find certain information easily. There are three main organizational structures: Hierarchical, Sequential, and Matrix.

Hierarchical: A well-known technique of content organization is visual hierarchy.. It is initially based on Gestalt psychological theory and its main goal is to present content on the carrier, be it a book page or poster, web page or mobile screen, in such a way that users can understand the level of importance for each element. It activates the ability of the brain to distinguish objects on the basis of their physical differences, such as size, color, contrast, alignment etc.

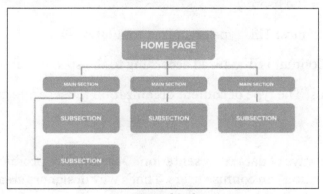

Hierarchical

Sequential: This structure creates some kind of a path for the users. They go step-by-step through content to accomplish the task they needed. This type is often used for the retail websites or apps, where people have to go from one task to another to make the purchase.

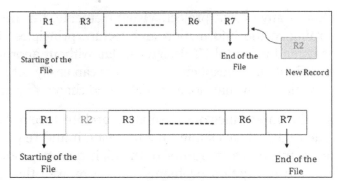

Sequential

Matrix: This type is a bit more complicated for the users since they choose the way of navigation on their own. Users are given choices of content organization. For example, they can navigate through content which is ordered according to date, or some may prefer navigation along the topic.

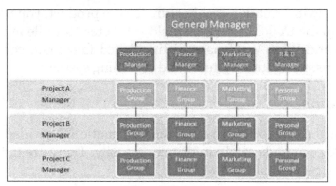

MoneyWise App

In addition, content can be grouped according to the organization schemes. They are meant to categorize content the product. Here are some of the popular schemes:

- Alphabetical schemes: Content is organized in alphabetical order. Also, they can serve as a navigation tool for the users.

- Chronological schemes: This type organizes content by date.

- Topic schemes: Content is organized according to the specific subject.

- Audience schemes: The type of content organization for separate groups of users.

Labeling Systems

This system involves the ways of data representation. Design of the product requires simplicity, so a great amount of information can confuse users. That's why designers create the labels which represent loads of data in few words. For example, when the designers give contact information of the company on the website, it usually includes the phone number, email, and social media contacts. However, designers can't present all of this information on one page. The button "Contact" in the header of the page is a label that triggers the associations in the users' heads without placing the whole data on the page. So, the labeling system aims at uniting the data effectively.

Navigation Systems

Navigation is the set of actions and techniques guiding users throughout the app or website, enabling them to fulfill their goals and successfully interact with the product. The navigation system, in terms of IA, involves the ways how users move through content. It's a complex system which employs many techniques and approaches, the reason why it's wrong to describe it in a short paragraph.

Searching Systems

This system is used in information architecture to help users search for the data within the digital product like a website or an app. The searching system is effective only for the products with loads of information when the users risk getting lost there. In this case, the designers should consider a search engine, filters, and many other tools helping users find content and plan how the data will look after the search.

References

- Piatetsky-shapiro, gregory; parker, gary (2011). "lesson: data mining, and knowledge discovery: an introduction". Introduction to data mining. Kd nuggets. Retrieved 30 august 2012

- Natural-language-processing-information-retrieval, natural-language-processing: tutorialspoint.com, Retrieved 14 July, 2019

- Mena, jesús (2011). Machine learning forensics for law enforcement, security, and intelligence. Boca raton, fl: crc press (taylor & francis group). Isbn 978-1-4398-6069-4

- Storage, definition: techtarget.com, Retrieved 17 May, 2019

- Lukasz kurgan and petr musilek (2006); a survey of knowledge discovery and data mining process models. The knowledge engineering review. Volume 21 issue 1, march 2006, pp 1–24, cambridge university press, new york, ny, usa doi:10.1017/s0269888906000737

- Information-technology-as-a-key-to-strategic-management-information-technology-essay, information-technology, essays: ukessays.com, Retrieved 19 April, 2019

- Content-management-system-cms, definition: techtarget.com, Retrieved 5 February, 2019

PERMISSIONS

INDEX